韵律研究
Prosodic Studies
（第一辑）

主编 冯胜利

科学出版社
北京

《韵律研究》编委会
Editorial Board of *Prosodic Studies*

主　编　冯胜利
(Chief Editor)

编　委（按姓名音序排列）
(Editorial Board Members)

Andrew Simpson	蔡维天	陈曙东
端木三	冯蒸	黄正德
Laura Downing	马秋武	Maria Luisa Zubizarreta
沈家煊	施向东	张健
赵敏俐	郑礼珊	

编辑部成员（按姓名音序排列）
(Editors)

黄梅　裴雨来　王丽娟　庄会彬

前　言

　　古人说："情发于声，声成文谓之音。"（《毛诗·序》）感情要通过声音来表达，声音有了结构（文理）才叫"音"。什么是声音的结构呢？最基本、最原始的声音结构是韵律（Llinás，2002：230；Fitch，2000）①。韵律是人们发音时，节奏的长短快慢和语音的高低强弱，一句话，就是语言的超音段语音现象。"韵律研究"就是以人类语言的超音段现象为对象。

　　中国古代学者很早就关注到韵律的现象。魏晋时的沈约（441—513）如是解释当时的韵文："欲使宫羽相变，低昂舛节；若前有浮声，则后须切响，一简之内，音韵尽殊，两句之中，轻重悉异"（《宋书·谢灵运传论》）。唐代的孔颖达（574—648）如是解释《诗经·邵南》的"羔羊之皮"："兼言羊者，以羔亦是羊，故连言以协句"。沈约的"前有浮声则后须切响"、孔颖达的"协句"、"足句"和"圆文"，都是中国文学史上著名的节律分析。

　　然而，长期以来，学界对语言韵律的研究，始终没有形成一个独立的学科。文学界里的韵律研究尤其如此。不仅汉语是这样，其他语言（如英文）也不例外。著名韵律学家 Bruce Hayes 一针见血地指出："韵文节律的研究，很不幸，还是一个支离破碎的领域，研究工作无法从学术的组织或刊物中获取教益"（Hayes，2010：2515）②。至今，国际学术范围内仍然没有一个专门以韵律为研究对象的独立刊物。毋庸置疑，《韵律研究》的创刊

---

　　① Llinás R. R. 2002. *I of the Vortex: From Neurons to Self.* Cambridge, MA.: MIT Press.
　　Fitch W. T. 2000. The evolution of speech: A comparative review. *Trends in Cognitive Sciences*, 4(7): 258-267.

　　② Hayes, B. 2010. Review of *Meter in Poetry* by Nigel Fabb and Morris Halle. *Lingua*, 120: 2515-2521.

填补了这一空白。

今天的韵律研究是幸运的,因为我们至少有了独立的韵律学(Metrical Phonology)。韵律音系学家 Ladd 说:"韵律学始于 Liberman 提出的新概念:语言学上的凸显最核心的是指双分枝结构节点之间的关系"(Ladd,2008:55)①。不仅如此,韵律和语言其他层面的接口研究也大为改观:曾经奉为圭臬的句法无语音原则(Principle of Phonology-Free Syntax)已不复存在;随之而来的是韵律构词学的独立成科,韵律句法学的蓬勃发展——不仅出现了韵律删除(prosodic blocking)和韵律启动(prosodic activating)的新兴研究,而且开始了"韵律-句法对应层(prosody-syntax co-hierarchy)"的新局面。更令人惊喜的是:韵律和文学的跨界互动的研究,无论是韵律文体学、韵律诗体学,还是韵律吟诵学,均如雨后春笋,破土而出:群山万壑赴荆门,一代新学在兴起。

语言学家 Simpson 说:"将来的韵律与语法的相互作用的研究,无论是跨方言的共时研究,还是历时的研究(这是可能的),都是未来汉语语言学研究中的一个丰富而内容充实的领域,是一个汉语可以为有关人类语言的普通语言学理论做出重要贡献的领域。"(Simpson,2014:489)②无疑,这是《韵律研究》的奋斗目标,同时也是《韵律研究》给同怀这一目标者搭建的历史舞台。

---

① Ladd, D. R. 2008. *Intonational Phonology* (2nd edition). Cambridge: Cambridge University Press.

② Simpson, A. 2014. Prosody and syntax. In C.-J. James Huang, Y.-H. Audrey Li & A. Simpson (Eds.) *Handbook of Chinese Linguistics* (pp. 465-491). Malden, MA.: John Wiley & Sons.

Preface

As is said in *Maoshixu* (Mao's Preface to the *Book of Songs*), "Emotions can be expressed through uttering sounds and the sounds will compose a rhythm when combined in an orderly regulated way." In other words, sounds contribute to emotional expression and have a structure of their own. What is then the structure of sounds? It is believed that the most fundamental primitive structure of sounds is prosody (Llinás, 2002: 230; Fitch, 2000) [①]. Briefly speaking, prosody is the suprasegmental feature of sounds which is concerned with different rhythms being fast or slow, long or short, and sound features like a high or low pitch, and a strong or weak stress. Prosodic studies is a thriving field of linguistic research that tries to explore the suprasengmeantal feature of human languages.

Scholars in ancient China have noticed the linguistic phenomenon of prosody long before. The scholar Shen Yue (441-513) of the Wei and Jin dynasties (220-420), when analyzing the verses of his time, held that: "we should make characters of different tonal patterns alternate with each other and ensure that the poetic couplet thus formed emerge in a relatively prominent manner. If the first line of the couplet contains characters of the level tone, then the second line must have characters of the non-level tone. The five characters of each line should differentiate one from another in terms of low and high pitch levels and the two lines must have completely different stress patterns." (Biographies and

---

① Llinás R. R. 2002. *I of the Vortex: From Neurons to Self.* Cambridge, MA: MIT Press.
Fitch W. T. 2000. The evolution of Speech: A Comparative Review. *Trends in Cognitive Sciences*, 4(7): 258-267.

Commentary of Xie Lingyun from *Songshu*). Furthermore, in order to explain "gaoyang zhi pi 羔羊之皮" 'lamb-sheep's skin "the skin of lambs' in *Shaonan* of the *Book of Songs*, the philologist Kong Yingda of the Tang dynasty proposed that "the text says lamb with sheep, because lamb is also a kind of sheep, in order to balance the sentence it mentions both lamb and sheep." Here, Shen Yue's proposal of "level and non-level tones" and Kong Yingda's analysis of "xie-ju 諧句" ' to balance the sentence', "zu-ju 足句" ' to fulfill the sentence', "yuan-wen 圓文" ' to round off the sentence' all constitute the well-known metrical study in the history of Chinese literature.

Nevertheless, prosodic studies of human languages have not become an independent field for quite a long time. This is particularly true for prosodic studies in the field of literature research. Such an awkward situation exists not only in the study of Chinese but also in the study of other languages including English. As is acutely pointed out by the famous metrical phonologist Bruce Hayes, "the field of metrics is, sadly, a fragmented one, conducted without benefit of an established scholarly association or journal." (Hayes, 2010: 2515) [①]. By far, there has not been a single specific journal on prosodic studies in the international academic circle. Now, the publication of *Prosodic Studies* has undoubtedly filled the gap.

We are lucky now to conduct prosodic studies since Metrical Phonology has emerged as a discipline in its own right. "Metrical Phonology begins with Liberman's notion that linguistic prominence crucially involves a relation between nodes in a binary-branching tree structure," says Ladd in *Intonational Phonology* (2008: 55) [②]. Moreover, the interface studies between prosody and other modules of linguistics have witnessed a dramatic development in recent years. On the one

---

[①] Hayes, B. 2010. Review of *Meter in Poetry* by Nigel Fabb and Morris Halle. *Lingua*, *120*: 2515-2521.

[②] Ladd, D. R. 2008. *Intenational Phonology* (2nd edition). Cambridge: Cambridge University Press.

hand, the principle of phonology-free syntax, once a well-accepted norm, has come to a dead end. On the other hand, Prosodic Morphology has gained its independence as a discipline and Prosodic Syntax has flourished with the recent study of "prosodic blocking" and "prosodic activating" as well as the proposal of "prosody-syntax co-hierarchy." There are even more remarkable achievements: Prosodic Stylistics, Poetic Prosody and Prosodic Chanting have sprung up like mushrooms after a rain. Thus, these different fields all converge to constitute the extensive range of prosodic studies just like different rivers flow together to form vast waters.

Simpson asserts that "the continued study of prosody and syntax interactions, whether as a study synchronically across different varieties of Chinese or (quite possibly) as a study diachronically, promises to be a rich and very informative area of future research for Chinese linguistics, and in ways that Chinese can also make important contribution to the general theories of human language" (Simpson, 2014: 489) [1]. This is the vision that *Prosodic Studies* is striving for and also the important stage set up by *Prosodic Studies* for all the researchers with the shared aspirations and interests.

---

[1] Simpson, A. 2014. Prosody and Syntax. In C.-J. James Huang, Y.-H. Audrey Li & A. Simpson (Eds.), *Handbook of Chinese Linguistics* (pp. 465-491). Malden, MA: John Wiley & Sons.

目　录

前言

The Prosodic Hierarchy in Chichewa: How Many Levels? ···· Laura J. Downing（1）

核心重音与信息结构···Maria Luisa Zubizarreta
（李　果　王　迟　王晓品　庄会彬 译）（45）

从音步和重音看语言的共性与任意性···端木三（73）

谈汉语焦点的韵律机制——句法韵律接口的个案研究·········蔡维天　李宗宪（98）

香港粤语句末助词声调与句调关系的初探··························张　凌　邓思颖（113）

先秦诗律探索···施向东（128）

Under the Microscope of Prosody: The Serendipitous Revelation of the
　Poetic Power and Beauty of "Function Words" ···············Shudong Chen（158）

《韵律研究》来稿须知···（186）

CONTENTS

Preface

The Prosodic Hierarchy in Chichewa: How Many Levels? ···· Laura J. Downing （1）

Nuclear Stress and Information Structure ··················Maria Luisa Zubizarreta （45）
    (Translators: Guo Li   Chi Wang   Xiaopin Wang   Huibin Zhuang)

Universal and Arbitrary Properties of Language: Perspectives from Foot
    Structure and Stress ·· San Duanmu （73）

On the Prosodic Nature of Chinese Foci: A Case Study of the
    Syntax-Prosody Interface ·· Weitian Tsai   Zongxian Li （98）

Preliminary Studies on Tones of Sentence-Final Particles and
    Intonation in Cantonese ································· Ling Zhang   Sze-Wing Tang （113）

A Research on the Versification in Pre Qin ································· Xiangdong Shi （128）

Under the Microscope of Prosody: The Serendipitous Revelation of the
    Poetic Power and Beauty of "Function Words" ························ Shudong Chen （158）

Prosodic Studies Notes for Authors ·· （186）

The Prosodic Hierarchy in Chichewa: How Many Levels?*

Laura J. Downing

Abstract Recent work (Itô & Mester, 2012, 2013; Selkirk, 2009, 2011) proposes that Prosodic Hierarchy is made up of only three levels of prosodic constituents, which are morpho-syntactically motivated and universally instantiated: Intonation Phrase, Phonological Phrase and Prosodic Word. This paper tests the validity of the three-level hypothesis by investigating the phonology of Chichewa, a Bantu language spoken in Malawi. Two challenges to the hypothesis emerge from this investigation. First, three levels of prosodic constituency is too parsimonious, as Chichewa, like many languages, provides evidence for another level, the Prosodic Stem (immediately dominated by Prosodic Word). The analysis also questions the universal validity of the three levels, as there is no strong evidence, at the phrasal level, for a Phonological Phrase domain distinct from Intonation Phrase. This paper argues for a middle path between extreme parsimony in the number of prosodic constituents admitted to the Prosodic Hierarchy and an empirically adequate theory which allows for more domains, when evidence for them

---

* I would first of all like to thank the many native speakers of Chichewa who have worked with me on their languages since I began in 2004. I am grateful to the Centre for Language Studies at the University of Malawi for their hospitality and support during my fieldwork stays. I owe many thanks to Lisa Cheng, Al Mtenje, Bernd Pompino-Marschall and Annie Rialland for hours of inspiring discussion and advice in analyzing parts of the data reported on here. I thank Diana Archangeli, Ricardo Bermudez-Otéro, Larry Hyman, Shin Ishihara, Maxwell Kadenge, Sara Myrberg, Tomas Riad, Marina Vigário, Irene Vogel and members of the BantuPsyn working group for comments on the work as it has developed over a number of presentations. This paper was improved by responding to the thoughtful comments of an anonymous reviewer. All remaining errors of fact or interpretation are my responsibility.

can be provided.

Keywords　Prosodic Stem, composite word group, Bantu languages, reduplication, tone domains, minimality, clitics, hiatus resolution.

1　Introduction

Prosodic theory proposes that phonological strings are parsed into a set of hierarchically arranged constituents—the Prosodic Hierarchy—which provide the domains for morpho-syntactically-conditioned phonological processes. (See, e.g., Inkelas, 1989; Nespor & Vogel, 1986; Selkirk, 1986, 1995; Hayes, 1989). A persistent research issue for the Prosodic Hierarchy is to determine what the cross-linguistically valid repertory of constituents should be. In addressing this issue, two conflicting considerations must be balanced (Inkelas, 2014): 1- The number of constituents should be as *parsimonious* as possible, as this is the best way to insure the posited constituents are of universal cross-linguistic relevance; and 2- The number of constituents must provide *sufficient* prosodic domains to account for morpho-syntactically conditioned phonological processes in all languages.

Selkirk (2009, 2011) and Itô & Mester (2012, 2013) have recently argued in favor of a parsimonious view. They make the strong claim that the Prosodic Hierarchy contains only the three universal, syntactically-defined constituents in (1):

(1) Prosodic Hierarchy (adapted, Itô & Mester, 2013: 26; Selkirk, 2011: 439)

Intonational Phrase	matches	syntactic clause (CP)
|		
Phonological Phrase	matches	syntactic phrase (XP)
|		
Prosodic Word	matches	syntactic word (X^0); i.e., a "word in syntactic constituent structure" (Selkirk, 2011: 439)

Any additional prosodic domains must, in their framework, be defined as recursions of one of these constituents. Further, all languages are expected to require this set of prosodic constituents, since they match universally instantiated syntactic constituents.

This paper investigates the cross-linguistic validity of the set of prosodic constituents in (1), based on a case study of Chichewa, a Bantu language (N.31) spoken mainly in Malawi. I argue, first, that this definition of the Prosodic Hierarchy is too parsimonious: an additional constituent, Prosodic Stem, is required to account for the distinction between stem- and word-level phonological domains that is motivated by Chichewa and has been demonstrated for many other languages. (See, e.g., Inkelas, 1989, 1993; Downing, 1999; Kiparsky, 2000; Bermudez-Otéro, 2011, 2012.) Secondly, I argue that this definition of the Prosodic Hierarchy is too inflexible: not every language has two levels of phrasing at the post-lexical level.

The paper is structured as follows. In section 2, I review arguments for prosodic constituents distinct from morphological ones, at the level of Prosodic Word (PWord) and also at the level of Prosodic Stem (PStem)—a sublexical constituent dominated by PWord—in Bantu and other languages. In section 3, I present data from Chichewa, showing that in this language, too, we find evidence for PWord distinct from grammatical word and also from PStem. Section 4 shows that alternatives to a PWord–PStem distinction are not workable. The distinction cannot be recast in terms of recursive Prosodic Word domains, following recent proposals by Itô & Mester (2012, 2013), Riad (2012), and Selkirk (2009, 2011). Another alternative approach (Vigário, 2010; Vogel, 2009, 2010) will also be shown to encounter problems in accounting for the data.

In section 5, we turn to post-lexical prosodic constituency. Previous work on prosodic phrasing in Chichewa (Kanerva, 1990; Truckenbrodt, 1995) argues for two levels of phrasing, Phonological Phrase and Intonation Phrase. However, once one includes a broader range of data in the prosodic analysis, it is more plausible to argue that Chichewa has only one level of prosodic phrasing, the Intonation Phrase. In section 6, I conclude by proposing a revised view of the number and the universality of the levels in the Prosodic Hierarchy.

2 Arguments for prosodic constituents distinct from morphological ones

Under the Indirect Reference Hypothesis (Nespor & Vogel, 1986; Selkirk, 1986) phonological processes apply with reference to prosodic constituents, not directly to morpho-syntactic ones. Evidence for prosodic constituents distinct from morpho-syntactic constituents comes from two sources: the constituent is a domain for phonological processes; and/or one finds mismatches between morpho-syntactic constituents and the prosodic constituent. In the default case, constituents such as Prosodic Word are coextensive with the corresponding morphological constituent: grammatical word. That is, as shown in (1), by definition prosodic constituents 'match' morpho-syntactic constituents (Inkelas, 1989, 1993; Itô & Mester, 2013; Selkirk, 2009, 2011). However, prosodic and morphological constituents may be misaligned, and these misalignments provide the best motivation for prosodic constituents. (See, e.g., Selkirk, 1986, 1995, 2011; Nespor & Vogel, 1986; Inkelas, 1989, 1993, 2011, 2014.) Before turning to the Chichewa data, we briefly review general evidence for mismatches between prosodic and morphological constituents, giving examples of mismatches at the word level and at the stem level.

2.1 Arguments for Prosodic Word: Sources of Misalignment

We begin by briefly reviewing common sources of misalignment between Prosodic Word and grammatical word. (Unless specified otherwise, prosodic constituency is indicated with parentheses throughout, while morphosyntactic constituency is indicated with square brackets).

2.1.1 Final extrametricality: ([xx) x]

It is very common for word-final syllables to be ineligible for stress or tone assignment. For stress, cross-linguistic surveys like Hyman (1977) and Goedemans & van der Hulst (2013) show that there are twice as many languages with penult stress as with final stress. For Bantu tone, surveys like Cassimjee & Kisseberth (1998) and Kisseberth & Odden (2003) show that it is common for the final syllable to be ineligible as a target of High tone spread. As Inkelas (1989) argues, the prosodic exceptionality of final syllables can be formalized by misaligning the Prosodic Word (the domain for stress or tone) and the grammatical word, excluding the final syllable or mora or Foot. To illustrate, in English, the final syllable is typically extrametrical for stress in nouns but not in verbs. This contrast in stress domain can be formalized as, for example: ([cón)tract] (noun) vs. ([contráct]) (verb). We can then make the generalization that main stress is assigned to the rightmost syllable in both types of words.

2.1.2 Initial vowel extrametricality: [V (xx)]

It is also fairly common for onsetless initial vowels to be excluded from the domain of parsing into stress feet or from tone association. Downing (1998a) provides a survey of such cases. (See, too, Goedemans, 1996; Odden, 2006.) As Downing (1998a, 1998b) argues, this generalization can be formalized in terms of PWord/grammatical word misalignment: optimal left-alignment of PWord is with the leftmost syllabically well-formed (onset-ful) syllable, leaving the initial vowel of the grammatical word unparsed by the corresponding PWord: [V (xx)].

2.1.3 Augmentation to satisfy Minimality: (x [x])

As work beginning with McCarthy & Prince (1986) has documented in some detail, it is very common, cross-linguistically, for words to be required to have a particular minimal size. One strong piece of evidence for a minimality requirement comes from languages where subminimal words are augmented through epenthesis of morphologically empty material. As Myers (1987, 1995) and Mudzingwa (2010) show, an example of this is provided by imperative verb formation in Zezuru Shona. In (2e-2h), below, we see that in minimally disyllabic stems, the imperative consists of the bare verb stem. However, in (2a-2d) we see that monosyllabic verb stems like -*pa* 'give' must be augmented with *i*- in the imperative form:

(2) Zezuru Shona imperatives; epenthetic elements are bolded; 'j' is the palatal glide (Downing & Kadenge, 2015)

Imperative	Infinitive	Gloss
a. **i**pá	ku-pá	'give'
b. **i**dyá	ku-dyá	'eat'
c. **i**nwá	ku-nwá	'drink'
d. **i**bvá	ku-bvá	'leave'
cf.		
e. ímbá	ku-**j**ímbá	'sing'
f. fámbá	ku-fámbá	'walk'
g. túmírá	ku-túmírá	'to send to'
h. verengerana	ku-verengerana	'read to each other'

The comparison between (2a-2d) and (2e) is instructive, as it shows that verb stems which begin with non-epenthetic *i*-(2e) retain it in the infinitive form (where a palatal glide - *j* - is inserted before the stem-initial vowel to resolve vowel hiatus). In contrast the epenthetic vowels in (2a-2d) do not occur in the infinitive, where the infinitive prefix allows the word to satisfy the disyllabic minimality requirement.

2.1.4 Clitics: ([x]x)

Clitics are defined as morphemes that are prosodically bound to an adjacent word, even though they are not necessarily morpho-syntactically dependent on that word. Cliticization can thus be formalized as a process that leads to misalignment between prosodic and morpho-syntactic constituency: e.g., ([[Base] clitic]) or ([clitic[Base]]), as argued for in work like Inkelas (1989), Selkirk (1995). For example, English enclitics—like possessive *s*, and the reduced forms of the auxiliary verb, *has* and *is*—are prosodically bound to a preceding word, whatever its lexical category. Evidence that these clitics are parsed into a Prosodic Word with their phonological host comes from the fact that they show voicing agreement with the final sound of their host, a process which only applies to coda consonants within the (P)word domain: e.g., Pat's ([Pat]s]) vs. Ed's ([ed]z]).

2.2 Arguments for Prosodic Stem: sources of misalignment

Empirical evidence for the Prosodic Stem (PStem)—distinct from both the morphological Stem and the Prosodic Word—has come from languages as diverse as:

(3)
- Salishan languages (Czaykowska-Higgins, 1996, 1998; Shaw, 2005),
- Athapaskan languages (McDonough, 1990),
- Chumash (Downing, 1998b; Inkelas, 2011, 2014; Inkelas & Zoll, 2005),
- Axininca Campa (Downing, 2006),
- Bantu languages (Downing, 1998a, 1998b, 1999, 2006; Hyman, 1987, 1998, 1999, 2009; Hyman & Inkelas, 1997; Jones, 2011; Mchombo, 1993; Mudzingwa, 2010; Mutaka, 1994),
- Bengali (Fitzpatrick-Cole, 1993),
- Japanese (Itô & Mester, 1996).

What many of the languages in (3) have in common is that words, especially verb words, consist of a string of inflectional prefixes, preceded or followed by a morphologically complex Stem:

(4) [Inflectional Prefixes [**Stem**]] OR [[**Stem**] Inflectional Prefixes]

The Bantu verb structures given in (5) illustrate in more detail the morphological complexity typical of these kinds of languages:

(5) Bantu verb structure; obligatory components are bolded (Meeussen, 1967; Myers, 1987, 1997; Downing, 1999; Hyman, 2009)

a. Verb word

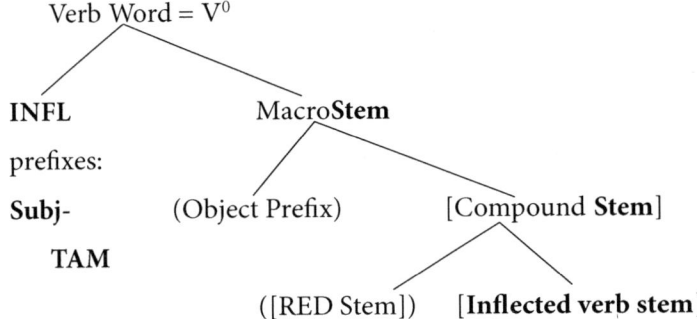

b. Inflected verb stem

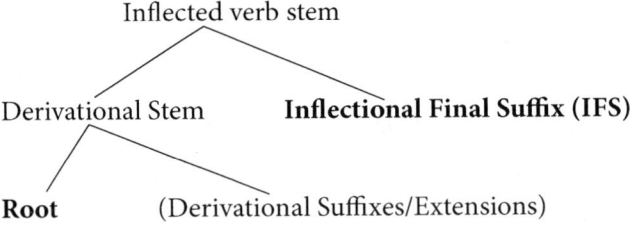

Morphologically, the Stem constituent recognized by Bantuists is defined as the word minus inflectional prefixes. This is a rather standard definition of stem: see, e.g., Bauer (2003), Bermudez-Otéro (2013), and Matthews (1991). Thus, in the Bantu verb structure in (5a), preverbal inflectional prefixes like Subject Agreement and Tense-Aspect-Mood (TAM) prefixes are not part of the

Stem. However, the Inflectional Final Suffix is traditionally included in the Stem.

Recent work in OT phonology like Kiparsky (2000) and Bermudez-Otéro (2011, 2012, 2013) explicitly proposes that a distinction between a stem vs. word domain (or stratum) is necessary to account for a wide range of phonological processes. For example, it is uncontroversial that many, if not most, languages have phonological processes that take some domain smaller than the morphological word, systematically excluding some affixes from the smaller domain. In many languages, we find the kinds of mismatches between the grammatical stem and the equivalent prosodic domain which motivate the Prosodic Stem as a distinct domain from the grammatical. The arguments for Prosodic Stem thus parallel those for the Prosodic Word.① We briefly review a couple of these arguments below.

2.2.1 Initial vowel extrametricality: [V (CV)]

As work like Hyman (2009) has demonstrated, the inflected verb stem in (5b) is the domain for verbal reduplication in most Bantu languages. This observation is reflected in the verb word structure in (5a), where the reduplicative morpheme forms a compound stem with the inflected verb stem. However, as Downing (1998a, 1998b) shows, it is rather common for (stem-)initial vowels to fail to reduplicate. (This is true not only in Bantu languages but also cross-linguistically.) The data from KiNande (Bantu D.41; Mutaka & Hyman, 1990), illustrate that with consonant-initial stems, the reduplicative morpheme copies the initial portion of the base stem. However, the stem-initial vowel is not reduplicated with the longer vowel-initial stems in (6c), and the reduplicative morpheme is infixed following the stem-initial vowel:

---

① See Inkelas (1989, 1993, 2014) for detailed conceptual arguments in favor of PStem.

(6) Kinande verbal reduplication (Mutaka & Hyman, 1990; Mutaka, 1994); *eri-* is the infinitive prefix; the reduplicant is underlined

Stem	Reduplicated Form	Gloss
a. *Consonant-initial*		
eri-huma	eri-<u>huma</u>=huma	to beat
eri-humira	eri-<u>huma</u>=humira	to beat for
eri-humirana	eri-<u>huma</u>=humirana	to beat for each other
b. *Monosyllabic*		
eri-swa	eri-<u>swa.swa</u>=swa	to grind
erí-ta	erí-<u>ta.ta</u>=ta	to bury
c. *Vowel-initial, infixing*		
ery-esera	ery-e=<u>sera</u>=sera	to play for
ery-óhera	ery-ó=<u>hera</u>=hera	to pick for
d. *Vowel-initial, prefixing*		
ery-esa	ery-<u>e.se.s</u>=e.sa	to play
ery-ôha	ery-<u>ó.ho.h</u>=o.ha	to pick

As Downing (1998a, 1998b, 1999) argues, this pattern of misalignment is best accounted for by proposing that initial vowels are not parsed into the PStem—e.g., [e (sera)]—allowing the PStem to begin with a well-formed onset-ful syllable. The reduplicative morpheme (RED) aligns with the PStem, not the grammatical stem, deriving infixation. Reduplication copies the PStem base.

2.2.2 Minimality

The forms in (6a) show that the reduplicative PStem is subject to a disyllabic maximality condition in Kinande. The forms in (6b) show that the reduplicative PStem is also subject to a disyllabic minimality constraint. In Kinande, this minimality constraint is satisfied by double reduplicating the base stem, leading to a mismatch between the base grammatical stem and the reduplicative PStem.

2.2.3 Left edge Onset requirement: (C [VCV...])

The requirement that the verb stem must begin with a well-formed onset-ful syllable is satisfied in other languages by epenthesizing an onset for the initial vowel. The Zezuru Shona infinitive form in (e) illustrates this strategy. An epenthesized palatal glide resolves vowel hiatus at the prefix-stem juncture, leading to misalignment between the PStem and the grammatical stem.

In the next section, we illustrate these kinds of misalignments at the word and stem level in detail with a case study of Chichewa prosody.

3 Prosodic Word and Prosodic Stem in Chichewa: a case study

This section builds on previous studies on prosodic domains for phonological processes in Chichewa, such as Downing & Mtenje (to appear), Hyman & Mtenje (1999), Kanerva (1990), Mchombo (1993), Moto (1989) and Mtenje (1988). As we shall see, Chichewa phonology provides evidence for two prosodic domains, Prosodic Word and Prosodic Stem, which roughly match grammatical word and grammatical stem but are sometimes misaligned with them.

3.1 Evidence for Prosodic Word

Kanerva (1990) provides several arguments in favor of a Prosodic Word (PWord) domain, distinct from grammatical word, in Chichewa. First, in Chichewa, as in Zezuru Shona, imperative verbs are subject to a minimality requirement.① The evidence is identical to Zezuru Shona: subminimal verb stems are augmented with an *i*- in the imperative which does not occur in the infinitive; note that penult vowels are predictably lengthened in Chichewa:

(7) Imperative verbs (Kanerva, 1990: 42ff)
   a. Stems with more than one syllable

Imperative	*Gloss*	*cf. Infinitive*
viina	'dance'	ku-víina
goóná	'sleep'	ku-góona
lemeérá	'get heavy'	ku-léméérá
yasamuula	'yawn'	ku-yásámuula

   b. Monosyllabic stems

ii-ba	'steal'	kuú-bá
ii-dya	'eat'	kuú-dyá
ii-gwa	'fall'	kuú-gwá
ii-mwa	'drink'	kuú-mwá

Again, it is instructive to compare imperative forms with an epenthetic *i*- with the imperative of verb stems like those in (8), which begin with non-epenthetic *i*-. As in Zezuru Shona, these verbs retain the initial vowel in the infinitive form, and a palatal glide – *y* – is inserted before the stem-initial vowel to resolve vowel hiatus:

---

① It is a matter of current debate how best to account for disyllabic minimality requirements like the one holding in Chichewa imperatives. Work like Kanerva (1990), McCarthy (2000) and McCarthy & Prince (1986) argues that minimality requirements are foot-based. However, a body of work has pointed out that the correlation between metrical foot size and minimal word size is very weak, cross-linguistically. See Downing (2006) and references therein for detailed discussion of this debate and of alternative proposals to account for word minimality requirements.

(8) Verb stems with an underlying initial *i*- (Kanerva, 1990: 43)

Imperative	Gloss	cf. Infinitive	
iika	'put'	ku-yíika	*kuú-ká
iima	'stand'	ku-yíima	
iimba	'sing'	ku-yíimba	
iwaálá	'forget'	ku-yíwáálá	

Surprisingly, the imperatives of monosyllabic stems do not lose the augmentative syllable when an enclitic, such as the 2nd person plural or =*nso*, is added to them, even though the enclitic alone would suffice to make the resulting output word form disyllabic:①

(9) Monosyllabic imperative verbs plus enclitics (Downing & Mtenje, to appear)
   a. i-phaa=ni 'kill, polite plural imperative'   *phaa=ni
   b. i-pháa=nso   'kill also, again, imperative'   *pháa=nso

Myers (1987) proposes for identical Zezuru Shona data that the augment is retained because the enclitics subcategorize for Prosodic Word, which, as we have just seen, is subject to a disyllabic minimality condition. These forms provide further evidence for PWord, since one must specify a minimal PWord, rather than a grammatical word, as the Base for cliticization.

The question now arises of what prosodic constituent the cliticized verbs in (9) are parsed into. Given the restricted set of prosodic constituents provided by the Prosodic Hierarchy in (1), the answer can only be that a word like *i-phaa=ni* forms a recursive Phonological Word: ((i-phaa)=ni). And, indeed, as Kanerva (1990) shows, there is tonal evidence in Chichewa that enclitics of different types have this prosodic parse. Three common enclitics— -*nso* 'even, also', -*di* 'indeed, truly, in fact' and -*tu* 'believe me, for sure, really'—contribute a High tone to

---

① The same facts hold for Zezuru Shona, as Myers (1987) shows, and for Swati, as Downing (1999) demonstrates. That is, imperatives of monosyllabic stems retain their minimality-motivated augment in these languages when certain clitics are added to them.

their host, which can be either a noun or a verb.① The High tone contributed by the enclitic does not surface on the enclitic itself, but rather surfaces on the preceding (penultimate) syllable:

(10) Toneless imperatives with High-toned enclitics (Downing & Mtenje, to appear)

  a. piita   'go'   pitáa=nso   'go again'
  b. yiimba   'sing'   yimbáa=di   'sing indeed'
  c. sangalaala   'rejoice'   sangalaláa=nso   'rejoice again'
  d. samaala   'take care'   samaláa=di   'take care indeed'

(11) Toneless nouns with High-toned enclitics (adapted, Kanerva, 1990: 152)

  a. nyaama   'meat'   nyamáa=nso   'meat=also'
  b. ma-deengu   'baskets'   ma-dengúu=nso   'baskets=also'
  c. ci-pataala   'hospital'   ci-pataláa=nso   'hospital=also'
  d. phiili   'mountain'   pilíi=di   'mountain=indeed'
  e. m̩-leenje   'hunter'   m̩-lenjée=di   'hunter=truly'
  f. nthiwatiiwa   'ostrich'   nthiwatiwáa=di   'ostrich=indeed'

However, when a High-toned enclitic is added to a noun with a High tone on its penult, such as *mfúumu* 'chief', the High tone of the enclitic does not surface on the penult of the encliticized form. If the enclitic's High tone were to be assigned to the penult of the encliticized form, an H-H sequence would be created—e.g., *mfúmú=nso* 'chief also'—yielding an OCP violation. In this case, as Moto (1989) and Kanerva (1990) show, the OCP violation is resolved by associating the enclitic's High tone with the enclitic itself (the final syllable of the form), as illustrated in the examples below:

---

① See Moto (1989: chapter 5) for a thorough discussion of the tonal properties of various enclitics in Chichewa.

(12) Examples of TONE SHIFT when enclitic is added to noun with penult High tone (adapted, Kanerva, 1990: 156)

    a. m-fúumu   'chief'   m-fúmúú=nsó

    b. ci-páatso   'fruit'   ci-pátsóó=nsó

    c. nkhúuku   'chicken'   nkhúkúú=dí

    d. mi-káango   'lions'   mi-kángóó=dí

Hyman & Mtenje's (1999b: 100) formulation of this process, which shifts (or 'bumps,' in their terms) a High tone from its usual association site, the penult, to the final syllable to avoid an H-H sequence, is given below:

(13) LOCAL TONE SHIFT (Hyman & Mtenje, 1999b: 100)

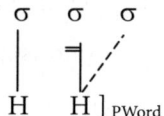

To illustrate:

(14)

    a. Input to TONE SHIFT: mfúmú=nso

    b. Local TONE SHIFT: mfúmu=nsó

    c. Output pronunciation: mfúmúú=nsó

    due to Penult lengthening and other tone processes; see section 5

As Kanerva (1990: 180, 181) shows, TONE SHIFT takes the Prosodic Word as its domain. First, as we have seen, "penult" and "final" refer to positions with the Prosodic Word, not the grammatical word, since an enclitic can be a target for "shifted" High tone. Furthermore, TONE SHIFT is Prosodic Word bound: encliticized forms with a High tone on the antepenult and penult have the same output tone pattern as uncontroversially word-internal sequences with the same input tone pattern. This is illustrated by the verbs in (15): a High tone lexically associated with the penult surfaces on the final syllable due to TONE SHIFT:

(15) Word-internal TONE SHIFT (adapted, Kanerva, 1990: sec. 6.2.1, 6.2.2); lexical High tone positions are underlined
a. a-dzá-chíí-bá   'S/he will steal it (cl.7).'
b. ndi-ná-chíí-dyá 'I ate it (cl.7).'

In contrast, TONE SHIFT does not apply across word boundaries in uncontroversially phrasal sequences such as those in (16) with the same input tone pattern: i.e., a High tone on the antepenult and High tone on the penult. Note we find a falling tone on the penultimate syllable of these phrases rather than a High tone on the final vowel, as we would expect if TONE SHIFT had applied (cf. the forms in (12) and in (15)):

(16) TONE SHIFT fails to apply across Prosodic Word boundaries (adapted, Kanerva, 1990); underlying High tone positions are underlined
a. ndí njúuchi   'by bees'   *ndí njúúchí
b. ti-tseké ndéege 'We should open the airplane.' *ti-tseké ndéégé

In sum, evidence for PWord (as opposed to grammatical word) in Chichewa comes from two sources of misalignment: to satisfy minimality and through cliticization.

3.2 Evidence for Prosodic Stem

To motivate Prosodic Stem (PStem) for any language, one must demonstrate, first, that some stem-external affixes are not included in the domain of some phonological processes, showing that the word and the stem are distinct phonological domains. Further, one must demonstrate that the grammatical stem is subject to prosodic well-formedness constraints that lead to misalignment with a PStem domain. The next two sections take up these arguments in turn.

3.2.1 Phonological processes that take stem (not word) as their domain

Verbal reduplication in Chichewa, as in Kinande (6) and most other Bantu languages (Hyman, 2009), takes the verb stem as its Base. Prefixes are not reduplicated. Reduplication expresses frequency or intensity of the action or state of the base verb, and it can also have the distributive meaning of doing the action "here and there." Unlike Kinande, there is no maximality condition on the reduplicative morpheme. As shown by the data below, the entire verb stem can be reduplicated, no matter how long it is:①

(17) Verbal reduplication in the remote past paradigm (adapted, Hyman & Mtenje, 1999b: 108; Moto, 1989: 278ff); '=' indicates the stem; the reduplicative morpheme is underlined②

    a. Low-toned stems

tí-náa=phá	tí-náa=phá-<u>íípha</u>	'we killed'
tí-náa=méenya	tí-náa=ményá-<u>meényá</u>	'we hit'
tí-náa=thandíiza	tí-náa=thandízá-<u>thandíiza</u>	'we helped'
tí-náa=vundikíila	tí-náa=vundikílá-<u>vundikíila</u>	'we covered'
tí-náa=fotokozéela	tí-náa=fotokozélá-<u>fotokozéela</u>	"we explained to'

    b. High-toned stems

tí-náa=péeza	tí-náa=pézá-<u>peézá</u>	'we found'
tí-náa=namíiza	tí-náa=namízá-<u>namíiza</u>	'we deceived'
tí-náa=thamangíila	tí-náa=thamangílá-<u>thamangíila</u>	'we ran to'
tí-náa=khululukíila	tí-náa=khululukílá-<u>khululukíila</u>	'we pardoned; forgave'

---

① See Hyman & Mtenje (1999b), Kanerva (1990: 48ff), Moto (1989: chapter 6), Mtenje (1988) and Myers & Carleton (1996) for detailed discussion and analysis of Chichewa reduplication.

② The data is adapted in order to indicate the surface, isolation pronunciation of words, including predictable phrase penult lengthening and its effect on the tone patterns.

Reduplication of monosyllabic verb stems like *-pha* 'give' emphasize that only the verb stem is the base for reduplication. As we can see, the reduplicative morpheme is subject to a disyllabic minimality condition. This condition is satisfied by augmenting the reduplicant with *i-*, not by copying prefixes outside the stem. (Recall, it is the prefixes which allow the verb word containing the base stem to satisfy disyllabic minimality.)

Vowel height harmony is another common Bantu phonological process that takes the stem (not the entire verb word) as its domain. Hyman's (1999) survey demonstrates that "canonical" Bantu VHH has the following characteristic properties:

(18) "Canonical" Bantu VHH (Hyman, 1999: 238)

    a. *Morphological conditioning*:

- It does not apply to the final vowel.
- It does not apply to prefixes.

That is, it applies roughly within the derivational stem (bolded):

[[Prefixes] [[**Root+Derivational Suffixes**] FV]; cf. (5b)

    b. *Front-back asymmetry*:

- Front vowel suffixes harmonize to both mid vowels, *e, o*;
- Back vowel suffixes harmonize only to the back mid vowel, *o*.

    c. *The low vowel a is also asymmetric*:

- It does not trigger harmony: like the high root vowels, it is followed by high vowels, not mid ones, for alternating suffixes.
- It is also opaque: it does not undergo harmony and blocks the spread of harmony.

Chichewa has all the properties of "canonical" Bantu VHH, as is well documented in work such as Kanerva (1990), Moto (1989), Mtenje (1985, 1986). What is relevant for our purposes is the morphological conditioning on the process: vowel harmony applies within the verb stem; it does not apply to prefixes. This is illustrated by the data below (cited from Downing & Mtenje, to appear). In comparing the data in (19a) vs. (19b), notice that the vowel of the infinitive prefix *ku-* is always [+high]; it does not harmonize with the root. However, the applicative suffix *-il-/-el-*, contained within the stem, does undergo harmony to agree with the root vowel:

(19)

a. Peripheral root vowels—i, u, a—are followed by peripheral suffix vowels

Applicative

ku=phíika	'to cook'	ku=phíkiila	'to cook for'
ku=túuma	'to send'	ku=túmiila	'to send for someone's benefit'
ku=gáawa	'to divide'	ku=gáwiila	'to share out; distribute'
ku=khúuta	'to be satisfied'	ku=khútiila	'to be satisfied with'
ku=líima	'to cultivate'	ku=límiila	'to farm for'
ku=váala	'to get dressed'	ku=váliila	'to put on'

b. Mid root vowels—e, o—are followed by mid suffix vowels

Applicative

ku=kóoka	'to pull out'	ku=kókeela	'to pull out for'
ku=tséeka	'to close'	ku=tsékeela	'to close for'
ku=méenya	'to hit'	ku=ményeela	'to hit someone with'
ku=góona	'to sleep'	ku=gónéélá	'to sleep on something'

Further, the subjunctive verbal final vowel suffix *-é* is always mid, no matter what vowel precedes (Mtenje, 1986: 113-114):

(20) Final vowels are outside the harmony domain

mu=won-eédw-é 'you should be seen (subjunctive)'   ti=namizaán-é 'we should deceive each other (subjunctive)'

	ndi=khululuk-iík-é	'I should be pardonable (subjunctive)'		
liimb-a		'be tough (imperative)'	mu=liímb-é	'you should be tough (subjunctive)'

In sum, one must be able to refer to a stem domain, distinct from the word, to define the context of reduplication and vowel harmony. Both processes ignore prefixes to the stem, even though the prefixes are part of the grammatical verb word. (We set aside here the complication that vowel harmony ignores final vowel suffixes, whereas these suffixes are copied in reduplication.)

3.2.2 Prosodic misalignment of PStem and grammatical stem

In Chichewa, as in other Bantu languages, vowel initial stems provide the context for processes to apply which lead to misalignment between PStem and the grammatical stem. The reason for this is that sequences of vowels in separate syllables are not found in Chichewa. Vowel sequences that arise across morpheme boundaries must be resolved by various morphologically-conditioned vowel hiatus resolution processes.① The relevant morphological domains for hiatus resolution are schematized below:

(21) Verb structure relevant for vowel hiatus resolution②

[$_{INFL}$SBJ - NEG2 - TAM = [$_{MACROSTEM}$ OM [$_{STEM}$ Root - extensions-FV]]

---

① Interestingly, both the morphological generalizations and the processes found to resolve hiatus are essentially identical to those described for Zezuru Shona by Myers (1987), Mudzingwa (2010) and Mudzingwa & Kadenge (2011). See Downing & Mtenje (to appear) for more detailed discussion and exemplification of vowel hiatus resolution strategies in Chichewa.

② The macro-stem is a Bantuist term for the constituent which comprises the object prefix (OM) and the verb stem.

One set of vowel hiatus resolution strategies applies within the inflectional prefix string: i.e., subject prefix, NEG2 and tense/aspect/mood prefixes (TAMs). Another set applies at the macro-stem and stem junctures and at the juncture between the word-initial negative prefix (NEG1) and a following subject marker. However, vowel hiatus is not resolved between words. Each of these contexts is illustrated below.

When vowel hiatus occurs between a CV subject marker and a vowel-initial TAM prefix, the first vowel deletes (unless it is a high, back vowel, which undergoes gliding). This process is illustrated by the data in (22):

(22)
    a. ti-a-bweél-á →ta-bweél-á   'we have come'
    we-PERF-come-FV
    cf. ti-ku-bwéel-a   'we are coming'
    b. ndi-a-lot-a → nda-loot-a   'I have dreamt'
    I-PERF-dream-FV
    cf. ndi-ná-loot-a   'I dreamt'
    c. a-a-dula →a-duula   'they have cut'
    cf. a-ku-dúula   'they are cutting'
    d. mu-a-gon-a →mwagoóná   'you have slept'
    e. mu-a-pit-a → mwapiita   'you have gone'

A different strategy for resolving vowel hiatus is found in the prefix=(macro)stem context, namely, a glide is inserted between the two vowels, thus preserving both the prefix vowel and the stem vowel and leading to misalignment between the grammatical (macro)stem and the prosodically well-formed PStem; inserted glides are bolded:

(23)
    ku= [imb-a →   kuyíimba   'to sing'

ku= [on-a →	kuwóona	'to see'
ku= [im-a →	kuyíima	'to stop'
ti= [end-e →	tiyeéndé	'let us walk'
ti= [imb-e →	tiyiímbé	'let us sing'
mu= [uluk-e →	muwuluúké	'you (pl.) should fly'
mu-a= [imb-a →	mwayiimba	'you have sung'
mu= [imb-a →	múyiimba	'you will soon sing'
ndi-ø-[a= [on-a →	ndíwáwoona	'I will soon see them (cl.6)'
	OR ndáawoona①	
ndi-a= [i-[on-a →	ndayíwoona	'I have seen it (cl.9)'
ndi-sa= [i-[on-e →	ndisayiwóone	'we should not see it (cl.9)'

Vowel hiatus is not resolved across word boundaries involving main lexical categories (i.e., XPs like nouns and verbs), whether by vowel deletion or by glide epenthesis, as illustrated by the data below:

(24)

a. *No vowel deletion*

mwaná a-kuú-dyá	*mwan' akudya	'the child is eating'
galú a-ná-thaaw-a	*gal' anathawa	'the dog ran away'

b. *No glide epenthesis*

nkhúkú i-ku-thámáángá	*nkhuku yikuthamanga	'a chicken is running'
mbulí í-ma-nyáad-a	*mbuli yimanyada	'an ignorant person brags'

In sum, hiatus resolution is a word bound process. Word-internally, hiatus is morphologically-conditioned, with one strategy—glide epenthesis—applying at

---

① This example illustrates that in this context hiatus can be resolved in one of two ways: either a glide is inserted before both the object marker and the stem OR vowel assimilation applies between the subject marker and the object marker.

主编 冯

陈曙东

黄正德

a Luisa Zubizarreta

健

the left edge of the (macro-)stem, and another strategy applying outside of this context. Thus, it provides further evidence for the stem as a phonological domain. Furthermore, glide epenthesis creates a prosodically well-formed PStem constituent, which is misaligned with the grammatical stem.

3.3 Summary of the evidence for two domains

We have shown that minimality restrictions, TONE SHIFT, vowel hiatus resolution, vowel harmony and reduplication motivate two phonological domains in Chichewa, one roughly corresponding to the word, and one roughly corresponding to the stem. The resulting overall prosodic structure of (verb) words is represented below, where parentheses indicate the smaller of the two domains while curly brackets indicates the larger one:

(25) Prosodic domains motivated by the data
{Infl (OM (Stem))} clitic}

Let us briefly summarize the evidence for two distinct domains. First, a disyllabic minimality requirement holds of words but not of stems. Further, vowel hiatus resolution strategies are word bound, and a different strategy is found at the left edge of the (macro-)stem than between other affixes. Word and stem are thus subject to different prosodic well-formedness conditions, which lead to misalignment between prosodic word and stem and grammatical word and stem.

Word and stem are also domains for different phonological and prosodic processes. TONE SHIFT is a word bound process. While it applies across word-internal morphological boundaries, including within the maximal PWord formed by enclitization, TONE SHIFT does not apply across word boundaries. In contrast, reduplication and vowel harmony are stem-bound processes. Prefixes contained within the verb word (and PWord) are not included in their domain.

The table in (26) summarizes these differences between stem and word domain:

(26) Contrasting prosodic domains in Chichewa

Process/Domain	max { }	(OM (Stem))
Minimality	√ (2 syllables)	X
Glide Epenthesis (left edge)	X	√
TONE SHIFT	X (across Word boundaries)	√ (across Stem boundaries)
Base for reduplication	X	√
Domain of vowel harmony	X	√

4 Labelling the domains

4.1 Why the two domains are best labelled PStem vs. PWord

I propose that it is best to label these two domains PWord – { } – vs. PStem – ( ) – as shown in (27). Note that the representation allows for some recursion, following standard practice since Inkelas (1989) in defining clitics as adjoined to PWord (i.e., recursively phrased with PWord to create a maxPWord). Similarly, Object Markers (OM) are clitics to PStem (i.e., recursively phrased with PStem to create a maxPStem):

(27) {$_{maxPWord}$ {$_{minPWord}$SBJ-TAM- ($_{maxPStem}$ OM ($_{minPStem}$ Stem))} clitic}

One argument in favor of this labelling is that it follows work like Inkelas (1989 ff), Kiparsky (2000) and Bermudez-Otéro (2011, 2012, 2013) in recognizing, to quote Kiparsky (2000: 362):

"The categories 'stem' and 'word' are special in being anchored in the universal prosodic hierarchy, their status in UG is comparable to the status of such categories as 'noun' and 'verb.'"

Indeed, the work cited in section 2.2 shows the broad cross-linguistic applicability of the PStem-PWord distinction. Furthermore, this labelling is transparent, respecting the requirement that the labeling of a prosodic domain should, all things being equal, match the label of the corresponding morpho-syntactic constituent. (See, e.g., Inkelas, 1989, 1993; Itô & Mester, 2012, 2013; Selkirk, 2009, 2011.) Finally—and most importantly—this labelling does not have the empirical or conceptual problems faced by two leading alternative approaches.

4.2 Alternative 1: Recursive PWord

As noted in the introduction, recent work on the Prosodic Hierarchy (Itô & Mester, 2012, 2013; Riad, 2012; Selkirk, 2009, 2011) makes the strong claim that it comprises only three universal constituents: Intonational Phrase, Phonological Phrase and Prosodic Word. (See (1), above.) In this framework, the Stem vs. Word domain distinction in Chichewa must be recast as a recursion of one of these constituents, most plausibly PWord. That is, this analysis would follow work like McCarthy (2000) in proposing Stem is parsed as the minProsodic Word. Other word-internal morphemes—like the object prefix (OM), tense/aspect/mood prefixes (TAM) and the subject prefix—are presumably parsed as non-maximal recursions of PWord. Clitics would be parsed into a maxProsodic Word. This alternative is formalized in the representation below, where ')' indicates PWord edges:

(28) Recursive PWords:($_{maxPWord}$ SBJ-(?TAM- (OM ($_{minPWord}$ Stem))) clitic)

That is, instead of defining two different prosodic domains, stem and word must be defined as recursive instantiations of the same prosodic domain type to achieve parsimony. This is the advantage of the approach.

However, the approach faces the disadvantage of suffering from both empirical and conceptual problems. First, it seems paradoxical to categorize Stem as a minPWord, when stem is not subject to a minimality constraint. This contradicts the usual definition of a minimal Prosodic Word. (See McCarthy & Prince, 1986 and much subsequent work.) Furthermore, the recursive PWord parse cannot account for why the innermost recursion of PWord—the constituent corresponding to the Macro-Stem domain—has distinct phonological properties: glide epenthesis applies at this edge but not at the edge of the other recursions of PWord, including the maximal PWord. 'First recursion of PWord' has no status as prosodic domain in this theory. The recursive PWord approach also cannot account for why inflectional prefixes count towards satisfying PWord minimality, whereas clitics do not. This is because it is not clear how to formalize the generalization that clitics subcategorize for a minimal PWord, whereas prefixes subcategorize for the stem (or PStem). As we have already noted, the minimal PWord parses the stem in this approach, yet the stem is not subject to disyllabic minimality.

In addition, the recursive PWord approach faces a serious conceptual problem. As Vigário (2010) and Vogel (2009, 2010) argue, recursive instantiations of the same prosodic constituent should, by definition, have the same prosodic properties. To quote Vogel (2010: 151):

" […] since constituents in linguistics are defined by a specific set of properties, if all of the strings in question are labeled as the same type of constituent, the expectation is that they will all behave in the same way phonologically."

However, as the table in (26) makes clear, the two domains have distinct phonological properties in Chichewa. Vigario (2010), Frota & Vigario (2013) and Vogel (2009, 2010) discuss in detail other problems with using recursion to give phonologically distinct domains similar labels in the name of parsimony.

In sum, even though their names partially overlap, we have established that minPWord and maxPWord in (28) are phonologically distinct. For this reason, it is not clear that the definition of recursion is met by a structure like the one in (28), which replaces PStem with minPWord. Even if this use of recursion were legitimate, it faces the empirical problem that it cannot identify phonologically significant word-internal morpheme boundaries, such as the one between the object prefix (OM) and the other prefixes, and it cannot distinguish clitics and prefixes. As a result, PWord recursion is not a viable strategy to replace the PStem vs. PWord domain distinction.

4.3 Alternative 2: Composite Word Group/Prosodic Word Group

Frota (2012), Frota & Vigário (2013), Kabak & Vogel (2001), Vogel (2009, 2010) and Vigário (2010) favor another definition of the Prosodic Hierarchy, based on studies of the phonology of compound-like and clitic-group like structures. They argue persuasively that these groupings should not be parsed as recursive Prosodic Words, but rather as a distinct prosodic constituent, called composite word group Vogel (2009, 2010) or prosodic word group Vigário (2010). One important argument in favor of this constituent is that many languages are like English in having special compound prosody (e.g., stress) that is distinct both from word stress and phrase stress: e.g., in American English: *I was stung by a yéllowjacket.* vs. *I love your yellow jácket.* Compound stress is at the left edge of a compound, but at the right edge of a phrase. Main stress at the word level also is at the right edge of a word, so one cannot properly define the domain of compound stress, if a compound is parsed as a recursion of prosodic word. The proposed revision of the Prosodic Hierarchy is given in (29):

(29) Adding CWG/PWG to the Prosodic Hierarchy

Intonation Phrase
|
Phonological Phrase
|
Composite Word Group
|
Phonological Word
|
~~Prosodic Stem~~

Both Vogel (2009, 2010) and Vigário (2010) suggest that Downing's (1999) PStem vs. PWord distinction (argued for on the basis of other Bantu languages) can be replaced by a PWord vs. Composite Word Group (or Prosodic Word Group) distinction. This suggestion is not worked out in detail by either author, though. I assume they would replace the representation in (27) with one like (30), which parses the Stem as a PWord and parses all prefixes and clitics into a Composite/Prosodic Word Group. Since these authors argue so strongly against the use of recursion, it is avoided in this representation:

(30) {$_{CWG}$SBJ-TAM- OM ($_{PWord}$ Stem) clitic}

This alternative approach has the advantage of respecting that a desire for parsimony should not lead to a misuse of recursive constituents. However, it faces the same empirical and conceptual problems in accounting for stem vs. word domains in Chichewa as the recursive PWord proposal. It seems paradoxical to categorize PStem as a PWord when it is not subject to a word minimality constraint. Further, this approach also does not distinguish object markers from other prefixes, nor does it distinguish clitics from affixes, even though, as we saw, these morpheme types have different phonological properties that are captured by the representation in (27). As a result, this approach is also not a viable alternative to one which appeals to a PStem vs. PWord distinction.

4.4 Interim summary

Chichewa data has been presented which motivates two constituents for phonological processes: stem vs. word. I follow earlier work like Inkelas (1989, 1993), Downing (1998a, 1998b, 1999, 2000, 2006), Mudzingwa (2010) and Downing & Kadenge (2015), among many others, in proposing that these two constituents are best categorized prosodically as PStem vs. PWord. Alternative labels and parsings have been shown to be empirically and conceptually inadequate.

Adding PStem to the Prosodic Hierarchy seems to go against the grain of Itô & Mester's (2012, 2013) and Selkirk's (2009, 2011) arguments in favor of being parsimonious with universal prosodic categories in the Prosodic Hierarchy. However, one might contend that it actually fits the spirit of their proposal. PStem is not a language-specific category. It has cross-linguistic validity because it is defined with respect to morphosyntactic structure. The Stem is an important sublexical morphological constituent in Bantu and other agglutinative languages. Further, it has been shown to account for phonological and prosodic processes in a number of unrelated languages. Indeed, Bermudez-Otéro (2013) identifies a cross-linguistic 'stem-level syndrome'. Adding PStem to the Prosodic Hierarchy allows phonological theory to better account for these phenomena.

5 Postlexical prosodic constituency

In this section, we turn to postlexical prosodic constituency in Chichewa and evaluate the number of levels in the Prosodic Hierarchy required to account for phrasal processes. Kanerva's (1990) original prosodic analysis of Chichewa argues for two levels of phrasing: Phonological Phrase and Intonation Phrase: the two phrasal constituents in (1). As we shall see, new data and new syntactic theories lead to a reconsideration of this proposal.

Kanerva (1990) and Bresnan & Kanerva (1989) demonstrate in some detail that lexical (and grammatical) High tone realization is conditioned by phonological processes which take the Phonological Phrase as their domain. Syntax is the main factor defining prosodic phrasing. In the analyses of Bresnan & Mchombo (1987) and Kanerva (1990), sentences have three main subconstituents—an optional subject noun phrase (NP), an obligatory verb phrase (VP), and an optional topic NP—which can be freely ordered. The VP consists of the verb and all its complements, as shown in (31a, 31d). According to these authors, each of the three constituents, when they co-occur, is parsed into its own Phonological Phrase. As shown in (30b) and (30c), topicalized NPs are in a distinct syntactic and prosodic phrase, and can occur in either order with respect to the VP. Phonological phrases are indicated with parentheses in the data below:[①]

(31)

    a. (Subj) (VP)—Kanerva (1990: 103, fig (114b))

    (mwaána)   (a-na-pézá   galú ku-dáambo)

    1.child   1SBJ-TAM-find 1.dog LOC-swamp

    'The child found the dog at the swamp.'

    b. (Subj) (VP) (Top)—(Kanerva, 1990: 107, fig (123b))

    (mwaána)   (a-na-ḿ -pézá   ku-dáambo)   (gaálu)

    1.child   1SBJ-TAM-1OBJ-find LOC-swamp 1.dog

    'The child found it at the swamp, the dog.'

    c. (Top) (VP) (Subj)—(Kanerva, 1990: 102, fig (110c))

    (a-leenje)   (zi-ná-wá-luuma)   (njúuchi)

---

① The following abbreviations are used in the morpheme glosses: numbers indicate noun agreement class; OBJ = object marker; SBJ = subject marker; TAM=tense-aspect marker; PERF = perfective; LOC = locative; REL = relative; COP = copula; INF = infinitive. Acute accents indicate High tone, and parentheses indicate prosodic phrasing.

2.hunter 10SBJ-SIMPLE.PAST-2OBJ-bite 10.bee
'The hunters, they bit them, the bees [did].'

d. (VP)—(Kanerva, 1990: 98, fig. (101))

(a-na-mény-á   nyumbá   ndí   mwáála)
1SBJ-RECENT.PAST-hit 9.house   with   3.rock
'S/he hit the house with a rock.'

Kanerva (1990) and Bresnan & Kanerva (1989) demonstrate that four phonological processes motivate the prosodic phrasing indicated in (31). First, the phrase penult vowel is lengthened. As noted above, Chichewa does not have contrastive vowel length, and penult lengthening is the only common vowel lengthening process in the language. While sequences of identical vowels arise across certain morpheme boundaries, all penult long vowels in the data are due to phrasal lengthening. Second, a High tone on a phrase-final vowel is retracted towards the penultimate mora. In the Nkhotakota variety (Kanerva, 1990), a High tone on a phrase-final vowel is completely retracted, as shown by the phrase-final tone pattern of the word for /galú/ 'dog' in (31b). In the Ntcheu variety (Downing & Mtenje, 2011a, 2011b), a phrase-final High tone is realized on both the penultimate and final moras: e.g., [gaálú] 'dog'. Third, within a prosodic phrase High tones double to the following syllable. However, the disyllabic window at the end of a prosodic phrase is a barrier to tone doubling. To see this, compare the tone pattern of /kálata/ 'letter' in phrase-medial (32b) vs. phrase-final (32a):

(32) Tone doubling blocked phrase finally (Downing & Mtenje, 2011a)

a. ((m-phunzitsi *a-méné* á-ná-kwiyá kwámbíiri) a-ná-wélengera
1-teacher   1-REL   1SBJ-TAM-be.angry very
1SBJ-TAM-read.to

aná   á súkúlú   kálaata)
2.child 2.of school 5.letter

'The teacher who was very angry read the students a letter.'

b. ((Káláta *i-méné* m-phunzitsi á-ná-weléenga) í-ma-néná m-fúumu)
5.letter 5-REL1-teacher 1SBJ-TAM-read 5SBJ-TAM-criticize 9-chief
'The letter which the teacher read criticizes the chief.'

There is one principled set of exceptions to the generalization that High tones do not double into the disyllabic phrase-final window, namely a process of High tone plateauing. A High tone can double into the phrase-final disyllabic window if it is followed by another High tone. This is illustrated by the phrase *[ndí mwáála]* 'with a rock' in (31d), where the High tone of the preposition *ndí* doubles onto the phrase-penult vowel, forming a High tone plateau with the (retracted) final High tone of /*mwalá*/ 'rock'. As Kisseberth & Odden (2003) show, High tone plateauing, tone doubling and avoidance of High tones on final vowels are, in fact, common tonal processes cross-Bantu.

Kanerva's (1990) prosodic analysis of Chichewa argues for two levels of phrasing: the Phonological Phrase is the domain of penult lengthening and tone processes, illustrated just above. The Intonation Phrase is the domain of culminative penult lengthening and downstep (= catathesis in Kanerva's terms). Kanerva, as was typical of his time, does not provide phonetic details of these correlates of the Intonation Phrase, but subsequent work confirms his observations. Myers' (1996, 1999) careful phonetic study provides an analysis of downstep in Chichewa sentences. Downing & Pompino-Marschall's (2013) phonetic analysis demonstrates that the penult vowel of an Intonation Phrase-final word is significantly longer than sentence-internal lengthened penults.

However, later work on the language has also led to some new generalizations about phrasing. Downing & Mtenje (2011a, 2011b) find that the subject NP is only variably followed by a prosodic phrase boundary. This variation in the phrasing of subjects is illustrated in the data below, where we see that the subject is not phrased separately in (33a), but it is in (33b):

(33)

    a. (Ma-kóló a-na-pátsíra mwaná ndalámá zá mú-longo wáake)
       6-parent 6SBJ-RECENT.PAST-give 1.child   10.money   10.of
       1-sister   1.her
       'The parents gave the child money for her sister.'

    b. (M-fúumu) (i-na-pátsá   mwaná   zóóváala)
       9-chief   9SBJ-RECENT.PAST-give 1.child   10.clothes
       'The chief gave the child clothes.'

As Downing & Mtenje (2011a, 2011b) and Cheng & Downing (2009, 2016) argue, a prosodic phrase boundary following the subject correlates with topicalization.

Moreover, it is not always true that all postverbal complements phrase with the verb. In relatively simple VPs, like those in (31), we do find that a verb and more than one following complement phrase together. In fact, this phrasing is the essential problem to be accounted for in any analysis of Chichewa. The Phonological Phrase which includes the VP is larger than we expect because there is no phrase break following the first XP complement of the verb. (Recall from (1), above, that a Phonological Phrase matches an XP.) The prosodic algorithm must therefore optimize a Phonological Phrase break setting off subject and topic noun phrases, yet it must not optimize a Phonological Phrase break following noun phrases internal to the verb phrase. Truckenbrodt's (1995, 1999) well-known WRAP constraint is a mechanism for achieving this. WRAP penalizes breaking the verb phrase into more than one Phonological Phrase.

Downing & Mtenje (2011a, 2011b) show, however, that WRAP predicts the incorrect phrasing when the first complement of a verb is modified by a relative clause. The verb plus the modified first complement plus a following complement should be WRAP-ed into a single Phonological Phrase. What we find instead is a prosodic phrase break following the relative clause.

(34) Phrasing of relative clauses violates WRAP; relative clause is underlined (Downing & Mtenje, 2011b)

a. ((Ma-kóló a-na-pátsíra <u>mwaná a-méné</u>
6.parent 6SBJ-TAM-give 1.child 1-REL

<u>á-ná-wa-chezéera</u>) ndalámá zá mú-longo wáake)
1SBJ-TAM-6OBJ-visit 10.money 10.of 1-sister 1.her

'The parents gave [the child who visited them] money for her sister.'

cf.

b. (Ma-kóló a-na-pátsíra mwaná ndalámá zá
6.parent 6SBJ-PST1-give 1.child 10.money 10.of

mú-longo wáake)
1-sister 1.her

'The parents gave the child money for her sister.'

c. (Ti-ku-gáníza kutí m-nyamatá á-pézá <u>galú</u>
we-TAM-think that 1-boy 1SBJ.TAM-find 1.dog

<u>a-méné á-ná-mu-sowéetsa</u>) ku dáambo)
1-REL 1SBJ-TAM-1OBJ-lose LOC 5.swamp

'We think the boy will find [the dog which he lost] at the swamp.'

cf.

d. (Subj) (VP) Kanerva (1990: 103, fig (114b))

(Mwaána) (a-na-pézá galú ku dáambo))
1.child 1SBJ-PST1-find 1.dog LOC 5.swamp

'The child found the dog at the swamp.'

Kanerva (1990) and Downing & Mtenje (2011a, 2011b) show that while all embedded complement clauses, including *think/say* clauses, phrase with what precedes in Chichewa, a break comes at the end of the most deeply embedded clause:

(35) Embedded and recursive clauses (underlined) (Downing & Mtenje, 2011a, 2011b)

a. (Mu-nthu <u>a-méné á-ná-bweréká búkhú</u>
1-man 1-REL 1SBJ-TAM-borrow 5.book
<u>li-méné ndí-ná-gulá ku Liloongwe</u>) w-a-pita ku Mzúuzu)
5-REL I-TAM-buy LOC Lilongwe 1SBJ-TAM-leave LOC Mzuzu
'The man who borrowed the book which I bought in Lilongwe has moved to Mzuzu.'

b. (Mu-nthu <u>a-méné á-ná-néná</u> kutí <u>m-balá</u>
1-man 1-REL 1SBJ-TAM-say that 9-thief
<u>i-ná-bá ndaláama</u>) a-ná-thaawa)
9SBJ-TAM-steal 10.money 2SBJ-TAM-run.away
'The man who said that the thief stole some money ran away.'

c. (Mu-nthu a-na-néná kutí m-balá <u>i-méné</u>
1-man 1SBJ-TAM-say that 9-thief 9-REL
<u>í-ná-bá ndaláama</u>) i-na-tháawa)
9SBJ-TAM-steal 10.money 9SBJ-TAM-run.away
'The man said that the thief who stole the money ran away.'

This range of data shows that prosodic phrases can be quite large in Chichewa, as they typically right-align with clauses (phases), rather than XPs, like noun phrases.

Based on this generalization, Chichewa prosodic phrases are best characterized as Intonation Phrases, since, by definition, this is the level of prosodic phrasing that aligns with the syntactic clause. Another motivation for identifying this prosodic constituent as an Intonation Phrase is that boundary tones often coincide with the right edge, as is expected for Intonation Phrases. For example, we find a continuation rise at the right edge of a relative clause, as illustrated in (36). Note in (36) that the words which end each of the Intonation Phrases— *kusáamba* 'swim' and *mtsíinje* 'river'—ave the same tone pattern: a HL on the lengthened penult syllable. But the final vowel of *kusáamba* rises in pitch, while the final vowel of *mtsíinje* falls in pitch due to the effect of intonational boundary tones. Notice, too, that High tones undergo downdrift, with the final High-toned string considerably lowered in pitch, typically barely rising above the level of a preceding Low tone:

(36)

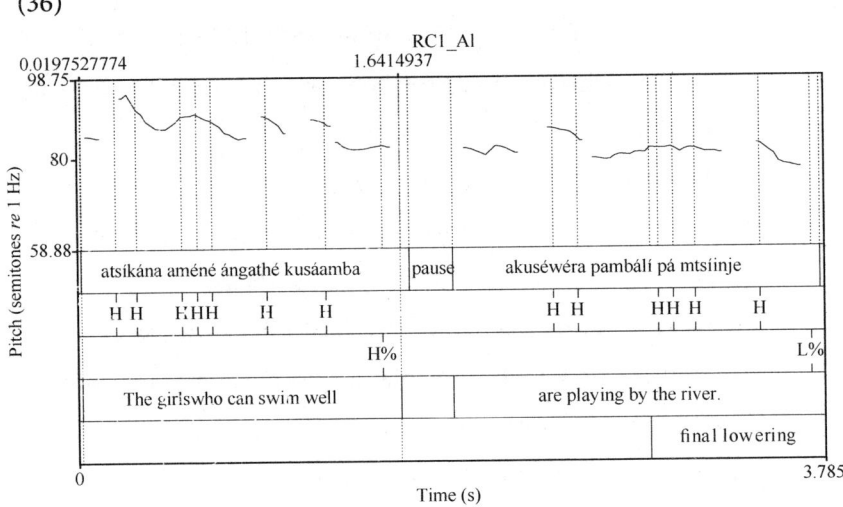

We also typically find a continuation rise following an initial Topic (in this case, a topicalized subject):

(37)

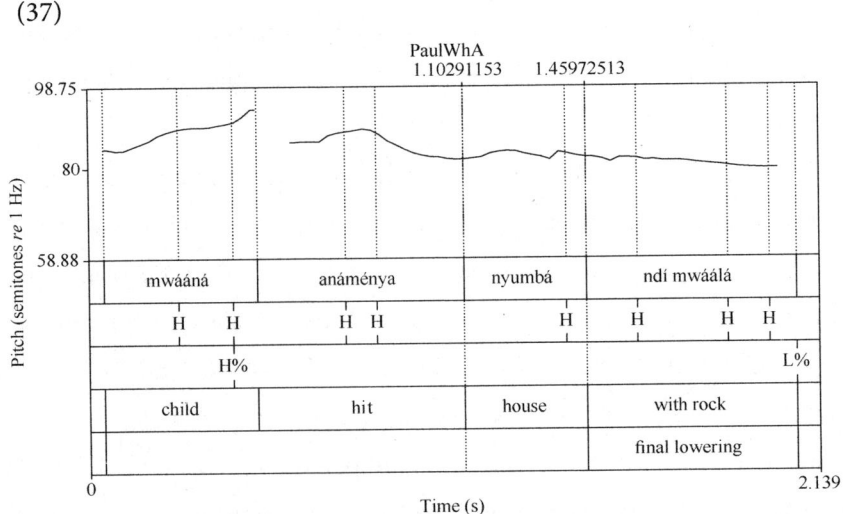

To sum up, there is no strong evidence for a distinction between Intonation Phrase and Phonological Phrase in Chichewa. Prosodic phrasing only seems to motivate an Intonation Phrase level, as phrasing targets clause edges and right edges of initial Topics. How then, can we define the domain for downstep and culminative penult lengthening, the correlates of Kanerva's (1990) Intonation Phrase? Following work like Itô & Mester (2012, 2013) and Selkirk (2009, 2011), I appeal to recursive levels of phrasing to maintain a parsimonious analysis. Adopting this view, Chichewa has recursive Intonation Phrasing and distinguishes a minimal and maximal Intonation Phrase. The minimal Intonation Phrase replaces the Phonological Phrase of earlier analyses, while the maximal Intonation Phrase replaces the Intonation Phrase.

6 Conclusion

In this article, arguments have been presented that the following recursive levels of the Prosodic Hierarchy are relevant to an analysis of Chichewa phonology:

(38) Levels of the Prosodic Hierarchy relevant for Chichewa
Intonation Phrase
|
Phonological Word
|
Prosodic Stem

Two differences can be noted from the standard Prosodic Hierarchy in (1), defended in recent work like Selkirk (2009, 2011) and Itô & Mester (2012, 2013). First, Chichewa requires reference to one fewer phrasal domain than is provided by the standard hierarchy, since Phonological Phrase plays no role in the language. Second, Chichewa requires reference to one more lexical domain than is provided by the standard hierarchy, since Phonological Word and Prosodic Stem are distinct phonological domains.

The analysis thus challenges the universality of the Prosodic Hierarchy in (1) in two ways. First, the set of prosodic constituents in the Hierarchy in (1) has been shown to be too parsimonious. While it might be sufficient to account for phonological processes at the phonology-syntax interface, the distinction between stem and word level phonology—widely attested in the world's languages—argues for an additional prosodic level to account for the interface between the phonological and morphological components of the grammar.① Second, the analysis questions whether the levels of the Prosodic Hierarchy are universally instantiated, since Phonological Phrase plays no role in Chichewa phonology. If the realization of the constituents in the Prosodic Hierarchy is mediated by Optimality Theoretic constraints, we actually do not expect constituents at all of the levels to be instantiated in every language. A prosodic constituent will only be found if the language provides overt phonological evidence for it. As Cheng & Downing (2016) argue, if there is no evidence, then the high-ranked constraint in (39) banning the insertion of prosodic structure without prosodic motivation, a variant of the general *STRUC(TURE) constraint (Prince & Smolensky, 2004: 30, fn 13), penalizes parsing a phonological string into that prosodic constituent type:

(39) *STRUC/PROSODY: Prosodic domain structure must have prosodic motivation.

So we end the paper still striving for a balance between a parsimonious theory and an empirically adequate theory of prosodic interface constituents. Em-

---

① Frota (2012), Frota & Vigário (2013), Kabak & Vogel (2001), Vogel (2009, 2010) and Vigário (2010) provide compelling arguments for adding the Composite Word Group or equivalent to the Prosodic Hierarchy. It is not discussed here, as Chichewa does not seem to provide evidence for this level.

pirical evidence clearly argues for more prosodic constituents than the three given in (1). However, Itô & Mester (2012, 2013) correctly caution against adding more constituents on a language-by-language basis. We want to be equally cautious about insisting that all constituents are realized in every language whether there is phonological evidence for them or not. This paper argues for a middle path: adding prosodic constituents to the Hierarchy only if they have morpho-syntactic correlates and are widely attested in the world's languages. And invoking, in an analysis, only the constituents for which phonological evidence can be provided. It is a matter for future research to determine whether the choice of levels relevant for a particular language falls out form independently-motivated syntactic or prosodic properties of the language.

References

Bermudez-Otéro, R. 2011. Cyclicity. In M. van Oostendorp, C. Ewen, E. Hume & K. Rice (Eds.), *The Blackwell companion to phonology,* vol. 4 (pp. 2019-2048). Malden, MA: Wiley-Blackwell.

Bermudez-Otéro, R. 2012. The architecture of grammar and the division of labor in exponence. In J. Trommer (Ed.), *The Morphology and Phonology of Exponence* (pp. 8-83). Oxford: Oxford University Press.

Bermudez-Otéro, R. 2013. The stem-level syndrome. UPenn Linguistics Dept. Speaker Series talk, 11 April 2013. Cassimjee, F. 1994. *Isixhosa Tonology.* Munich: Lincom Europa.

Bermudez-Otéro, R. & Luís, A. R. 2009. Cyclic domains and prosodic spans in the phonology of European Portuguese functional morphs. Talk presented at OCP6, Edinburgh, 24 Jan. 2009.

Bresnan, J. & Kanerva, J. 1989. Locative inversion in Chichewa: A case study of factorization in grammar. *Linguistic Inquiry*, 20: 1-50.

Bresnan, J. & Mchombo, S. 1987. Topic, pronoun and agreement in Chichewa. *Language, 63*: 741-782.

Cassimjee, F. & Kisseberth, C. W. 1998. Optimal Domains Theory and Bantu Tonology: A Case Study from Isixhosa and Shingazidja. In L. Hyman & C. Kisseberth (Eds.), *Theoretical Aspects of Bantu Tone* (pp. 33-132). Stanford: CSLI.

Cheng, L. L.-S. & Downing, L. J. 2009. Where's the topic in Zulu? In H. de Hoop & G. van

Bergen (Eds.), *The Linguistic Review* (Special Issue on *Topics Cross-linguistically*), *26*: 207-238.

Cheng, L. L.-S. & Downing, L. J. 2016. Phasal syntax = cyclic phonology? *Syntax*, *19*: 156-191.

Czaykowska-Higgins, E. 1996. *What's in a Word? Word Structure in Moses-Columbia Salish (Nxaʔamxcin)*. Winnipeg: Voices of Rupert's Land.

Czaykowska-Higgins, E. 1998. The morphological and phonological constituent structure of words in Moses-Columbia Salish (Nxaʔamxcin). In E. Czaykowska- Higgins & M. D. Kinkade (Eds.), *Salish Languages and Linguistics: Theoretical and Descriptive Perspectives* (pp. 153-195). Berlin: Mouton de Gruyter.

Downing, L. J. 1998a. On the prosodic misalignment of onsetless syllables. *NLLT*, *16*: 1-52.

Downing, L. J. 1998b. Prosodic misalignment and reduplication. In G. Booij & J. van Marle (Eds.), *Yearbook of Morphology 1997* (pp. 83-120). Dordrecht: Kluwer Academic Publishers.

Downing, L. J. 1999. Prosodic stem ≠ Prosodic word in Bantu. In T. Alan Hall & U. Kleinhenz (Eds.), *Studies on the Phonological Word* (pp. 73-98). Amsterdam: John Benjamins.

Downing, L. J. 2000. Morphological and prosodic constraints on Kinande verbal reduplication. *Phonology*, *17*: 1-38.

Downing, L. J. 2006. *Canonical Forms in Prosodic Morphology*. Oxford: Oxford University Press.

Downing, L. J. & Kadenge, M. 2015. Prosodic stems in Zezuru Shona. *SALALS*, *33*(3): 291-305.

Downing, L. J. & Mtenje, A. 2011a. Prosodic phrasing of Chichewa relative clauses. *Journal of African Languages and Linguistics*, *32*: 65-111.

Downing, L. J. & Mtenje, A. 2011b. Un-WRAP-ing prosodic phrasing in Chichewa. In N. Dehé, I. Feldhausen & S. Ishihara (Eds.), *Lingua* (Special issue on *The Phonology-Syntax Interface*), *121*(13): 1965-1986.

Downing, L. J. & Mtenje, A. to appear. *The Phonology of Chichewa*. Oxford: Oxford University Press.

Downing, L. J. & Pompino-Marschall, B. 2013. The focus prosody of Chichewa and the Stress-Focus constraint: A response to Samek-Lodovici (2005). *NLLT*, *31*: 647-681.

Fitzpatrick-Cole, J. 1994. The prosodic domain hierarchy in reduplication. Ph.D. dissertation, Stanford University.

Frota, S. 2012. Prosodic structure, constituents and their implementation. In A. C. Cohn, C. Fougeron & M. K. Huffman, with assistance from Margaret E. L. Renwick (Eds.), *The Oxford Handbook of Laboratory Phonology* (pp. 255-265). Oxford: OUP.

Frota, S. & Vigário, M. 2013. Review of *Prosody Matters: Essays in Honor of Elisabeth Selkirk*.

Phonology, 30: 165-172.

Goedemans, R. 1996. An optimality account of onset sensitivity in quantity-insensitive languages. *The Linguistic Review, 13*: 33-48.

Goedemans, R. & van der Hulst, H. 2013. Fixed stress locations. In M. S. Dryer & M. Haspelmath (Eds.), *The World Atlas of Language Structures Online*. Leipzig: Max Planck Institute for Evolutionary Anthropology. (Available online at http://wals.info/chapter/ 14, Accessed on 2014-03-09.)

Hayes, B. 1989. The prosodic hierarchy in meter. In P. Kiparsky & G. Youmans (Eds.), *Rhythm and Meter (Phonetics and Phonology I)* (pp. 201-260). New York: Academic Press.

Hyman, L. M. 1977. On the nature of linguistic stress. In L. Hyman (Ed.), *Studies in Stressand Accent. SCOPIL* 4, 37-82. Los Angeles: USC Linguistics Department.

Hyman, L. M. 1999. The historical interpretation of vowel harmony in Bantu. In J.-M. Hombert & L. M. Hyman (Eds.), *Bantu Historical Linguistics* (pp. 235-295). Stanford: CSLI Publications.

Hyman, L. M. 2009. The natural history of verb-stem reduplication in Bantu. *Morphology, 19*: 177-206.

Hyman, L. M. & Inkelas, S. 1997. Emergent templates: The unusual case of Tiene. *University of Maryland Working Papers in Linguistics, 5*: 92-116.

Hyman, L. M., Inkelas, S. & Sibanda, G. 2009. Morphosyntactic correspondence in Bantu reduplication. In K. Hanson & S. Inkelas (Eds.), *The Nature of the Word: Essays in Honor of Paul Kiparsky* (pp. 273-310). Cambridge, MA: The MIT Press.

Hyman, L. M. & Mtenje, A. 1999b. Prosodic Morphology and tone: The case of Chichewa. In R. Kager, H. van der Hulst & W. Zonneveld (Eds.), *The Prosody-Morphology Interface* (pp. 90-133). Cambridge: Cambridge University Press.

Inkelas, S. 1989. Prosodic constituency in the lexicon. Ph.D. dissertation, Stanford University.

Inkelas, S. 1993. Deriving cyclicity. In S. Hargus & E.M. Kaisse (Eds.), *Studies in Lexical Phonology, Phonetics and Phonology* 4 (pp. 75-100). San Diego: Academic Press.

Inkelas, S. 2011. The Interaction Between Morphology and Phonology. In J. Goldsmith, J. Riggle & A. C. L. Yu (Eds.), *The Handbook of Phonological Theory* (2nd Ed.). Oxford: Wiley-Blackwell.

Inkelas, S. 2014. *The Interplay of Morphology and Phonology*. Oxford: Oxford University Press.

Inkelas, S. & Zoll, C. 2005. *Reduplication*. Cambridge: Cambridge University Press.

Ito, J. & Mester, A. 1996. Stem and word in Sino-Japanese. In T. Otake & A. Cutler (Eds.), *Phonological Structure and Language Processing: Cross-Linguistic Studies* (pp. 13-44). Berlin: Mouton de Gruyter.

Ito, J. & Mester, A. 2012. Recursive prosodic phrasing in Japanese. In T. Borowsky, S. Kawahara, T. Shinya & M. Sugahara (Eds.), *Prosody Matters: Essays in Honor of Elisabeth Selkirk* (pp. 280-303). Sheffield: Equinox Publishing.

Ito, J. & Mester, A. 2013. Prosodic subcategories in Japanese. *Lingua, 124*: 20-40.

Jones, P. 2011. New evidence for a Phonological Stem domain in Kinande. *Proceedings of WCCFL 28*, 285-293.

Kabak, B. & Vogel, I. 2001. The phonological word and stress assignment in Turkish. *Phonology, 18*: 315-260.

Kadenge, M. 2010. Hiatus contexts and hiatus resolution strategies in Zezuru. *Southern African Linguistics and Applied Language Studies, 28*(1): 1-11.

Kanerva, J. 1990. *Focus and Phrasing in Chichewa Phonology*. New York: Garland Publishing.

Kiparsky, P. 2000. Opacity and cyclicity. *The Linguistic Review, 17*: 351-367.

Kisseberth, C. W. & Odden, D. 2003. Tone. In D. Nurse & G. Philippson (Eds.), *The Bantu Languages* (pp. 59-70). London: Routledge.

McCarthy, J. J. 2000. The prosody of phrase in Rotuman. *Natural Language and Linguistic Theory, 18*: 147-197.

McCarthy, J. J. & Prince, A. 1986. *Prosodic Morphology 1986*. Report no. RuCCS-TR-32. New Brunswick, NJ: Rutgers University Center for Cognitive Science (http://ruccs.rutgers.edu/tech_rpt/pm86all.pdf. Accessed on 10 March 2014.)

McDonough, J. 1990. Topics in the morphology and phonology of Navajo verbs. Ph.D. dissertation, University of Massachusetts, Amherst.

Matthews, P. H. 1991. *Morphology* (2nd edition). Cambridge: CUP.

Mchombo, S. 1993. Reflexive and reciprocal in Chichewa. In S. A. Mchombo (Ed.), *Theoretical Aspects of Bantu Grammar* (pp. 181-207). Stanford, CA: CSLI.

Meeussen, A. E. 1967. Bantu grammatical reconstructions. *Annales du Musée Royal de l'Afrique Central, Série 8. Sciences Humaines, 61*, 81-121.

Moto, F. 1989. Phonology of the Bantu lexicon. Ph.D. dissertation, University College London.

Mtenje, A. D. 1985. Arguments for an autosegmental analysis of Chichewa vowelharmony. *Lingua, 66*: 21-52.

Mtenje, A. D. 1986. Issues in the Nonlinear Phonology of Chichewa. Ph.D. dissertation, University College London.

Mtenje, A. D. 1988. On tone and transfer in Chichewa reduplication. *Linguistics, 26*: 125-155.

Mudzingwa, C. 2010. Shona morphophonemics: Repair strategies in Karanga and Zezuru. Ph.D. dissertation, University of British Columbia.

Mudzingwa, C. & Kadenge, M. 2011. Comparing hiatus resolution in Nambya and Karanga:

An Optimality Theory account. *Nordic Journal of African Studies, 20*(3): 203-240.

Mutaka, N. M. 1994. *The Lexical Tonology of Kinande*. Munich: Lincom Europa.

Myers, S. 1987. Tone and the structure of words in Shona. Ph.D. dissertation, University of Massachusetts, Amherst.

Myers, S. 1995. The phonological word in Shona. In F. X. Katamba (Ed.), *Bantu Phonology and Morphology* (pp. 69-92). Munich: LINCOM EUROPA.

Myers, S. 1996. Boundary tones and the phonetic implementation of tone in Chichewa. *SAL, 25*: 29-60.

Myers, S. 1997. OCP effects in Optimality Theory. *NLLT, 15*: 847-892.

Myers, S. 1998. AUX in Bantu Morphology and Phonology. In L. Hyman & C. Kisseberth (Eds.), *Theoretical Aspects of Bantu Tone* (pp. 231-264). Stanford: CSLI.

Myers, S. 1999. Downdrift and pitch range in Chichewa intonation. In J. Ohala, Y. Hasegawa, M. Ohala, D. Granville & A. Bailey (Eds.), *Proceedings of the XIVth International Congress of Phonetic Sciences* (pp. 1981-1984). Linguistics Department, University of California, Berkeley.

Nespor, M. & Vogel, I. 1986. *Prosodic Phonology*. Dordrecht: Foris.

Odden, D. 2006. Minimality and onsetless syllables in Zinza. *Phonology, 23*: 431-441.

Prince, A. & Smolensky, P. 2004. *Optimality Theory: Constraint Interaction in Generative Grammar*. Malden, MA: Blackwell.

Riad, T. 2012. Culminativity, stress and tone accent in Central Swedish. *Lingua, 122*: 1352-1379.

Selkirk, E. 1986. On derived domains in sentence phonology. *Phonology, 3*: 371-405.

Selkirk, E. 1995. The prosodic structure of function words. *Papers in Optimality Theory. UMOP* 18, 439-469.

Selkirk, E. 2009. On clause and intonational phrase in Japanese: The syntactic grounding of prosodic constituent structure. *Gengo Kenkyuu, 136*: 35-73.

Selkirk, E. 2011. The syntax-phonology interface. In J. Goldsmith, J. Riggle & A. C. L. Yu (Eds.), *The Handbook of Phonological Theory* (2nd edition) (pp. 435-484). Malden, MA: Wiley-Blackwell.

Shaw, P. 2005. Non-adjacency in reduplication. In B. Hurch with the assistance of Veronika Mattes (Ed.), *Studies on Reduplication* (pp. 161-210). Berlin: Mouton de Gruyter.

Truckenbrodt, H. 1995. Phonological Phrases: Their relation to syntax, focus and prominence. Ph.D. dissertation, MIT.

Truckenbrodt, H. 1999. On the relation between syntactic phrases and phonological phrases. *Linguistic Inquiry, 30*: 219-255.

Vigário, M. 2010. Prosodic structure between the prosodic word and the phonological phrase: Recursive nodes or an independent domain? *The Linguistic Review, 27*: 485-530.

Vogel, I. 2009a. Universals of prosodic structure. In S. Scalise, E. Magni & A. Bisetto (Eds.), *Universals of Language Today* (pp. 59-82). Dordrecht: Springer.

Vogel, I. 2009b. The status of the Clitic Group. In J. Grijzenhout & B. Kabak (Eds.), *Phonological Domains: Universals and Deviations* (pp. 15-46). Berlin: Mouton de Gruyter.

Vogel, I. 2010. The phonology of compounds. In S. Scalise & I. Vogel (Eds.), *Cross- disciplinary Issues in Compounding* (pp. 145-163). Amsterdam: John Benjamins.

齐佩瓦语的韵律层级：几个层次？

Laura J. Downing

摘要 近来的研究（Itô & Mester，2012，2013；Selkirk，2009，2011）认为，韵律层级由三层韵律成分构成，即语调短语、音系短语以及韵律词。它们为形态-句法所激发且在各种语言中皆有例示。本文通过调查齐佩瓦语的音系来检测该三层级假说的效度问题。齐佩瓦语是班图语的一支，使用于马拉维共和国。通过此次调查，我们发现，该假说面临着两个挑战，第一，三层的韵律层级设置过于俭省，因为齐佩瓦语（及其他许多语言）都表明，有必要在韵律词之下设置另一层级，韵律词干。第二，这一分析还对三层级假说的普遍效度问题提出了质疑，因为在短语层面，没有足够的证据来对韵律短语与语调短语做出鲜明的区分。对于韵律层级成分的数目问题，本文既不支持过于俭省的做法，亦对按需设置韵律域的观点持保留态度。

关键词 韵律词干 复合词组 班图语系 重叠 调域 最小限度 黏附词 间断分辨率

Laura J. Downing

Professor, Institute for Languages and Literatures, University of Gothenburg

E-mail: laura.downing@sprak.gu.se

核心重音与信息结构*

Maria Luisa Zubizarreta

李 果 王 迟 王晓品 庄会彬 译

摘要 鉴于宽域焦点语境("无标记"重音模式)下德语和英语中特定结构所观察到的重音模式的可变性,以及与之对立的西班牙语和意大利语中的核心重音的固定性(核心重音总是落在最右侧的成分上),本文讨论并评价在重音模式下计算核心重音(简称 NS)的不同方法。此外,文章简要讨论在窄域焦点语境下("有标记"重音模式)核心重音的具体情况,指出最近的研究表明"无标记"核心重音与"有标记"核心重音模式源自截然不同的机制。

关键词 核心重音 照应性音高重音删略 节律结构 韵律短语划分

1 引 言

在塑造句子的韵律结构尤其是凸显关系方面,信息结构发挥了十分重要的作用。这已为人所知。例如,早期对英语的研究:Bolinger(1958,

---

* 原文题目为 Nuclear Stress and Information Structure,刊于 2016 The Oxford Handbook of Information Structure,Edited by Caroline Féry and Shinichiro Ishihara。本文由四川大学李果、香港中文大学王迟、北京语言大学王晓品和河南大学庄会彬共同翻译。文章翻译过程中得到冯胜利先生的指导,但囿于译者的水平和眼光,在翻译过程中难免存在对原作理解不到位的地方以及理解上的偏差。由此导致的所有讹误,概由译者负责。

1972），Halliday（1976），Chomsky（1971）和 Jackendoff（1972）。^①然而在信息结构和韵律中，哪些方面属于语法的范围仍然存在争议。在上述早期论著中，Chomsky（1971）和 Jackendoff（1972）引人注目，他们都注意到焦点概念（句中非预设部分或断言部分）用语法手段进行表达^②，而且注意到在确认焦点时句子的核心重音（NS）发挥了十分重要的作用。^③该制约条件如（1）所述，核心重音与句子的语调核心校齐（align），这一现象称为"核心音高重读"（Nuclear Pitch Accent，NPA）^④；也可参考 Zubizarreta（1998）和 Reinhart（2006）。

(1) The focused constituent must contain the rhythmically most prominent word, i.e. the word that bears the Nuclear Stress.

成为焦点的成分一定包含节奏中最凸显的一个词，亦即承担核心重音

---

① 跨语言韵律音系学的研究（如 Jun，2005）已发现两种典型的方法用以表达凸显的音系概念：一是*在顶点实现*（通过核心音高重音实现，核心音高与它对应的节律成分核心重读音节校齐）；另一种是*划出边界实现*（通过韵律音渡实现，它和句法范畴的边界校齐），例如韩语、日语、孟加拉国语和许多班图语，也见于 Féry（2001）对法语的研究。本文只关注在顶点实现凸显的类型，具体来说是日耳曼语（即英语、德语）和罗曼语（例如西班牙语、意大利语）。见 Jun（2016）。

② Rochemont（1986）根据新信息与旧信息（或已知信息）的二分定义焦点。但是其他的研究已经指出立足于语篇的"焦点/预设"二分存在语义输入（Rooth（1985））。它必须和"新信息/旧信息"二分区别开。后者是语言概念，可能影响句子的韵律但是没有语义输入。实际上，焦点成分可以包含旧信息（或已知信息）。见 Ladd（1980，1996）和本章第 4 节。

③ 如（1）中所述，在使用音高重音定义凸显（见尾注①）的语言中，根据核心重音直接确认焦点成分。这条理设也面临挑战。Selkirk（1984，1995），Gussenhoven（1984），支持焦点确认与句中音高重音的分布直接相关，与 NPA 的概念或 NPA 对应的节律成分——句中的核心重音无关。更具体地说，这些学者认为使用焦点投射规则或焦点-范围形成规则条件音高-重音的指派和谓语-论元结构。核心音高重读（对应的是节律概念"核心重音"）是语调范域（Newman（1946），把 NSR 视为后期韵律规则）中最后一个音高重读的词，但是对定义句中焦点可能的范围不发挥重要作用。又见 Nespor 和 Vogel（1986）（他们支持"**音高重读优先**"的焦点-凸显关系）与 Féry（2011）（在本文第 2 节讨论过）。本文不会讨论 Selkirk 与 Gussenhoven 的观点，但可看看 Zubizarreta（1998：78-85）对他们的评述，也可以参考 Myrberg 和 Riad（2016）。

④ 作为语调曲拱的中心，NPA 对限制出现在它前后的语调曲拱的类型起了非常重要的作用。（见 Ladd 1980，1996 的评述。）

的词。

因此，在（2a）这类**宽焦**例子中，全句成为焦点，核心重音落在最右侧的成分上（例如宾语的介词短语补述语）。一般称之为"无标记"重音模式。**只要承担无标记核心重音的词语包含在焦点成分中，无标记核心重音就能将全句视为焦点（宽焦），也能表达不同程度的窄焦如动词短语、限定词短语（DP）直接宾语或修饰名词的介词短语补述语**。因此（2a）既可以回答"怎么回事"（宽焦），也可以回答"猫做了什么"（动词短语作为窄焦）或者"猫读了什么"（直接宾语作为窄焦）。倘若焦点缩窄为句中不包含无标记核心重音的一部分，如（2b）中的主语，那么节奏中最凸显的重音必须移到主语上。这种句子只能回答"谁读了一本关于老鼠的书"。这类重音不允许"焦点投射"（focus projection）①，称为"有标记"重音。②这是任何关于确认焦点的理论都必须给予解释的基本事实。

　　（2） a. The cat read a book about <u>rats</u>.
　　　　 b. The <u>cat</u> read a book about rats.

本文用术语"无标记重音模式"指称未受语篇因素影响的重音模式，语篇因素包括焦点/预设二分和已提及的信息或旧信息（或对话双方共同分享的信息）。尽管"容纳"（accommodation）因素导致有时可能很难找到定义无标记模式所依赖的"纯化"语境，但我们相信从理论上对这些模式的认识对深入理解"有标记重音模式"是重要的。认识到短语重音在确定句中焦点范围起作用的学者对短语重音自身的计算范域一直存在分歧。有些学者支持根据句法结构直接计算核心重音如 Cinque（1993），Kahnemuyipour（2004/2009），Reinhart（2006）。我们把这种观点称为"严格句法说"（strictly syntactic approach）。从事韵律音系学的学者支持根据韵律适用域计算短语

---

① 关于"焦点投射"理论，见 Arregi（2016）。
② 这里我们只关注宽焦语境下的主要重音，不关心次要重音。在及物句中次要重音总是落在主语上（如正文中 2a 中的 cat）。与主要重音不同，"无标记重音"模式中的次要重音是完全，至少是部分由韵律节奏决定的。见 Zubizarreta（1998：38-40，166）。
　　我们注意到上文提到的观点和其他理论的观点不同。其他观点认为在宽焦语境下使用同样的一个算法生成主要重音和次要重音。具体论述见 Chomsky 和 Halle（1968），Halle 和 Vergnaud（1987），Cinque（1993），Reinhart（2006），Kahnemuyipour（2004/2009）。

重音，具体来说是根据音系短语（phonological phrase）或主短语（major phrase，记作 p-短语），它们是根据自身和句法范畴的关系来定义的，更准确地说是根据它们和词汇的句法范畴定义的，如 Selkirk（1995），Kratzer 和 Selkirk（2007），Féry（2011）等的论述。我们把这种观点称为"韵律短语划分说"（prosodic-phrasing approach）。①Truckenbrodt（2006）提出了"综合说"：一方面他根据句法结构直接计算短语重音，另一方面他把核心重音定为韵律语调域中的最后一个短语重音。其他学者支持根据节律解释过的句法结构计算核心重音，句法结构的特定成分可能在节律上是隐形的（Halle 和 Vergnaud（1987），Zubizarreta（1998），Zubizarreta 和 Vergnaud（2005），Nava 和 Zubizarreta（2010），Zubizarreta 和 Nava（2011））。我们把这种观点称为"经过节律解释的句法说"（metrically-interpreted syntactic approach）。

在应用方面，有两个重要的议题已引起越来越多的讨论。一个是在宽焦语境中（无标记重音模式）日耳曼语的核心重音的定位具有可变性；另一个是核心重音在句中的位置存在跨语言的差异。具体来说，日耳曼语和罗曼语类型是对立的，如 Ladd（1996）、Samek-Lodovici（2005）、Vallduví（1995）、Zubizarreta（1998）、Nava 和 Zubizarreta（2010）、Zubizarreta 和 Nava（2011）。在第 2 小节和第 3 小节中，我们讨论上述研究中的一些方法如何解决无标记重音模式下一种语言类型内部和跨语言中核心重音定位的可变性，即 Kratzer 和 Selkirk（2007）（她们源自 Kahnemuyipour（2004/2009）的深刻见解）、Féry（2011）以及 Zubizarreta 和 Nava（2011）（他们的研究立足于 Zubizarreta 和 Vergnaud（2005））的提议。

另一个存在分歧的重要问题是在"有标记"重音模式和"无标记"重音模式的计算中是否牵涉到不同的算法，也许是性质完全不同的算法。有些论著猜测存在这种差异，如 Cinque（1993），Kahnemuyipour（2004/2009），Selkirk 和 Kratzer（2007），另外一些则明确支持存在这种差异，如 Reinhart（2006），Zubizarreta 和 Nava（2010），而 Bolinger（1972）以及 Schmerling（1976），Selkirk（1984，1995）和 Gussenhoven（1984）则明确否认这种差异。在第 4 小节，我们讨论 Reinhart（2006）提出的观点，她认为有标记重

---

① 关于韵律短语划分，见 Jun（2016）。

音模式的产生是照应性重音删略（anaphoric deaccenting）（即 A-重音删略促发核心重音移动）的结果，同时讨论 Féry 和 Kügler（2008）提出的替代观点，语篇概念如新信息、旧信息以及窄焦直接调整全句的音高范围（这个过程称为"调准"（scaling））。最后，我们简要回顾一些研究结果，它们支持"窄焦的韵律确实是由不同的机制产生的"，这一机制直接参照了信息结构，并受制于方言/个人言语的偏好，与之截然对立的是"无标记重音模式"下的核心重音，它是根据概括性的语法运算规则生成的。但针对有标记与无标记重音模式来源的争论仍然是个尚未解决的问题，有待进一步的深入研究。[①]

2　短语重音的计算域

在这一节，我们简要回顾宽焦语境下计算"无标记"重音的一些更新的方法。我们集中讨论这些方法如何处理日耳曼语中核心重音位置的可变性。

2.1　严格句法说与韵律短语划分说

Halle 和 Chomsky（1968）提出了经典核心重音规则（NSR）。遵循特定的传统，循环使用这一规则可以预测到核心重音落在全句的最后一个成分上，符合在及物性主谓宾（SVO）句中主要凸显落在宾语上的事实，如（2a）所示。有一个对经典核心重音规则的重要挑战（尽管它肯定不是唯一的一个），是在动词居末的日耳曼语中（如（3a）和（3b））核心重音没有落在

[①] 一位评议人提出另一个重要的问题，我们在本文无法给出完全的判断。这个问题是：是否核心重音的位置确认了在宽焦和类似的窄焦语境下（本文假定的观点）焦点可能的范围，或者是否与窄焦相关的句法结构需要用一个在韵律上可以解释的"焦点"特征来标注。一个与之相关的理论问题是：核心句法的简约性到底可以达到何种程度？在 Chomsky（1995，1999/2001）提出的最简方案理论框架下，假定短语的句法属性只由组成短语的词汇形式的属性决定。在这个语法概念下，"焦点"句法特征是一个奇怪的特征。

最后一个成分（即动词）上，而是分别落在直接宾语和介词短语补述语上。

（3）a. Hans hat [[ein [Buch]]gelesen].
　　　　Hans has　a　book　　read
　　　　'Hans has read a book.'
　　b. Peter hat [[an [einem [Papier]]]gearbeitet].
　　　　Peter has　on　a　paper　　worked
　　　　'Peter has worked on apaper.'

Cinque（1993）提出一个建议，他试图不考虑语序而完全利用句法结构提供的结构信息计算核心重音。更具体地说，Cinque 提出的算法是把句法结构中嵌入最深（*the most deeply embedded*）的节点视为核心重音的位置。无论是在动词居末还是在动词居前的语言中，作为动词短语中嵌入最深的节点，补述语承载主重音。如果认为附加语是附接在动词的投射上，而补述语是动词的姊妹节点如（3b）和（4），那么 Cinque 的观点也解释了由 Krifka（1984）发现的补述语和附加语的差异。因为附加语和指示语不属于小句句法结构的"主路径"（main path），所以它们的内部结构对计算核心重音来说是隐形成分。

（4）Peter hat [vP an einem kleinen Tisch [vPgearbeitet]].
　　　Peter has　on　a　small　table　　　worked
　　　'Peter worked on a small table.'

引入"语段"（phase）概念作为语法接口部分的相关句法范域后（Chomsky1999/ 2001，2005），一个关于句法与短语重音相互作用的新思路变得明晰起来。Chomsky（1999/2001，2005）把两种句法范畴定义为"语段域"：句标词短语（CP）和轻动词短语（vP），把它们的姊妹节点时态词短语（TP）和动词短语（VP）分别定义为拼出（spell-out）和解释（interpretation）的范域（即接口域）。Adger（2006）在（5）中提出：

（5）The spell-out domain of a phase is the domain for phrasal stress assignment.

语段的拼出域就是指派短语重音的范围。

为了解释在中心语居前和中心语居末的语言的及物句中宾语都具有优先性，Kahnemuyipour（2004/2009）进一步优化了这个规则：①

（6）Assign phrase stress with in the highest constituent within the spell-out domain.

把短语重音指派给拼出范域中最高的成分。

如果认为在计算核心重音的拼出范域中，（3a）中限定词短语的宾语和（3b）中地点介词短语在比动词高的位置，那么（6）的规则就解释了（3）中核心重音的位置；因为使用了动词到轻动词（V-to v）的移位规则，使得直接宾语或介词短语论元成为结构中最高的成分。②另一方面，如果（4）中介词短语附加语在拼出范域之外，那么它不会承载核心重音。假定存在动词到轻动词的移位，拼出范域（动词短语）不包含语音材料。可以假定在这些例子中，核心重音落到最近的非空形式上。在（4）的例子中，最近的非空形式是动词。③

针对 Kahnemuyipour 提出的以语段为基础的短语重音指派说，Kratzer 和 Selkirk（2007）提出一个修订的、韵律的版本。按照她们的观点，短语重音的范围是音系短语（或主短语），主短语本身被定义为语段拼出范域中位置最高的短语（见（7））。进而假定主短语的韵律中心语承担短语重音，且最后一个短语重音被定为核心重音。

---

① 注意，关于一个复杂限定词短语中核心重音的最终位置需要进一步的假设。立足于波斯语，Kahnemuyipour（2004/2009）认为在一个限定词短语中指派短语重音的算法独立于决定句中核心重音的算法。

② 见 Kahnemuyipour（2004：128）对 Larson（1988）双及物结构分析的详细讨论。

③ 在英语中，无论句末成分是补述语还是附加语，核心重音都落在句末成分上（例如"约翰写了论文"和"约翰在办公室工作"）。为了解释这个现象，Kahnemuyipour 采纳 Cinque 对副词的分析。这种分析把副词统一视为动词短语之上功能词投射的指示语。英语的词序是把动词短语移到包含副词的功能词投射之上得到的。如正文中前面提到的，进一步假定，如果拼出域中是空的（在这里指最低的动词短语），核心重音就落在最近的非空形式上。在介词短语作为地点附加语的英语不及物句中，最近的非空成分是地点介词短语。见 Kahnemuyipour（2004），4.5.2 有进一步的详细讨论。

(7) The highest phrase within the spell-out domain of a phase corresponds to a prosodic major phrase in phonological representation.

语段拼出范围中最高的短语即音系表征式中的韵律主短语。

（3a）的直接宾语和（3b）的介词短语组成一个主短语，即短语重音的范围，作为语调短语（或 i-短语）的最后一个主短语，最终它们承载核心重音。假设在韵律上，介词短语附加于轻动词短语的拼出范围—动词短语—之外，这个理论框架可以解释（3b）与（4）的对立。

基于韵律短语划分指派短语重音规则的另一个版本是由 Féry（2011）提出的，他把概念"韵律范域整合"（prosodic domain integration）加入系统中。与 Kratzer 和 Selkirk 的分析不同，Féry 的观点建立在一个限制-排序的优选论理论框架下。①我们深入挖掘两种方法的异同，不考虑这些理论差异。正如 Kratzer 和 Selkirk 的分析，在 Féry 的规则中句法短语被映射到韵律短语上（见（8）），每个韵律范域的核心（p-短语和 i-短语）重读，而 i-短语的韵律核心是最右侧的中心语（见（9））（等同于经典核心短语规则中的核心重音成分）。Féry 观点的创新在于在韵律上一个短语论元可以与其相邻的中心语合并为一个更大的音系短语（p-短语，见（10a）），因而导致一个音系短语（p-短语）嵌入另一个音系短语（p-短语）。进而针对附加语概念引入"韵律从属"（*prosodic subordination*），见（10b），这为使用一个不同的解释说明（3）和（4）中论元-附加语的对立铺平了道路。在韵律上，（3b）中介词短语补述语与其相邻的中心语整合，但（4b）中则不然，它被分析为"从属"于论元-谓语韵律范域。②

(8) A syntactic maximal projection including at least a <u>prosodic word</u> is contained in its own prosodic domain.

包含至少一个韵律词的句法的最大投射被包含在它的韵律范域中。

---

① 有关基于"限制"的优选论理论框架下韵律与信息结构的互动，见 Samek-Lodovici（2016）。

② 我们后面会看到，（10a）的规则应该是"与其相邻的中心语合并为一个更大的 p-短语或 i-短语"，（10b）应该是"从属于论元-谓语复杂结构的 p-短语或 i-短语。"

(9) Align the right boundary of every i-phrase with its head.
把每个语调短语（i-短语）的右边界和它的中心语校齐。

(10) a. An XP argument can be prosodically integrated with its adjacent head into a larger p-phrase.
在韵律上一个短语论元可以与其相邻的中心语一起并入一个更高层级的音系短语（p-短语）中。

b. The p-phrase of an adjunct is subordinated to the p-phrase of an argument-predicate complex.
一个附加语的音系短语（p-短语）从属于一个论元-谓语复杂结构所在的音系短语（p-短语）。

在下一小节，我们将进一步详细讨论 Kratzer 和 Selkirk（2007）、Féry（2011）提出的系统以及他们如何解决在特定结构语境中核心重音位置的可变性。

2.2　日耳曼语中核心重音位置的可变性

2.2.1　不及物动词情况

众所周知，日耳曼语的"主-谓"不及物动词情况呈现重音位置的可变性（Chafe（1974）；Schmerling（1976）；Selkirk（1984，1995）；Sasse（1987）；Zubizarreta（1998）；Nava 和 Zubizarreta（2010）；Irwin（2012））。核心重音指派到主语位置抑或动词都能用宽焦语境中"主-谓"不及物的情况加以验证。尽管已有学者将这种可变性同非作格（unergative）/非宾格（unaccusative）联系到一起（例如 Zubizarreta（1998）；Kahnemuyipour（2004/2009）；Irwin（2012）），但核心重音的可变性似乎并不受这两种不及物类型的限制。

基于对 34 位英语母语者的问答调查，Zubizarreta 和 Nava（2011）认为，单就非作格动词而言，可变性是成系统的（例如，an actress was crying *vs*. an <u>actress</u> was crying；a guest sang *vs*. a guest <u>sang</u>；下划线指示重音位置，下同），而非宾格的情况则不够齐整。尤为明显的是，在"出现动词"（verbs of appearance）的情况下，核心重音系统地落在主语上（例如，the <u>aliens</u> arrive, the police came, a rabbit appeared），其他非宾格动词（sub-classes of unac-cusative）则又呈现一些可变性（例如，the major fell; the magician disap-peared）。Chafe（1974）及 Sasse（1987）除了指出交替性不及物动词（alternating intransitives）会系统地将其核心重音指派在主语上（如 a window broke），还指出与动词词类（verb class）相关的核心重音的变化。通过细致地分析不及物动词核心重音可变性相关语境，Sasse（1987）认为这种差异同直接判断（thetic）（eventive：事件性）与主题判断（话题-述题）（categorical）（topic-comment）的区别有关。有代表性的情况是"出现动词"（arrive, come, appear）常与事件性谓语（eventive predicates）相关联，因此其核心重音系统地落在主语位置上。

Kratzer 和 Selkirk（2007）根据阶段性谓语（stage-level predicates）与个体性谓语（individual-level predicates）的差异重新分析了直接判断与主题判断的不同。他们认为阶段性谓语的主语占据的是时态词短语（Tense Phrase）指示语（Spec）的位置（没有语音形式的时空话题被假定出现在这样的结构中），而个体性谓语的主语占据了更高话题短语（TopP）的指示语位置。他们进一步提出了一些设想。具体而言，他们假定当动词（或复杂动词 verb cluster）为拼出域的唯一成分时，它会移到轻动词（ν）投射，从而空出动词短语；而韵律的拼出则会跳过空的范域。因此，例（11a）的结构如（11b）所示，核心重音落在主语上。其动词短语为空，并不构成一个韵律上的拼出域。下一个拼出域是时态词短语①；根据规则（7），时态词短语的指示语（Spec，TP）位置的主语被确定为一个主短语，也就是语调短语（i-domain）上的最后一个主短语，因此重音落在此处。②

（11）a. Ich hab' gehört, dass Mettallarbeiter gestreikt haben.
　　　　I have heard　that metal workers　gone-on-strike have

---

① 假定话题短语（像句标词短语）构成了一个语段，时态词短语是它的拼出域。
② 要注意的是，为了解释短语重音落在主语上这一事实，在（11）中，作出词汇动词已经从动词短语结构中移出的假定至关重要。如果动词仍然在动词短语结构里，那么动词将携带短语重音，而且当动词短语包含音系材料时，动词短语自身就是一个拼出域。

b. [TopP pro [TP Metallarbeiter_i [vP e_i [VP ~~gestreikt~~]gestreikt haben]]]

（12a）给出了主语在话题短语的指示语位置上的一个例子，（12b）则是其相关结构。话题短语被假定为构成了一个语段，时态词短语是它的拼出域。此外，假设一例外条件（*Elsewhere Condition*），即带有合格材料的拼出域必须包含一个主短语重音。（12b）中，时态词短语拼出域中唯一合格的成分是动词，所以由它构成一个音系短语，并最终承担核心重音（成为语调短语内的最后一个音系短语）①。

(12) a. Ich hab' irgendwo   gelesen, dass der König von Bayern   spinnt.
   I have somewhere read   that the king of Bavaria   is.crazy
b. ...[TopP der König von Bayern_i [TP e_i [vPe_i[VP ~~spinnt~~] spinnt]]]

需要注意的是，当动词是动词短语中的唯一一个音系材料，动词移出动词短语结构进入轻动词投射（这是描述核心重音位置在主语上的关键假定，见（11）），这一假设不无后果。尤其是，它破坏了一个对（4）中 Krifka 事实的可能解释。结果，根据（12）中的逻辑，作为动词短语拼出域的唯一成分，该动词移出到 v 投射，从而腾空出了动词短语。上文曾指出韵律拼出域会越过空的范域。结果，（4）中动词和介词短语附加语将不再属于独立的韵律拼出域，它们都是时态词短语拼出域的一部分。根据规则（7），我们期望短语重音要么落在主语上（如果主语被置于时态词（T）的指示语位置，如下文 4'i)，要么可能落在介词短语（PP）附加语上（如果主语在话题（Top）的指示语位置，并且附加语被视为时态词范域的一部分（见 4'ii)），但我们不期望短语重音落在被认为处于 *v*P 范域的动词分词（verbal participle）上。因此，需要更多的假设来阻止动词从动词短语内部移出。逻辑上的一种可能是处所附加语会迫使动词留在动词短语之内（其原因还有待了解）；它将构成一个主要的音系短语，并且根据上述例外条件承载

---

① 有一位外审专家指出，在 Kaynemuyipour 的系统里，可以依据更低一层短语范域的存在与否区分个体层面与阶段性层面。

短语重音。

  （4'）（i）[TopP pro [TP Peter hat [an einem kleinen Tisch [vP e_i [VP gearbeitet] gearbeitet]]]

    （ii）[Top Peter_i hat [TP e_i [an einem kleinen Tisch [vP e_i [VP gearbeitet] gearbeitet]]]]

  为了解释"主-谓"不及物情况下核心重音位置的可变性，Féry 也求助于主题判断陈述主语的话题地位，它占据一个与直接判断陈述的主语不同的句法位置。他认为韵律短语切分和韵律整合都对句法的区分敏感。因此，在（11b）的情况中，处在时态词的指示语的主语 XP 被映射到一音系短语上，并且在韵律上被归并到一个包含动词的更大的韵律范域中（见规则 10a 和注释 13），从而产生单一的语调短语，正如（13a）所示（小型的大写字母标示音高重读词（pitch-accented word））。因为主语是语调短语中唯一的音系短语，由此它充当了语调短语的核心，并且在短语中承担唯一的音高重音（pitch accent）（相当于核心重音）。另一方面，（12b）的话题本就构成语调短语。所以，（12b）中主语和的动词被映射到两个不同的语调短语上，每个携带一个音高重读核心（或核心重音），如（13b）所示。

  （13）a.（_{ip}（p-p METALLARBEITER）gestreikt haben）
     b.（_{ip} der König von BAYERN）（_{ip} SPINNT）

2.2.2 地点和方向介词短语

  关于日耳曼语中核心重音位置可变性的另外一个现象，是带有地点短语（如 14a）和方向短语（如 14b）的及物结构，由 Féry 带向了讨论的前沿。Kratzer 和 Selkirk 就直接宾语系统地携带短语重音（和最终的核心重音）的情况作出了明确的分析。回想在（6）的分析中，只有拼出域中位置最高的短语被解析为主短语（在（6）中是动词短语），进而被确定为包含短语重音。在（15）中，直接宾语被假定为是拼出域中最高的短语；因此它组成了一个主短语并且携带短语重音，而随后的介词短语和动词则不携带短语重音。

（14）a. ...dass ein JUNGE eine GEIGE im Supermarkt kaufte.
　　　　　that a boy　a violin　in. the supermarket bought
　　　　　'that a boy bought a violin in the supermarket'

　　　b. ...dass MARIA KINDER in die Schule fuhr.
　　　　　that Maria　children　in the school drove
　　　　　'that Maria drove children to school'

Féry 指出存在可以适用于（14）的另外一种韵律模式，即直接宾语和介词短语都得到音高重音。而介词短语作为处于句子的最末成分承载核心重音，如（15）所示[①]。

（15）a. ...dass ein JUNGE eine GEIGE im SUPERMARKT kaufte
　　　b. ...dass MARIA KINDER in die SCHULE fuhr.

值得注意的是，通常假设，（15b）方向介词短语为动词 drive 的词汇意义蕴含的一部分，因此它是动词"drive"的"论元"[②]。另一方面，（15a）的处所成分跟（4）中 Krifka 例子中的处所成分一样，都不是论元。事实上，（15a）与（15b）的模式相似，因此也引人入胜。这也许还说明了在饰谓性副词（VP adverbs）的句法结构划分中采用 Larson（1988）的方案是正确的。根据 Larson 的方法，句法（而非动词的词汇义）决定了动词域（verbal domain）中短语（XP）的结构[③]。Larson 的建议是，当直接宾语引发双分支动词短语壳结构（binary VP-shell structure），表示处所的介词短语和时间副词可以并入动词短语壳分析（VP-shell analysis），如（16）所示（以德语词序呈现）：

---

① 此外，Féry 也谈及了一种较少的选项，其中动词也携带一个音高重读。在此，我们将不考虑这种情况。

② "开车送（drive）"像"去（go）"一样，都包含一个有向的运动义，也就是说，它必然产生目标。

③ Larson 进一步假定：一般的题元层级决定句法结构层面动词论旨角色的映射。

（16） a. [vP [VP DP[VP PP$_{Loc}$ V]]v]

b. [vP [VP DP[VP PP$_{Temp}$ V]]v]

于是，由于直接宾语可以充当动词短语的指示语，如（17）所示，（15a）和（15b）中的介宾短语自动整合进一个"动词短语壳"的双层句法分析。换句话说，句法上（4）中的介词短语充当附加语，而（15a）中的处所短语是动词谓语的一部分，（15b）中的介词短语也同样如此。这样的介词短语可以称为"谓语性介词短语"（predicative PPs）。如果 Féry 的分析是正确的，需要根据这些原则提出一些假设。

（17） a. ...dass ein JUNGE$_i$ [vP e$_i$ [VP eine GEIGE [im SUPERMARKT kaufte]] v]

b. ...dass MARIA$_i$ [vPe$_i$ [VP KINDER[in die SCHULE fuhr]]v]

根据上述分析，（15）中的模式源自这一典型分析：动词短语之内的每个短语都组成了"同一层次"的音系短语（p-phrase），而最后一个短语则被确定为语调短语的核心，并承担核心重音，见（18a）。至于（14）中的模式，Féry 认为在这种情况下，根据（10b）中的"附加语从属规则"，介词短语"在韵律上从属"于"论元-谓语"复杂体（直接宾语—动词），因此产生了（18b）的模式。①这一韵律从属关系，可以通过区分音系短语的不同层次，如 P$_1$、P$_2$（其中 P$_2$ 从属于 P$_1$）等来标示。（18b）中，P$_1$ 在韵律上从属于由宾语和动词所形成的论元-谓语复杂体，在这个例子中就是一个语调短语。因此 P$_1$ 承担"核心音高重读"（=核心重音），而且由于 P$_2$ 处于核心重音之后的位置，它的音高重音会被删除。Féry 认为，德语偏好（18b）的模式，是因为这种语言里存在着动词与其非邻接直接宾语论元进行韵律整合的倾向。②

---

① 注意（18）中就介宾短语这一"附加语"术语是学术上的一种误称。正如早期认为的：更恰当的术语应该是"谓语性介宾短语"。

② 需要进一步开展有关双宾语的研究，以确定动词选择其直接宾语的预测能力适用于判断指派于直接宾语上的核心重音（例 18b）还是介宾结构的核心重音（例 18a）。英语亦亟需类似研究。

(18) a.（ip（P1 eine GEIGE）（P1 im SUPERMARKT）kaufte）
　　b.（ip（P1 eine GEIGE）（P2 im Supermarkt）kaufte）

(10b) The p-phrase of an adjunct is subordinated to the p-phrase of an argument-predicate complex.（but see note 13）.
附加语的音系短语从属于论元-谓语复杂结构所在的音系短语。

　　(10b) 的意图很清楚。它旨在说明，既然句法中心语会在韵律上从属于短语论元，那么及物句中的介词短语同样可以发生韵律从属，尽管事实上它不是句法核心。也许我们可以推断：直接宾语、"谓语性介词短语"发生"韵律从属"，很可能是因为在及物结构中介词短语打破了动词短语内部直接宾语和动词之间的自然邻接关系。

　　另一方面，在中心语居首的语言如英语中，如果及物结构的语序是"动词-限定词短语-介词短语"，那么核心重音通常会落在全新宽域焦点结构中的介词短语上（如 *they bought a violin at the market*），与不及物动词的介词短语附加语的情况一样（如 *he worked at the office*）。①

　　总而言之，在日耳曼语中的句法结构会允许在宽焦语境下核心重音位置的可变性。两个代表性的例证是，主谓不及物结构和及物动词携带地点性介词短语或方向性介词短语。一个解释方案必须能够说明这种可变性，才算得上是充分的。②

3　经节律解释的句法结构分析法

　　以 Halle 和 Vergnaud（1987）为基础，Zubizarreta（1998）提出了一个根据（抽象）句法结构运算核心重音的体系，该体系可以忽略某些句法成

---

① 参看 Zubizarreta 和 Nava（2011）就英语双宾语的数据，但是注释 21 所提及的预测问题仍然将被探讨。
② 另外的语法因素，如"预测性"和"标明-有价值"可能影响与其对立面相对的一种韵律模式的运用，并且引发了"如果你是一个能测人心思者，那么重音位置是可以预测"的错误观念。

分，尤其是功能范畴。功能范畴节律的显隐特征既可解释本文第二节所列的语言内部核心重音指派差异，也可解释该方面的跨语言差异，如日耳曼语和罗曼语之间的不同（尤以西班牙语为代表）。Zubizarreta（1998）的理论在 Nava 和 Zubizarreta（2010）以及 Zubizarret 和 Nava（2011）之中得到了进一步修正。本节将介绍修正后的理论，并称其为"经节律解释的句法结构分析法（metrically-interpreted syntactic approach）"①

在西班牙语类的语言中，核心重音总是落在语调短语的右边界。因此，在西班牙语的限定词短语-动词结构里，核心重音总是落在动词上。这一现象不仅见于前文所讨论的"主语-动词"不及物结构里（a dog's barking vs. un perro está ladrando），也出现于不定式关系从句中；试比较英语例句 there are problems to solve/there are problems to compute（Bolinger(1972)）和对应的西班牙语例句 Hay problemas que resolver/ Hay problemas que computarizar 。MI-S 主要依靠两个特征来解释日耳曼语（而非罗曼语）在新信息宽焦语境下短语内部核心重音的韵律模式。第一个特征前文已经提及，复述如（19）。

（19）In Germanic, functional categories may be interpreted as metrically invisible, while in Romance, functional categories are always metrically visible.

在日耳曼语中，功能范畴在节律上可被视作隐形，而在罗曼语中，功能范畴在节律上总是显性的。

MI-S 的第二个特征是，核心重音规则由两部分构成：一部分对"中心语-论元"敏感，另一部分对"线性顺序"敏感。上述核心重音规则示于（20），可见核心重音承载成分总是被节律重的成分所统制（dominate）（Liberman

---

① 两个版本之间的一个重要的区别在于节律的非可见性。在 Zubizarreta（1998）中，所有音高重音删略成分都被认为是节律隐形成分。在此后的几个版本里，音高重音删略并不会直接影响句法范畴的节律地位；出于计算核心重音的需要，只有功能中心语可能会被界定为节律上不可见的成分。

（1975））[①, ②]。此处"论元"是 Hale 和 Keyser（2002）意义上的词汇-句法论元，而不是词汇-语义论元[③]。

（20）Given two metrical sister nodes A and B：(i) If A is a head and B is its argument，assign S to B（*specific-NSR*）. Otherwise，(ii) assign S to the right-most constituent node in the phrase（*general-NSR*）.

对于两个节律姊妹节点 A 和 B：(i) 若 A 为中心语，B 为其论元，则将核心重音指派给 B（特殊核心重音规则）。如若不然，(ii) 将核心重音指派给短语内最右侧的成分（一般核心重音规则）。

试看例（21）中"主语-动词"不及物句的节律结构。若时态词节律隐形，根据（20i）将核心重音指派给主语，因为主语为其节律姊妹节点动词的论元，故可作为核心重音承载成分。若时态词节律显性，限定词短语和动词不是节律姊妹节点，则（20i）不适用；则启用规则（20ii），将核心重音指派给动词（见 21b）。该分析亦适用于（13）中的德语"主语-动词"不及物句，以及（22）中的不定式关系结构。（22a）中，不定式中心语 T 节律隐形，关系小句中的核心承载核心重音。（22b）中，时态词节律显形，则关系小句中的动词承载核心重音。对比之下，在罗曼语中，功能范畴节

---

① 根据 Kayne（1994），Zubizarreta（1998）认为"最右端的"成分即"嵌入最深的"成分（亦同 Cinque（1993））。Szendröi（2001）不予赞同，因为在有些语言，如匈牙利语里存在"其他"类型的计算法则，将核心重音指派给最左端的成分。

② 节律栅可由节律树推导出来，其中核心重音是节律栅上最高的节拍（Liberman 和 Prince（1977）；Selkirk（1984）；Halle 和 Vegnaud（1987））。有关节律栅的讨论，亦见 Myrberg 和 Riad（2016）。按照 Zubizarreta 的观点，句子层面的节律树只能部分影响句子的节律栅。节律栅剩下部分的形状则由基于短语切分以及韵律的其他规则决定，其中核心重音为节律栅的中心锚定点。见注释 6。

③ 事实上，相关关系并不完全是中心语与语义论元的关系，而是中心语与词汇-句法（l-s）论元的关系。当且仅当一成分包含于一词汇中心语的词汇句法结构中，该成分称作该中心语的词汇-句法论元（依据 Hale 和 Keyser（2002））。此次修正的重要意义在于，它顾及了动词性中心语投射内较低位置的方式性副词吸引核心重音这一事实。例如，Hans hat ein Gedicht gut gelesen 'Hans has read the book well'；Kahnemuyipour（2004：117）亦谈及波斯语中类似的现象。

律上总是显性的,因此一直呈现句末核心重音的韵律模式(即在当前讨论的结构中,核心重音落在动词上)①。

(21) a.

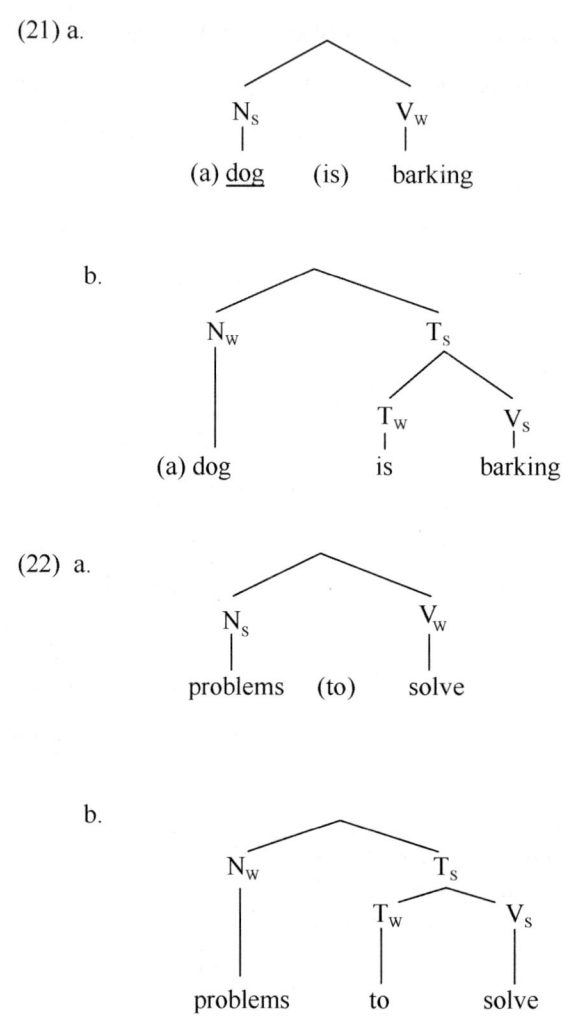

---

① 在特定情况下,英语中的功能词也会重读。和我们现在的研究直接相关的功能词——助动词在三种情况下会重读:出现在句末位置,由词汇后规则赋予重音(见 Inkelas 和 Zec(1993));出现在表强调的语境中,由强调重音规则(Emphatic Stress Rule)赋予重音(见 Zubizarreta(1998));当它右侧的承载核心重音的成分作为已知信息进行音高重音删略,促发核心重音转移到助动词之上(有关照应性音高重音删略以及核心重音转移的讨论见第 4 小节)。按照经节律解释的句法结构分析法,这类情况表明英语的功能范畴节律上可见。

上述分析最终旨在解释语言中基本层级（低层）节律特征与短语（高层）节律特征之间的联系，而其关键之处则在功能范畴的节律特征。在日耳曼语中，各类功能范畴均发生语音弱化，包括承载时态的助动词。在罗曼语中，情况却不同。甚至在元音弱化普遍的加泰罗尼亚语（Catalan）中，情况也非如此。加泰罗尼亚语里，许多限定词和介词都发生语音弱化，而承载时态的助动词从不弱化（见 Solà 等（2002））。功能范畴的节律显隐与功能词的韵律特征之间存在间接关系，即功能范畴的节律隐形取决于各类功能范畴（如 D，P，T，C）整体上发生弱化，而不与个别案例相关。这一点在 MI-S 分析法中容易理解，因为核心重音运算作用于（基于抽象句法结构的）抽象的节律结构，而不是音系词（phonological words）[①]。

需要指出的是，尽管理论有别，Féry 所提出的体系与 MI-S 在概念上存在一定的相似之处。前者将（21a）和（22a）描述为"韵律整合"，后者则依靠"节律成分"的概念。值得注意的是，Féry 的分析将（21b）中的主语限定词短语置于一个独特的话题位置，主语限定词短语必须分析成一个语调短语，动词则构成另一个语调短语（各有自身的核心重音）。而目前尚不清楚这种分析如何解释例（22b）。相比之下，MI-S 分析法在（21b）、（22b）中仅指派一个核心重音，即重音落在动词上；主语限定词短语则根据另外的节律规则获得次重音（见注释 5）。请注意，MI-S 分析并未讨论核心重音位置与音系短语划分之间的关系。因此，并不能排除（21b）只有一个音系短语。有趣的是，同一音系短语内两个相邻重音成分引发的重音回移（stress retraction）现象支持了上述分析的可行性。如（ip Ànne Marie bícycled ）（本例取自 Inkelas 和 Zec（1993））。然而，在后期于主语之后插入一个具有独立核心重音的语调短语边界，也是可行的，如（ip Anne Maríe）（ip bícycled）。

现在讨论介词短语。德语（3b）和（4）之间的差异可以根据（20）的

[①] 在 Nava 和 Zubizarreta（2010）以及 Zubizarreta 和 Nava（2011）的版本中，（20）中的核心重音规则并没有做参数化处理。因为在罗曼语中功能范畴在节律上可见，从而成为节律树计算的一部分，所以完全可以推出在罗曼语中只有规则的第（ii）部分适用。

核心重音规则得到直接解释。(3b) 中的介词短语是动词的一个词汇-句法论元，因此根据（20i）承载核心重音。而（4）中的介词短语是附加语，因此（20i）不适用，根据（20ii）将核心重音指派给 V (*Hans hat (an einem Papier gearbeitet)*)。

  对于含有位置和方向介词短语的及物句，如果将介词短语分析为动词的词汇-句法论元，或者更精确地说，将介词短语看作动词所在"动词短语壳"的一部分（如例 16a），则核心重音规则将核心重音指派给介词短语。因此，(17) 中的结构会呈现 (15) 所示的重音模式。至于 (14)，分析上则需要有所补充（正如 Féry 的体系所遇到的情况）。鉴于介词 P 的节律隐形特征，可以认为介词短语与动词发生了"节律并入"（事实上，同一类型的分析 Zubizarreta（1998：65）已提出）。若介词短语"节律上并入"动词，则宾语限定词短语和动词成为节律姊妹节点，根据（20i）将核心重音指派给宾语。

  与 Féry 提出的"韵律从属"机制一样，究竟"节律从属"因何触发，仍有待解答。前文曾提及，可能在中心语居后的德语（而非英语）中，及物句中的介词短语打破了动词短语中未提升的直接宾语与动词之间原本存在的相邻性。某种程度上，韵律通过将核心重音指派给宾语（可能通过将间隔的短语并入动词 V 所在的节律域这一方式）弥补了宾语和动词之间所缺乏句法（结构）相邻性。如果这一假设是正确的，则可预测节律并入（或韵律从属）只会发生在（17）一类的结构之中。核心重音不可能落在已经移出动词短语的宾语之上。此种情况下，宾语无核心重音这一现象本身也会说明它已经移出动词短语。

  总之，日耳曼语内部以及跨语言的核心重音指派差异说明，对于核心重音指派最好采取一种灵活的方式进行分析。Féry 所提出的韵律短语划分方法以及本节所介绍的 MI-S 方法在处理核心重音指派差异方面本质上都具备这样的灵活性。然而，两种体系在核心重音的理论地位方面却有根本不同的立场。

  在韵律短语划分的体系中，核心重音是划分韵律短语后的副产品。而在 MI-S 方法中，核心重音运算不需要划分韵律短语，并且它所确定的是无标记情形下的核心音高。

4　语篇旧信息及重音删略

我们接下来讨论日耳曼语中"有标记"的核心重音。在日耳曼语中，语篇在决定核心重音的位置方面起着主要作用。迄今，学者们已经识别出两种"有标记的"韵律模式：一个是在宽域焦点语境中，另一个是在窄域焦点语境中。在这些语境中，承载无标记核心重音的成分，因是语篇旧信息（即在前文中已经提到的信息）而失去音高重音。① 由于核心重音无法与重音删略材料相结合，它只能左移（Ladd（1980，1996），Reinhart（2006）；Nava 和 Zubizarreta（2010）；Zubizarreta 和 Nava（2011）等）。我们把这一现象称作（照应性）音高重音删略及核心重音转移（*NS-Shift*）。

有关"窄域"焦点"有标"重音模式的例子，可见（23）（其中斜体标记重音的部分）。

（23）a. <u>Mary</u> *bought that old stamp*. [Who bought that old stamp？]
　　　b. I am drawing <u>pictures</u> *on the cover*. [What are you drawing on the cover？]

音高重音删略触发了节律结构中韵律重量的改变。为说明这一点，我们不妨一起看一下（23b）中动词短语的节律树。（24a）是核心重音规则生成的节律树。介词的宾语的重音删略触发了核心重音转移，节律树上的轻（w）重（s）被重新标注（如 24b）。确切说来，那就是，原本携带无标记核心重音的介词宾语被重新标记为 W。结果，其姊妹节点（动词直接宾语）被重新标记为 S，并被解释为携带（有标记的）核心重音（即为 S 所统治的唯一节点被认为承载核心重音）。所以，介词宾语被认为是在节奏上（rhythmically）属于直接宾语。同样的道理，（23a）中重音删略后的 VP 被重新标记为 W，而其姊妹节点（主语）则被重新标记为 S；而且主语被认为是承载主要（有标的）重音，宾语则被认为节奏上处于从属性地位。

---

① 有关已知信息的讨论，见 Rochemont（2016）。有关德语中与各类已知信息相关的音高重音的细致讨论，亦见 Baumann（2006）。

(24)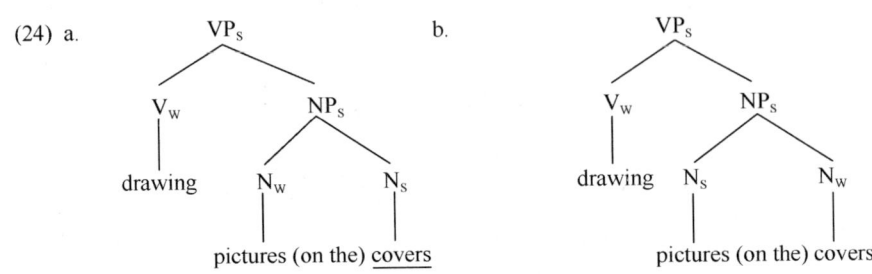

对窄域焦点而言，鉴于（1）中的常规核心重音-焦点对应限制，"有标记的"模式为其唯一选择，如（23）所示：如果焦点成分必须在韵律上识别为自然焦点的承载者，就必须采用照应性重音删略以及核心重音转移。①

我们再接着谈"宽域焦点"语境中"有标记的"韵律模式，如（25）所示（引自 Nava 和 Zubizarreta（2010）；Zubizarreta 和 Nava（2011）），其建立模型的例子则最早来自于 Ladd）。其中，经过了核心重音删略后的部分以斜体标示，而语篇语境则以括号标示。（25a）中，核心音高重音在动词上，动词短语为焦点成分；（25b）中，核心音高重音在直接宾语上，整个句子都是焦点成分。

（25）a. Because I <u>collect</u> *stamps*. [Why are you buying that old stamp？]

　　　b. Because I'm drawing <u>pictures</u> o*n the covers*. [Why are these notebooks missing their covers？]

（25）中的"有标记"模式（宽域焦点语境）不同于（23）的（窄域焦点语境）。如前所述，在具有"有标记"焦点的情况下，为使"有标记"焦点成分与核心重音相重合，根据（1）的要求，必须使用音高重音删略手段。另一方面，如果一个宽域焦点句中包含信息已知材料，对于标准英语而言，就存在重音删略的倾向。但仅此而已，未成系统：Zubizarreta 和 Nava（2011）调查了 35 位英语母语者（ENC），其中，75% 的被试会对（25a）的宾语进行重音删略，88%的被试则会对（25b）的介词短语进行重音删略。②此外，

---

① Reinhart（2006）提出，焦点组成的集合通过竞争满足韵律界面的要求，未经核心重音迁移而获得的核心重音模式比经由核心重音迁移获得的核心重音模式更受青睐。

② 与 Nava 和 Zubizarreta（2010）的研究相比，Zubizarreta 和 Nava（2011）的研究的被试更多。

据 Ladd（1996）的报告，有些英语方言（如夏威夷英语）并不对"宽域焦点"语境的已知信息进行音高重音删略。

根据以上讨论，核心重音规则是通过一种语法囊括机制（grammatically encapsulated mechanism）来决定中性语境下核心重音位置的（一句之中韵律上最为突显的词）。另一方面，核心重音转移由语篇因素触发（也就是说，由旧信息的音高重音删略导致）。根据这一观点，核心重音转移的运作触发节律结构的改变。此外，还有一种替代性的观点引人入胜，是由 Féry 和 Kügler（2008），Féry（2011）提出的，该观点认为，语篇概念直接导致了音高重音的缩减，而不致影响底层的节律结构。目前，有一种被称为"降阶"（Downstepping）的广为人知的现象，在无标记的语调模式中（皆为新信息）导致音高重音缩减，在一个调域中降阶从左向右应用，利用前面紧邻的高调降低后面的高调，有关英语降阶的文献见 Pierrehumbert（1980），Liberman 和 Pierrehumbert（1984）；德语降阶方面的文献则有 Féry 和 Kügler（2008），Féry（2011）及其所引用文献。根据后面几位学者的意见，这种降阶声调的默认序列可以受到语篇因素的进一步影响，如窄域焦点可能会导致音高重音的升阶，而已知信息则会使之在核心之前下降，在核心之后压缩。①

倘若采用 Féry 和 Kügler 的提议，我们就会得到这样一种观点：在"有标记"模式的情况下，音高重音（更确切地说，是核心音高重音）与核心重音（由节奏上的核心重音规则决定）分道扬镳（这一观点可见于 Kahnemuyipour（2004，2009））。具体而言，核心重音与核心音高重音会在中性语篇（宽域焦点）的情况下重合；在语篇因素触发承载核心重音成分的音高删略时，则不然。这一观点与经典的观点截然不同，值得进一步探讨。

且不论"有标"模式具体如何获得，需要记住的是，"有标记"模式是通过一种明确的语法囊括机制生成；而"无标记"模式则由其他机制生成

---

① 能够在两种方案之间作出抉择的关键问题在于，在确定"迁移的核心重音"的位置时是否与节律上的姊妹节点相关；相关讨论见 Ladd（1996），Green 等（2006）则提供了一些相关的试验数据。

（这些机制对语篇因素敏感）。最近有关西班牙语方言研究以及西班牙语母语者的英语（English of native Spanish speakers）研究为这一结论提供了进一步的支持。

经常有报道称，罗曼语族如西班牙语、意大利语等不会对已知材料进行音高重音删略操作，这些语言中句内的核心重音则会被识别为强调成分，见 Ladd（1996），Cruttenden（1997），Zubizarreta（1998）。有研究认为，就句内窄域焦点而言，这些语言会使用其他策略，如语序，令焦点成分与核心重音重合（见 Zubizarreta（1998）；Samek-Lodovici（2005））。最近的研究则认为，西班牙语并不完全排除句内窄域焦点，事实上在某些情况下还颇受偏爱。Gabriel（2010）所报道的一些阿根廷方言语料表明，不及物动词结构——V*S*[1]以及及物动词带附着宾语时——cl.V*S*[2]（26a）（也就是对"谁买了那本书"的一种回答）偏向于使用句末主语承载信息窄域焦点。另一方面，当信息上承载窄域焦点的主语出现在及物结构中且宾语为词汇词时，*SVO* 语序（26b）比 *VOS* 语序（26c）更受偏爱（下划线部分指的是焦点，可理解为最为突显部分，斜体则表示音高重音删略）。对于这些方言，照应性音高重音删略及核心重音转移（在西班牙语中这是有标记选择）更多地应用于 *V-XP-S* 语序（可能是出于"重量"的考虑）。然而，在其他方言，**信息上承载窄域焦点的主语**倾向于使用（26c）这种表达，（26b）的情况则被理解为是一种更正或对比焦点的情况（Zubizarreta（1998））（例如，*JOHN bought the book*，*not PETER*）。Zubizarreta（1998）认为，更正/对比的重音是通过强调重音规则生成的，它也能用于词的下一层面（与核心重音或核心重音转移规则（NS-Shift）不同）。这一规则可同 Féry & Kügler 的音高升阶规则（pitch-upstepping）相媲美；但它仅用来辨识窄域对比焦点（更广泛地说是更正）而不是信息焦点。窄域对比与窄域信息（或者新信息）焦点的区分，亦见 Katz 和 Selkirk（2011）。

---

[1] 即不及物动词加主语。
[2] 即附着宾语、及物动词加主语。

（26）a. El libro, locompró Juan.
　　　The book ACC Cl bought Juan
　　　'The book, Juan bought it."
　　b. Juan *compró el libro.*
　　c. Compró el libro Juan.

　　总而言之，虽然在语篇中性的语境中核心音高重音并不存在方言的差异（核心音高重音呈系统地占据语调范围的末尾位置），在有标记的情况下核心音高重音的位置表现出方言差异（甚至可能有个体的差异），而且在某些方言中这种偏好依赖于其他与重音相关韵律考虑。这一点支持了"有标记"模式与"无标记"模式是通过某种不同机制获得的观点。

　　Nava 和 Zubizarreta（2010）以及 Zubizarreta 和 Nava（2011）针对母语为西班牙语、英语为二语者产出的语料的研究，指向同样的结论。该研究表明，对二语学习者来说，产出句内"有标记的"核心重音（（23）那样的窄域焦点以及（25）那样的宽域焦点）要比产出句内"无标记的"核心重音明显简单（即在宽域焦点语境的事件性 SV 结构中核心重音落在主语上，如 2.1 所议）。作者的结论是，西班牙语语法与照应性音高重音删略及核心重音转移兼容，另外习得二语中的照应性音高重音删略及核心重音转移并不抑制母语的任何语法运算；所以说，讲西班牙语人容易把这一机制融合到他们的二语英语语法中。另一方面，母语为西班牙语的人在习得日耳曼语非句末核心重音这一"无标记的"韵律模式时会非常困难。在上述研究中，很少有二语习得者会为事件性 SV 不及物结构产出日耳曼语式的重音模式（而且从未达到母语的程度）。我们也期待"有标记的"重音类型更容易在语言接触中受到影响。

　　这一推理也适用于另一种观点（Féry 和 Kügler（2008）；Féry（2011）），该观点认为"有标记的"模式是通过直接缩减音高重音生成的。对于西班牙语母语者、德语或英语二语者，后一种机制（依赖于语篇的机制）比概括性的语法短语切分规则（10a）更容易习得。

5 结　　语

本文伊始即已指出，一句之中的突显与信息结构密切相关。我们已经根据实际语料，尤其是日耳曼语中与核心重音可变性相关的语料，对最近的一些研究进行了比较。无论语法中核心重音的最终状态如何（无论它是韵律切分的副产品还是在计算节律结构中有其优越性），它都需要一个语法系统成功地解释某些日耳曼语结构中核心重音位置的多样性以及罗曼语中核心重音位置的固定性。最近有关西班牙方言差异的研究，以及一语西班牙语/二语英语者的产出支持"无标记"（宽焦）模式是通过一种不同于"有标记"（窄焦）模式的规则生成（例如前者通过核心重音规则完成，后者则通过照应性音高重音删略及核心重音转移完成）这一观点。至于窄信息焦点和窄对比焦点是否在韵律上不同（前者以核心重音辨识，后者则通过强调重音辨识），则是另外一个问题，本章对其仅是浅议，它仍是当前热议的话题。

参　考　文　献

Baumann, S. 2006. *The Intonation of Givenness*. Tübingen: Max Niemeyer Verlag.

Bolinger, D. 1958. A theory of pitch accent in English. *Word*, 14: 109-149.

Bolinger, D. 1972. Accent is predictable (if you're a mind-reader). *Language*, 48: 633-644.

Chafe, W. 1974. Language and Consciousness. *Language*, 50(1): 111-133.

Chomsky, N. 1971. Deep Structure, Surface Structure and Semantic Interpretation. In D. Steinberg & L. Jakobovits (Eds.), *Semantics: An Interdisciplinary Reader in Philosophy, Linguistics and Psychology* (pp. 183-216). Cambridge: Cambridge University Press.

Chomsky, N. 1999. Derivation by Phase. *MIT Occasional Papers in Linguistics 18*. Also in M. Kenstowicz (Ed.), *Ken Hale: A Life in Language* (pp. 1-52). Cambridge, Mass: MIT Press, 2001.

Chomsky, N. 1995. *The Minimalist Program*. Cambridge, MA: MIT Press.

Chomsky, N. & Halle, M. 1968. *The Sound Pattern of English*. New York: Harper Row.

Cinque, G. 1993. A Null Theory of Phrase and Compound Stress. *Linguistic Inquiry*, 24: 239-298.

Cruttenden, A. 1997. *Intonation*. Cambridge: Cambridge University Press.

Féry, C. 2001. Focus and Phrasing in French. In C. Féry & W. Sternefeld (Eds.), *Audiatur Vox Sapientiae: A Festschrift for Arnim von Stechow*. Berlin: Akademie Verlag, 153-181.

Féry, C. & Kügler, Frank. 2008. Pitch Accent Scaling on Given, New and Focused Constituents in German. *Journal of Phonetics, 36*: 680-703.

Féry, C. 2011. German sentence accents and embedded prosodic phrases. *Lingua, 121*: 1906-1922.

Gabriel, C. 2010. On Focus, Prosody, and Word Order in Argentinean Spanish: A Minimalist OT Account. *ReVEL, 4* (Special edition): 183-222.

Gussenhoven, C. 1984. *On the Grammar and Semantics of Sentence Accents*. Dordrecht: Foris.

Green, J. P. & S. Kaufman. 2006. Evidence for phonological constraints on nuclear accent placement. *Language, 82*(1): 151-168.

Hale, K. & Keyser, S. J. 2002. *Prolegomenon to a Theory of Argument Structure*. Cambridge, MA.: MIT Press.

Halle, M. & Vergnaud, J.-R. 1987. *An Essay on Stress*. Cambridge, MA.: MIT Press.

Halliday, M. 1967. Notes on Transitivity and Theme in English, part II. *Journal of Linguistics, 3*: 199-244.

Inkelas, S. & Zec, D. 1993. Auxiliary Reduction without Empty Categories: A Prosodic Account. *Working Papers of the Cornell Phonetics Laboratory, 8*: 205-253.

Irwin, P. 2012. Unaccusativity at the interfaces. Ph.D. dissertation, New York University.

Jackendoff, R. 1972. *Semantic Interpretation in Generative Grammar*. Cambridge, MA.: MIT Press.

Jun, S. A. 2005. Prosodic Typology. In S. Jun (Ed.), *Prosodic Typology: The Phonology of Intonation and Phrasing* (pp. 430-458). Oxford: Oxford University Press.

Kayne, R. 1994. *The Antisymmetry of Syntax*. Cambridge, MA.: MIT Press.

Katz, J. & Selkirk, E. 2011. Contrastive focus vs. discourse new: Evidence from phonetic prominence in English. *Language,* 87(4): 771-816

Krifka, M. 1984. *Fokus, Topik, Syntaktische Struktur und Semantische Interpretation*. Tübingen: University of Tübingen.

Kahnemuyipour, A. 2004. *The Syntax of Sentential Stress*. Ph.D. dissertation, University of Toronto. Published (2009). Oxford: Oxford University Press.

Kratzer, A. & Selkirk, E. 2007. Phase Theory and Prosodic Spellout: The case of verbs. *The Linguistic Review, 24*: 93-135.

Ladd, R. 1980. *The Structure of Intonational Meaning: Evidence from English*. Bloomington:

Indiana University Press.

Ladd, R. 1996. *Intonational Phonology*. Bloomington: Indiana University Press.

Larson, R. 1988. On the Double Object Construction. *Linguistic Inquiry*, *19*: 335-391.

Liberman, M. 1975. *The Intonational System of English*. Cambridge, MA.: MIT Press.

Liberman, M. & Pierrehumbert, J. 1984. Intonational Invariance under Changes in Pitch Range and Length. In M. Aronoff & R. Oehrle (Eds.), *Language sound Structure* (pp. 157-223). Cambridge, MA.: MIT Press.

Liberman, M.& Prince, A. 1977. On Stress and Linguistic Rhythm. *Linguistic Inquiry*, *8*: 249-336.

Nava, E. & Zubizarreta, M. L. 2010. Deconstructing the nuclear stress algorithm: Evidence from second language speech. In N. Erteschik-Shir & L. Rochman (Eds.), *The Sound Patterns of Syntax* (pp. 291-316). Oxford: Oxford University Press.

Nespor, M. & Vogel, I. 1986. *Prosodic Phonology*. Dordrecht: Foris.

Newman, S. 1946. On the Stress System of English. *Word*, 2: 171-187.

Pierrehumbert, J. 1980. *The Phonology and Phonetics of English Intonation*. Cambridge, MA.: MIT Press.

Reinhart, T. 2006. *Interface Strategies: Optimal and Costly Computation*. Cambridge, MA.: MIT Press.

Rochemont, M. 1986. *Focus in Generative Grammar*. Amsterdam: John Benjamins.

Rooth, M. 1985. *Association with Focus*. Ph.D. dissertation. Department of Linguistics, University of Massachusetts, Amherst.

Samek-Lodovici, V. 2005. Prosody Syntax Interaction in the Expression of Focus. *Natural Language and Linguistic Theory*, *23*: 687-755.

Sasse, H.-J. 1987. The Thetic/Categorical Distinction Revisited. *Linguistics*, *25*: 511-580.

Schmerling, S. 1976. *Aspects of English Sentence Stress*. Austin: University of Texas Press.

Selkirk, E. 1984. *Phonology and Syntax: The Relation between Sound and Structure*. Cambridge, MA.: MIT Press.

Selkirk, E. 1995. Sentence Prosody: Intonation, Stress, and Phrasing. In J. A. Goldsmith (Ed.), *The Handbook of Phonological Theory* (pp. 550-569). Cambridge: Blackwell.

Szendröi, K. 2001. *Focus and the Syntax-Phonology Interface*. Ph.D dissertation, University College London.

Solà, J., Lloret, M. R., Mascaró, J. & Pérez-Saldanya, M. 2002. *Gramàtica Del Català Contemporani*, vol. 1, Barcelona: Empúrie.

Truckenbrodt, H. 2006. Phrasal stress. In Keith Brown (Ed.), *The Encyclopedia of Languages and Linguistics* (2nd edition) (Vol. 9) (pp. 572-579). Oxford: Elsevier.

Vallduví, E. 1995. Structural Properties of Information Packaging in Catalan. In K. Kiss (Ed.), *Discourse Configurational Languages*. Oxford: Oxford University Press.

Zubizarreta, M. L. 1998. *Prosody, Focus, and Word Order*. Cambridge, MA.: MIT Press.

Zubizarreta, M. L. & Vergnaud, J.-R. 2005. Phrasal stress, focus, and syntax. In M. Everaert & H. van Riemsdijk (Eds.), *The Syntax Companion*. Cambridge: Blackwell.

Zubizarreta, M. L. & Nava, E. 2011. Encoding discourse-based meaning: Prosody vs. syntax: Implications for second language acquisition. *Lingua, 121*(4): 652-669.

Nuclear Stress and Information Structure

Maria Luisa Zubizarreta

Abstract This paper discusses and evaluates different approaches to the nuclear stress (NS) algorithm in light of the variability in stress pattern observed for certain constructions in German and English in wide focus contexts ("unmarked" stress patterns), in opposition to the rigid (right-most) nature of NS in Spanish/Italian. The paper also briefly discusses the case of nuclear stress in narrow focus contexts ("marked" stress patterns), and points to recent research that suggests that "unmarked" and "marked" stress patterns originate through distinct mechanisms.

Keywords Nuclear stress, Anaphoric Deaccenting, Metrical structure, Prosodic phrasing.

Maria Luisa Zubizarreta

Professor, Linguistics Department, University of Southern California

E-mail: zubizarr@usc.edu

从音步和重音看语言的共性与任意性*

端木三

摘要 不同语言既有特性（任意性）也有共性，但是遇到语言之间有不同现象时，往往很难知道这种现象体现了语言的任意性，还是掩盖着语言的共性。Duanmu（2000）提出一个假设，即语言的任意性仅限于词汇的音义结合，其他方面都应该以共性为主。本文以音步和重音为例，为上述假设提供证据，同时演示如何寻找语言的共性。

关键词 音步 重音 音系 语言的共性 语言的任意性

1 引言：语言的特性（任意性）和共性

不同的语言既有特性（即任意性），也有共性。共性的例子可见（1），特性的例子可见（2）。

（1）已知的语言共性举例：
  a. 句子由词（语素）组成。
  b. 词（语素）由语音组成。
  c. 诗歌的押韵，以韵母相同为基础，声母、介音不必相同，如"晒-帅-外"[ṣai]-[ṣwai]-[wai] 押韵。

（2）已知的语言特性（任意性）举例：

---

* 本文内容曾在"第二届汉语韵律语法研究国际研讨会"上宣读，感谢会议的邀请、香港中文大学的热情接待以及与会者的讨论。因篇幅所限，本文只包括会议发言的音步和重音部分，有关声调、音位、音节的讨论可见端木三（2016b）。

a. 汉语用声调区别词义，英语不用。
　　b. 普通话的音节没有塞音结尾，而英语的有。
　　c. 有的语言音位多，有的语言音位少。
　　d. 有的语言词重音在第一音节，有的语言词重音在最后一个音节。
　　e. 英语的单音节词少，汉语的单音节词多。

　　以上例子都是一些常见性质，学者们有共识也许不奇怪。遇到不常见的情况时，比如（3）所列举的例子，人们的看法就很不一样。

　　（3）共性还是特性答案不清楚的情况举例：
　　a. 升调、降调，是否都是平调（高、低）的组合？
　　b. 所有语言是否都以元音、辅音为音位？
　　c. 所有语言是否都有音节结构？
　　d. 所有语言是否都有重音？

　　关于升调，我们知道，非洲语言的升调是"低+高"两个平调的组合，降调是"高+低"两个平调的组合（Leben, 1972; Williams, 1976; Goldsmith, 1976, 1981）。这个性质是不是语言的共性？如果是，汉语也应该如此。如果分析不适合汉语，那么这个性质就没有普遍性。在这个问题上，有人认为汉语的升调、降调也是平调的组合，有人认为不是，一直没有统一看法。又如，西方传统描写某个语言，一般从音位开始，首先要弄清该语言有什么元音、辅音。音位分析，有没有普遍性？如果有，汉语是不是也应该从音位入手？如果汉语不适合用音位分析，那么音位分析就没有普遍性（游汝杰等，1980；Ladefoged, 2001）。再如，中国传统描写某个语言，一般从音节开始，首先要问的是该语言或方言有什么声母、韵母，有多少音节。音节分析，有没有普遍性？如果有，英语是不是也应该用音节分析？可是英语的音节分析问题不少，以致有的学者认为音节分析不适合英语（Chomsky 和 Halle，1968；Steriade，1999），认为音节理论没有普遍性。关于重音，我们知道英语有，可是汉语有没有，意见至今仍然不一致。

　　对于未知问题有不同看法，本来很正常。只要不影响研究、不影响我们寻求答案，什么样的态度似乎关系不大。可是，以上两种态度对研究产生的影响很不一样。为了方便，我们把两种观点称为"普遍论"和"分类论"。普遍论在看到语言之间有不同时，一般会继续探讨这种不同是否掩盖了语言的共性。分类论在看到语言之间有不同时，一般只是给有关语言冠以不同类别，研究也就到此为止。因为分类论不要求对表面现象加以深究，所以很难有新发现。而普遍论力求透过表面现象继续寻找普遍规律，所以发现新规律的机会也相对更多。

可是，语言之间的确有任意性的区别，如（2）所列的例子。这些区别没有共性可寻，也没有进一步的原因可寻。如果见到这些区别时，继续盲目寻找共性，恐怕只是徒劳。那么有没有一个指导性的标准，可以让我们知道，什么样的语言区别是任意的、不用继续深究，什么样的语言区别可能只是表面现象、后面掩盖着语言的共性？

语言的任意性，最常见的表现是词或语素的音义结合。对于一个事物（或动作、概念、等），一个语言可以任意选用一组语音来表达。比如，莎士比亚说，一朵玫瑰无论你怎么称呼它，都丝毫不会影响它的香味。那么除了词汇的音义结合以外，语言还有哪些任意性？要想出一个可靠的例子，似乎并不容易。所以，Duanmu（2000：v）说，"除了词汇以外，各种语言都惊人的相似"（Beyond the lexicon, languages are strikingly similar）。我们将这个观点进一步明确化，见（4）。

（4）语言任意性的限定：

　　　语言的任意性仅局限于造词，即词（或语素）的音义结合。

虽然语言的任意性只有一条，但是我们可以从中推出语言之间的一系列其他区别，包括（2）列举的所有例子。比如，一个语言是否用声调别义，可以归因于音义结合的任意性。一个语言的音节是否用塞音结尾，也可以归因于音义结合的任意性。因为造词可以（无计划地）任意选音位，所以有的语言音位用得多、有的用得少，这也可以归因于音义结合的任意性。词的重音在哪个音节，也属于音义结合的一个方面，所以也是任意的。最后，词的长短（音节数），也是音义结合的一个方面，所以也是任意的。因此，（2）所列的区别全部可以归因于造词过程的音义结合，无需其他解释。

值得指出的是，虽然音义结合是任意的，但是词的语音仍然必须符合音系的普遍规则，比如语音必须组成音节，音节不能超过 CVX（Duanmu，2008），重音必须由长音节负载（端木三，2014，2016a）等。

当然，以上的假设需要证实。比如，(3) 所列的例子都不属于音义结合，根据我们的假设，都应该有共性可寻，我们能证实吗？关于（3a-c），端木三（2016b）逐条进行了讨论，本文不重复。下面我们只考虑两个题目，即音步结构和重音的体现。这两个题目，几乎所有学者的态度都属于"分类论"，而根据我们的假设，它们应该属于共性。因此，我们对它们进行比较详细的讨论。

2 音步结构

音步理论来自西方，最初源于对诗歌节奏的研究。最常见的节奏是节拍的轻重交替，音步也就是交替重复的单位，即一个音步就是轻重节拍的一次交替。因此，每个音步都有且仅有一个重音，而每个重音来自一个音步。因为音步跟重音直接有关，音步也广泛用于词重音的研究。

音步研究多以"分类论"为主，可能因为诗歌的节奏看起来十分多样，如一首诗有几行、每行有多长（多少音节）、每行是重拍起还是轻拍起等。各种语言的词重音，看起来也十分多样，比如有的语言词重音一般在第一个音节（如匈牙利语），有的一般在第二个音节（如印第安语 Paiute），有的一般在末尾音节（如法语），有的根据音节长短而有所变化（如英语），等等。

Hyman（1977）收集了 444 个语言的词重音，根据词重音是否有固定的位置，将这些语言进行了分类，结果见（5）。

(5) Hyman（1977：58）对词重音的分类：

重音位	语言数
第一音节	114
第二音节	12
倒数第三音节	6
倒数第二音节	77
倒数第一音节	97
其他情况	138
共计	444

词重音有固定位置的有 306 个语言，其他 138 无固定位置。后者包括三类（Hyman，1977：66-68）：(i) 以音节长短决定重音的语言（9 个），如阿拉伯语；(ii) 无词重音的语言（16 个），如韩语；(iii) 无固定词重音位置的语言（113 个），如汉语、英语。

Hayes（1985，1995）认为，因为重音跟音步有关，即每个音步都有一个重音，而每个重音都来自一个音步，因此除了考虑词重音的位置以外，还需要考虑音步的种类。Hayes 提出，词首、词尾有时会多出一个音节，如果我们排除多余音节，基本音步只有三种，见（6），其中 M 表示莫拉，S 表示音节，下横线表示重音。

(6) Hayes（1985, 1995）提出的三种基本音步：

音步种类	符号表示
莫拉左重步（moraic trochee）	(<u>M</u>M)
音节左重步（syllabic trochee）	(<u>S</u>S)
音节右重步（syllabic iamb）	(S<u>S</u>)

莫拉指韵母位置的数量，冯胜利（1997，2015）称之为"韵素"。一个长音节有两个莫拉，一个短音节只有一个莫拉。长音节的韵母有三种：双元音、元音加辅音、或长元音，如普通话的 [mai]"买"、[man]"慢"、[ma：]"骂"。因为长音节有两个莫拉，每个长音节都可以组成一个莫拉步。

Halle 和 Vergnaud（1987）提出一个不同的音步分类法。他们认为，每种音步都是一组基本参数的组合。他们提出的参数有三项，见（7）。

(7) Halle 和 Vergnaud（1987）提出的音步参数及选择值：

参数	选择值
节拍单位	两项：莫拉、音节
音步长短	三项：两拍、三拍、无限制
重音位置	三项：左、右、中

如果参数值可以自由搭配，一共可以产生 2 × 3 × 3 = 18 种音步。不过，莫拉步一般只有两拍，而且重音位置的"中"只适合于三拍音步，所以音步种类一共不到 18 个。即使如此，Halle 和 Vergnaud 的音步种类仍然大大超过 Hayes 提出的三个种类。不过，三拍音步和长度无限制的音步都不多

（或者是可以用两排步来分析）；如果排除这两类，那么音步长短只有一类，重音位置也只剩两类（重音在"中"的也排除了）。这样，Halle 和 Vergnaud 的音步就只有四类，即左重莫拉步、右重莫拉步、左重音节步、右重音节步，只比 Hayes 多了一个右重莫拉步。

如果词重音的位置是音义结合的一个方面，那它基本属于语言的任意性，所以语言之间词重音的位置的区别不用进一步解释。如果音步是节奏的单位，而节奏不限于单词，经常可以出现在更大的语法单位上，如诗句，那么，音步就不应该属于语言的任意性，而应该属于语言的共性。换言之，根据我们的假设（4），音步的"分类论"是值得质疑的。

Hayes（1985，1995）提出一个理论来限制音步的分类，他称之为"右重/左重法"（the Iambic/Trochaic Law）。他说，音步的种类跟节拍有关。如果节拍不分长短，就应该是左重步，否则就是右重步。莫拉不分长短，因此莫拉步都是左重。如果一个语言的音节不分长短，而且这个语言选择音节步，它的音步也是左重步。如果一个语言的音节要分长短，而且这个语言选择音节步，它的音步就是右重步。根据"右重/左重法"，音步类型看起来有了限制，其实分类的本质不变，即语言可以选择音节是否分长短，还可以选择节拍单位是莫拉还是音节。这些选择都被认为是任意的、不用进一步解释的。

音步理论认为，对词重音来说，一个语言只能选择一种音步。可是一个语言选的是什么音步往往不容易判断。比如，英语是人们研究得最多的语言之一，可是有人认为英语用的是音节步（Halle 和 Vergnaud，1987），有人认为是莫拉步（Mester，1994；Hayes，1995）。可见，就连这个最基本的问题也无共识。对其他语言来讲，我们对事实的了解往往更少，其音步分类的可信度也可想而知。因此，对音步的研究，还是应该从我们比较熟悉的、有足够语料的语言做起。

汉语的重音，感觉上往往没有英语的明显。汉语诗歌的传统研究也从来不谈重音或音步（王力，1958）。不过，汉语也有一系列迹象，说明重音和音步仍然存在。

首先，汉语有个普遍现象，即轻声音节（轻声字）跟普通音节的重音区别很明显（Chao，1968），而且，前者的平均时长明显短于后者。还有，轻声音节一般没有声调，而普通音节有声调。原来有声调的音节，变成轻声以后，也会失去原来的声调，而且韵母也会有相应的简化。我们用普通话举例，见（8），引自高名凯、石安石（1963：84-85），其中横线后的数字表示声调，2 表示上声，4 表示去声，0 表示轻声。

（8）轻声音节韵母简化、失去本调（高名凯和石安石，1963：84-85）：

汉字	非轻声	轻声	轻声使用举例
头	[tʰou]-2	[tʰo]-0	木头
袋	[tai]-4	[te]-0	脑袋

以上现象，可以用"声调-重音连接律"（Tone-Stress Principle）来解释，见（9）。该规律被用来分析各种语言，包括英语（Goldsmith，1981；Liberman，1975；Pierrehumbert，1980），日语（Pierrehumbert 和 Beckman，1988），汉语（Yip，1980；Duanmu，1999），以及各种非洲语言（Goldsmith，1976）。

（9）声调-重音连接律（Tone-Stress Alignment）：
　　声调必须和有重音的音节连接（边界调除外）。

普通话的轻声音节只有一个莫拉，不足以组成一个莫拉步，所以无重音、不能保留本调。其他音节都有两个莫拉，可以组成莫拉步，进而有重音，可以保留声调。

因为音步是韵律的最小单位，应该可以单独使用，由一个音步组成的词也叫"最小词"（minimal word）。如果汉语的非轻声音节是个莫拉步，这样的单音节词应该可以单独使用。可是，汉语的最小词一般需要两个音节。比如，高本汉（Karlgren，1918，1923）发现，汉语很多动词不能单独使用，而必须增加一个语义多余的词，例子见（10）、（11）。

（10）汉语单音节动词一般不单用：
　　问：你想做什么？
　　回答：教书/写字/走路/吃饭。
　　不答：教/写/走/吃。

（11）英语单音节动词可以单用：
　　问：What do you want to do?

"你想做什么？"
回答：Teach/Write/Walk/Eat.
"教/写/走/吃。"
不答：Teach books/Write words/Walk roads/Eat meal.
"教书/写字/走路/吃饭。"

汉语的例子，回答不能只用"教"、"写"、"走"或"吃"，而必须用双音节的"教书"、"写字"、"走路"或"吃饭"。从语义来看，这里的宾语完全是多余的，或者是无用的。比如，"教书"就是"教"，用不用书完全无关；"写"的一定是字，所以"字"完全多余。相应的英语例子，进一步显示了这些宾语的多余性：英语的回答只用动词，不用宾语，用了宾语反而显得臃肿。当然，对"普遍论"来说，为什么汉语需要用双音节，而英语不需要，也是个需要解释的问题，我们下面还会讨论。

吕叔湘（1963）也举过不少例子，姓名、地名、国名、都不用单音节，必须加一个字凑成双音节，而双音节的名词就不用加多余的字，例子见（12）、（13）。

（12）汉语单音节名词一般不单用：
问：他是谁？
回答：老王/小王/欧阳。
不答：王/老欧阳。

（13）汉语单音节地名、国名一般不单用：
问：你去哪儿？
回答：泰山/华山/沙市/上海/法国/荷兰。
不答：泰/华/沙/上海市/法/荷兰国。

回答姓名时，如果是单音节，习惯要加个"老"、"小"等，凑成双音节；如果姓名是双音节，就可以直接用，一般不加"老"、"小"，如一般不说"老欧阳"。同样，地名、国名如果是单音节，必须加个语义多余的"山"、"市"、"国"等；如果地名是双音节，习惯就不加，如不说"荷兰国"。

有人可能会说，使用双音节是为了避免歧义。比如，如果只说"我去泰",也许听话人不知道你去"泰山""泰国",还是"太湖",说"我去泰山"就清楚了。不过,在没有歧义时,汉语仍然需要双音节。比如,如果别人知道你要去爬山,但是不知道是去泰山还是华山,这时"山"字的语义完全多余,但是你还是得用双音节,见(14)。

(14) 无歧义时汉语仍然需要双音节:
问:你去华山还是泰山?
回答:泰山。
不答:泰。

因此,汉语对双音节的要求,主要出于韵律的考虑,而不是语义的考虑。而最自然的韵律单位就是一个音节步,即一个双音节单位。

可是我们在前面说了,汉语已经有莫拉步,用于区分无调的轻声音节和有调的其他音节。如果汉语既有莫拉步,又有音节步,这就违反了前人的一个根本假设,即一个语言只能选择一种音步(Hayes,1995)。Duanmu(1999,2007)、Duanmu et al.(2005)提出,前人的假设应该修改。对英语和汉语来讲,左重莫拉步和左重音节步都需要,两者组成"双重左重步"(dual trochee)。莫拉步用于区别长音节(有重音)和短音节(无重音),音节步用于解释最小自由词对双音节的要求。"双重左重步"必须符合"双拍步"(Foot Binarity)的要求,见(15)。

(15) "双拍步"(Foot Binarity,Prince,1980):
音步必须有两拍。

双拍步的要求源于节奏的本质,即轻重交替:交替一次需要两拍,也即一个音步。双重左重步的结构见(16),其中"M"表示莫拉,"X"表示重音音节位,"。"表示无重音音节位,"|"表示音节界。

(16) 双重左重步(Duanmu,1999,2007;Duanmu et al.,2005):
a. 合理结构:长长
```
        X
(   X        X    )   音节步
( MM   ) | ( MM   )   莫拉步
```

b. 合理结构：长短

```
               X
   (   X          。   )    音节步
   (   MM    ) | M         莫拉步
```

c. 不合理结构：短长（问题：第一音节是单拍莫拉步）

```
               X
   (   X          X    )    音节步
   (   M    ) | (  MM  )    莫拉步
```

d. 不合理结构：短短（问题：第一音节是单拍莫拉步）

```
               X
   (   X     。   )    音节步
   (   M   ) | M       莫拉步
```

e. 不合理结构：长（问题：单拍音节步）

```
       X
   (   X    )    音节步
   (   MM   )    莫拉步
```

f. 不合理结构：短（问题：单拍音节步、单拍莫拉步）

```
       X
   (   X    )    音节步
   (   M    )    莫拉步
```

如果音节分长短，两个音节有四种搭配：长长、长短、短长、短短。其中"长长"、"长短"中的长音节分别是个莫拉步，短音节不是。然后，两个音节再组成一个左重音节步。这两种搭配中的莫拉步、音节步都符合双拍步。

"短长"中的长音节是个莫拉步，短音节也有重音，来自左重音节步。这个重音使得短音节也成为一个莫拉步，而这个莫拉步只有一排，因此违反了双拍步。同样，"短短"的第一音节也是一个单拍的莫拉步，因此也违反双拍步。还有，单音节一般不能组成双重音步，无论是长音节还是短音节。

汉语"长长"音步的例子很多，多数双音节单位都是。在北京话里，"长长"音步在非停顿前一律是"重中"（Chao, 1968），即第一音节最重、第二音节次重，如"大学教师"中的"大学"，跟音步结构的分析一致。在停顿

前（包括单独出现时），北京话的"长长"音步经常由"重中"变为"中重"，如单读的"大学"，或"北京大学"中的"大学"。端木三（2014）认为，北京话的基本音步一律是左重，不过"长长"音步在停顿前可以产生重音右移，进而产生结构变化，分析见（17）。

（17）普通话停顿前的重音右移，产生"长短"型音步（S0）：

```
           X                           X
    (  X       X   )          X   (    X     。 )  音节步
    (  MM  )(  MM  )        (  MM  )(  MM  )   0   莫拉步
       大      学      →       大       学
```

新结构的第一音节仍然是莫拉步，但是不再处于音节步内。新的音节步往右移了一位，产生一个"长短"型音步，其中的第二拍是停顿，也称"空拍"或"休止"。这种音步，我们用（S0）表示，其中 S 指音节（syllable），0 指空拍。空拍的概念在韵律研究中经常用到，包括对各国诗歌韵律的研究（Burling，1966；松浦友久，1992；Hayes，1995；川本皓嗣，2004；端木三，2016a）。值得注意的是，汉语的 S0 音步很受限制，一般只用于重音右移时，以及少数可以单用的词，如"好！"、"对！"等。

汉语"长短"音步的例子也很多，如北京话的"妈妈"、"西瓜"、"来了"等，其中第一个音节有重音，第二个音节是轻声、无重音。"长短"音步不能产生重音右移，否则重音会落在单莫拉的短音节上，违反双拍步要求。

汉语没有"短长"、"短短"音步，跟音步分析的预测相符。汉语的事实说明"短长"、"短短"音步的结构的确有问题。

英语的"长长"音步例子有 congress [kɔŋ][grɛs]"会议"、content [kɔn][tɛn]<t>"内容"等，其中方括号表示音节界、尖括号表示末尾可以不计的辅音（Hayes，1982；Duanmu，2008）。这类单词的主重音在第一音节、次重音在第二音节，跟音步分析的预测相符。值得指出的是，英语词典对次重音的标注不大一致，比如，很多词典都不给单音节单词标重音（如 ten [tɛn]"十"），主重音右边的音节一般也不标次重音（如 yellow [jɛlou]"黄"的第二音节）。Chomsky 和 Halle（1968）认为，英语无重音的元音一般都是 [ə]，有

时也可以是 [ɪ]（如 Michigan [mɪʃɪgən]的第二个元音），而双元音以及[aʊ ɔ ɛ æ ʌ ɪ]等一律都有重音。因为无重音的[ə]与[ɪ]很少有对立，我们也可以不必区分两者，一律写成[ə]（如 Michigan [mɪʃəgən]的第二个元音），这样英语无重音的元音都是[ə]，而双元音以及[aʊ ɔ ɛ æ ʌ ɪ]等一律都有重音。

英语"长短"音步的例子有 panda [pæn][də]"熊猫"、Texas [tɛk][sə]<s>"德克萨斯"等。这类单词的第一音节有重音，第二音节无重音，跟音步分析的预测相符。

英语的单音节词很多，也可以分析为"长短"音步（S0），其中第二拍是个空拍，例子见（18）。

（18）用"长短"音步（S0）分析英语的单音节词：
　　　　fan [fæn][0]"扇"

英语的空拍，经常不以停顿出现，而是使前面的音节拉长。这个现象，一般称为"顿前拖延"（pre-pause lengthening），也称"末尾拖延"（final lengthening），初敏等（2003）称之为"停延"。根据 Price et al.（1991）的研究，在主要边界前（语调短语以及更大边界前），顿前拖延跟音节重音的关系见图 1。该图显示，有重音的末尾音节比其他音节（即有重音的非末尾音节、无重音的末尾音节以及其他无重音音节）平均长出一倍。而且，在主要焦点位置，前者延长更多。

顿前拖延为 S0 音步提供了支持，而 S0 音步对顿前拖延提供了解释。不过，英语的事实也提出一个新问题。如果英语的单音节词可以和空拍组成 S0 音步，进而可以单用，为什么汉语的单音节词一般不能单用？

我们认为，英语、汉语对 S0 音步使用之所以不同，在于它们的顿前拖延不同。学过英语的中国人恐怕都有同感，英国人（或美国人）讲话时，单音节词特别容易拖长，而中国人讲话时，单音节词很少拖长。试比较英语的 My name is John 和汉语的"我姓姜"，其中的 John [dʒɒn] 和"姜" [tɕɑŋ]发音基本相同，可是前者一般明显拖长，而后者则不然。同样，中国学生学英语的一个难点，就是要学会在什么地方把音节拖长。

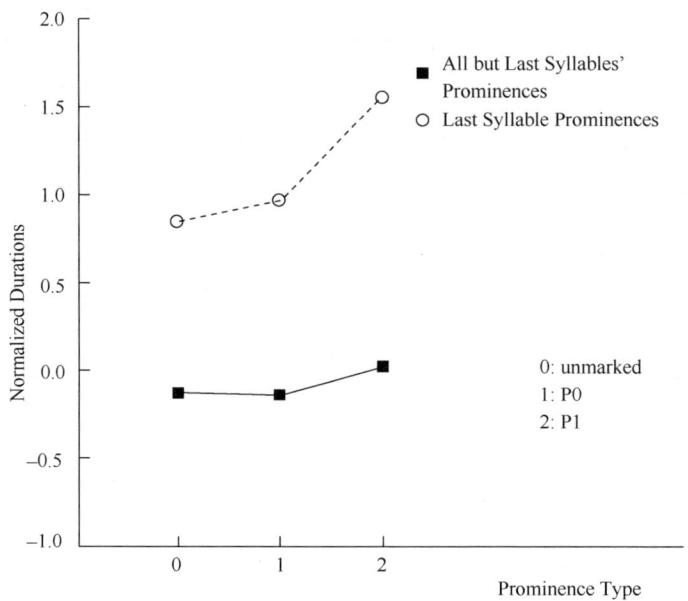

图 1　语调短语（intonational phrase）以及更大边界前的顿前拖延跟音节重音的关系
（经 Acoustical Society of America 同意，摘自 Price et al. 1991：2966）

注：图中虚线表示有重音的末尾音节、实线表示其他音节。横坐标的 0 表示无焦点，1 表示次要焦点，2 表示主要焦点。纵坐标表示相对时长。上图显示，有重音的末尾音节（虚线）比其他音节（实线）长出一倍。而且，在主要焦点位置，前者延长更多。

实验数据也支持同样的结论。上面看到，英语的顿前拖延可以使音节长度增加一倍以上（Price et al.，1991）。而汉语的情况却不然。比如，林茂灿等（1984）的研究发现，北京话的后重音节，在停顿前只是略微延长，平均不到 15%，远远低于英语的拖延幅度，数据见（19）。

（19）北京话的顿前拖延（103 个两字组，单独发音，多数是后重）：

发音人	第一音节平均时长	第二音节平均时长	延长比例
男	265 毫秒	301 毫秒	13.5%
女	249 毫秒	283 毫秒	13.6%

为什么汉语的音节没有英语的容易拖延？一个可能是，汉语是有调语言，英语不是。有调语言的音节长度跟声调的识别有关。比如，普通话的阳平跟上声（全上）有时长上的区别，阳平读长了容易跟全上混淆，全上读短了容易跟阳平混淆。另一个可能是，汉语经常通过延长音节并额外加

调来表达语气，Chao（1933）称之为声调语调的"连续叠加"（successive addition）。比如，"坏"的声调（降调）加"疑问"语调（高调）产生"降+升"调，如"坏？"。同样，"高"的声调（高调）加"确定"语调（低调）产生"高+降"调，如"高！"。如果把音节随便拉长，普通话的有些声调就有可能被理解为声调语调的"连续叠加"。比如，"告"拉长了就有可能跟有确定语调的"高！"（高+降）相混淆。当然，这两种可能的解释都有待进一步证明。

跟汉语一样，英语没有"短长"的左重音步，也没有"短短"的左重音步。看似"短长"的左重单词，如 rabbi [ræ][bai] "拉比"，应该分析为"长长"音步，即 [ræb][ai]（Duanmu, 2008）。看似"短短"的左重单词，如 villa [vɪ][lə] "别墅"，应该分析为"长短"音步，即[vɪl][ə]（Duanmu, 2008）。

剩下还有一个音步没有讨论，即"右重音节步"（也称"抑扬"步）。首先，根据 Hayes（1985）的统计，右重音节步的例子比左重音步少得多。而且，有学者已经指出，右重音节步可以看成左重音节步（Abercrombie, 1965；Kager, 1993；Vijver, 1998；端木三, 2014）。有关例子见（20）、（21），其中小 x 表示无重音音节，大 X 表示有重音音节，括号表示音步界。诗歌例子取自莎士比亚的《国王理查德二世》。

（20）用左重音步分析右重音步，诗歌举例：
　　　右重音步　（xX）（xX）（xX）（xX）（xX）
　　　左重音步 x（Xx）（Xx）（Xx）（Xx）（X0）
　　　诗句　The lion dying thrusteth forth its paw
　　　"垂死的雄狮猛地伸出前爪"

（21）用左重音步分析右重音步，单词举例：
　　　右重音步　（xX）
　　　左重音步 x（X0）
　　　单词　today "今天"

Abercrombie（1965）认为，英语的所谓"抑扬五步格"诗歌（即每行有五个右重音步），如果第一个音节不计、末尾加一个空拍，就变成了"扬抑五步格"（即每行有五个左重音步）。同样，一个右重的双音节单词，看上去像个右重音步（xX），但是如果第一个音节不计、末尾加一个空拍，就成了一个左重音步（X0）。

以上讨论说明，英语、汉语的音步结构有惊人的相似之处，两者都使用左重莫拉步和左重音节步，即"双重左重步"，两者的最小词都是左重音节步。而且，尚无明确证据需要增加右重音步。这个结论，从英语本身很难看出，而通过汉语和英语的比较，就清楚多了。

我们的分析，仅限于英语和汉语。有什么理由认为，我们的结论有普遍意义、其他语言也都如此？我们认为，起码有三条理由。第一，英语和汉语是两个完全独立的语言，历史上没有同源关系。它们之间能找到的共性，说明其他语言中也有可能找到。第二，英语是否有双重音步，并不是一目了然的事，至今还没有其他学者提出来过。因此，这样的规律很可能来自人的自然本能，很难想象是任意造出来的。同样，汉语是否有音步或重音，学者们长期意见不一，因此，这样的规律也很难想象是任意造出来的。第三，虽然有很多语言尚待研究，我们没有证据认为它们肯定不适合我们发现的规律。从科学的方法论来说，在没有见到反例以前，我们的基本假设应该是，现有的理论是正确的，是能够适用于新情况的。

3 重音的体现

关于重音，端木三（2014，2016a）有较详细的综述。限于篇幅，这里我们只讨论一个问题，即为什么从语感上来说，英语的重音比较明显，特别是词重音，而汉语的却不明显。这个事实，应该是有共识的。比如，讨论汉语重音的文献一方面不多，一方面争议比较大。而且还有人认为，汉语根本就没有重音（高名凯、石安石 1963；Selkirk 和 Shen，1990）。

关于重音的存在和重音的体现，前人的观点几乎都是"分类论"。比如，Hyman（1977）认为，有的语言有重音，有的语言无重音。Hayes（1995：7）

说,"重音的语音体现形式,各个语言皆可不同"(stress is phonetically realized on a language-specific basis)。Kager(1995:366)说,"我们至今没有发现重音有任何固定的语音特征"(an unambiguous phonetic correlate has not yet been discovered)。陈渊泉(Chen,2000)说,有的音步有重音(如上海话),有的音步无重音(如普通话)。王洪君(2004)说,英语的音步以重音为基础,汉语的音步以音节之间的松紧为基础。

对"分类论"来说,问题到此结束:有的语言有重音,有的没有;有的语言这样体现重音,有的那样体现。这都是任意的选择、都不需要任何其他解释。而对"普遍论"来说,重音的不同体现需要有个解释。首先,我们必须要问,为什么英语的重音明显,而汉语的不明显?

如果我们全面考察事实,就会发现英语的重音并不是任何时候都明显,尤其是次重音(Wang,1962)。比如,canteen"食堂"的第一个音节、rabbi"拉比"的第二个音节、multiply"乘"的第三音节有没有次重音,意见并不一致。Chomsky和Halle(1968)认为,这样的长音节一律都有次重音。可是在英语词典CELEX里(Baayen et al.,1995),跟主重音相邻的长音节一般不标次重音,如canteen的第一个音节、yellow的第二个音节、rabbi的第二个音节等,而跟主重音不相邻的长音节,主重音左边的一般要标,如kangaroo"袋鼠"的第一音节,主重音右边的却不标,如bungalow"平房"、multiply"乘"的第三音节。不过,英语单词的主重音,一般都比次重音清楚的,下面我们主要讨论主重音。

根据Fry(1958)的研究,英语重音主要体现在声调变化(这里的"声调"泛指音节上的调形,无论是否可以区别词义)。比如,英语的subject [sʌbdʒɛkt],可以是名词"题目",也可以是动词"附属于",前者重音在第一音节,后者重音在第二音节。如果我们通过语音合成,仅仅变化其声调,就可以使这个单词在名词、动词之间来回变化:声调是"高-低"时,听起来是名词,声调是"低-降"时,听起来是动词。英语重音,也可以通过时长来体现。比如,如果声调保持一样,把subject的两个音节变成"长-短",听起来就像名词,把两个音节变成"短-长",听起来就像动词。不过,时长对重音的影响没有声调那么大。

了解了英语的情况，我们也可以解释为什么汉语的重音不明显。首先，上面说过，汉语非轻声音节的长度变化不大（林茂灿等，1984），远远小于英语（Price et al.，1991），因此我们不容易根据时长来辨别汉语的重音。还有，汉语是有调语言，每个普通音节都有声调，因此不能通过改变声调来表示重音，从而不容易听出谁的重音大，谁的重音小。当然，汉语重音"不容易"判断并不等于"不可能"判断。比如，赵元任（Chao，1968）认为，如果排除轻声，北京话双音节的重音一般是"中-重"，三音节一般是"中-轻-重"，这个说法也有一些语言学家支持（如Hoa，1983）。不过，正如赵元任指出，这种相对重音，一般人感觉不清楚，所以不容易取得一致意见。

赵元任（Chao，1968）还指出，汉语（普通话）既有重音区别不明显的例子，也有重音区别明显的例子。我们发现英语也如此，既有重音区别明显的例子，也有重音区别不明显的例子。汉语的例子见（22）、（23），英语的例子见（24）、（25）。

（22）音节间重音区别不明显的汉语（普通话）例子：

	音标	音节	声调	重音标记
大路	[ta:][lu:]	长-长	有-有	音节、声调皆无别

（23）音节间重音区别明显的汉语（普通话）例子：

	音标	音节	声调	重音标记
妈妈	[ma:][ma]	长-短	有-无	音节、声调皆有别

（24）音节间重音区别明显的英语例子：

	音标	音节	声调	汉译	重音标记
today	[tə][dei]	短-长	无-有	"今天"	音节有别、声调有别
kangaroo	[kæŋ][gə][ru:]	长-短-（长）	无-无-（有）	"袋鼠"	音节有别、声调无别
canteen	[kæn][ti:n]	长-长	无-有	"食堂"	音节无别、声调有别
shoe store	[ʃu:][stoɚ]	长-长	有-无	"鞋店"	音节无别、声调有别

(25) 音节间重音区别不明显的英语例子：

	音标	音节	声调	汉译	重音标记
real deal	[ri:l][di:l]	长-长	有调-有调	"好买卖"	音节无别、声调无别
Red Cross	[rɛd][krɔs]	长-长	有调-有调	"红十字"	音节无别、声调无别

普通话的"大路"（及多数双音节词语），音节无别（两个音节皆长），声调也无别（两个音节皆有声调），因此，重音区别不明显。普通话的"妈妈"（以及其他有轻声音节的例子），音节有别（前长后短），声调也有别（前有后无），所以，无论母语是汉语还是英语，听上去都是第一音节重，第二音节轻。

英语重音区别明显的例子，要么声调有别（如"[kæn][ti:n]/食堂"、"[ʃu:][stoɚ]/鞋店"），要么音节有别（如"[kæŋ][gə]/袋鼠的前两音节"），要么音节、声调皆有别（如"[tə][dei]/今天"）。而重音区别不明显的例子，两个音节都长，而且两个都有声调。因为体现重音的两个标记皆无别，所以无论母语是汉语还是英语，听上去都不容易判断哪个音节更重。这类例子（包括多数"形名"词组），有人认为是"中-重"，即第二个单词略微更重（Chomsky 和 Halle，1968），有人认为是"等重"或"双重"，即两个音节皆重（Kenyon 和 Knott，1944），说明重音区别的确不明显。

以上例子说明，英语的重音并不是所有时候都清楚，汉语的重音也不是什么时候都不清楚；两个语言都有重音清楚的时候，也有重音不清楚的时候。两个语言在重音的体现上实际上是一样的，我们用（26）来总结它们的共性。值得指出的是，无重音的音节虽然没有单词调，但是可以有语句调（也称"边界调"boundary tone）。比如，虚词"了"是个无重音的短音节，在陈述句"关了"里，它有个语句调（低调），而在疑问句"关了？"里，它有个不同的语句调（高调）。

(26) 重音的体现规则：
    a. 有重音的音节长；无重音的音节短。
    b. 有重音的音节可以有单词调；无重音的音节没有单词调。

两个音节之间，只要长短有区别，或者声调有区别（即声调的有无），重音区别就明显，否则就不明显。英语和汉语的区别，不在于重音体现的不同，而在于英语重音明显的情况多、汉语重音明显的情况少。

那么，为什么英语重音明显的情况多、汉语重音明显的情况少呢？我们认为，主要原因在于汉语的有调音节远远多于英语。而汉语有调音节多的原因有两点，见（27）。

(27) 汉语有调音节多于英语的原因（可用下面的（29）来解释）：
    a. 英语短音节多，汉语短音节少，而短音节在两个语言里都无调。
    b. 英语长音节有的有调、有的无调，汉语每个长音节都有调。

首先，根据我们对英语词典的抽样估计，英语的短音节占音节总数的四分之一到三分之一。而汉语词典里，短音节（轻声音节）的数量不到百分之一，远远小于英语的比例。其次，英语的长音节有时候有调，有时候没有，具体情况见（28）。

(28) 英语长音节的有调环境（黑体表示有关重音）：

环境	声调	例子（下横线表示有关音节）
有词重音	有	can**teen** [kæn][ti:n] "食堂" **con**tract [kɔn][trækt] "合同" **cat** [kæt] "猫"
无词重音	无	can<u>teen</u> [kæn][ti:n] "食堂" con<u>tract</u> [kɔn][trækt] "合同"
有复合词重音	有	**pan**cake [pæn][keik] "烙饼"
无复合词重音	无	pan<u>cake</u> [pæn][keik] "烙饼"
"等重"短语	皆有	**Red Cross** [rɛd][krɔs] "红十字"

一般来说，英语的长音节，必须是有词重音、复合词重音或短语重音时，才有声调。而汉语的长音节每个都有声调。比如，英语的 Timbuktu [tɪm][bʌk][tu:] "廷巴克图"（地名）是一个单词，有三个长音节，但只有词重音所在的末尾一个音节有声调，其他两个音节没有。而在汉语里，"廷巴克图" [tʰin][ba:][kɤ][tu:]有四个长音节，每个都有声调。

(27) 所列的两项区别，实际上可以归因于一个区别，即（29）。这个区别是个熟知的事实,而且属于词汇音义结合的任意性,所以不用进一步解释。

(29) 英汉的词长区别:

英语的多音节单词很多,汉语的多音节单词很少。

我们首先考虑(27a),即英语、汉语音节长短的比较。一个语言的单词大多数都是实词,而每个实词都有重音。因为汉语的单词(复合词除外)基本都是单音节,所以多数音节都有重音,都是长音节。英语的多音节词很多,而每个词只需一个重音,其他可以是非重音(也即短音节),因此,英语的单词有很多短音节。下面我们考虑(27b)。有理由认为,每个实词都需要一个词调。汉语多数音节都是词,所以都有词调。英语的多音节词里,只有一个词调,落在有词重音的音节上,其他音节无词调——无论音节长短。因此,汉语的词调多,英语的词调少。

以上讨论说明,在重音的体现方面,英语、汉语没有根本的区别,都遵循(26)所示的普遍规律。有重音的音节都是长音节,无重音都是短音节。而且,有的长音节有声调(单词调),有的长音节没有单词调(没有词重音的长音节,如 canteen "餐厅" 的第一个音节)。两个音节有声调区别时(即一个有调、一个无调),无论音节长短有区别(如汉语的"妈妈"、英语的 today "今天")还是无区别(如英语 canteen "餐厅"),重音区别在两个语言里都清楚。音节有长短区别时,无论声调有区别(如汉语的"妈妈")还是无区别(如英语 kangaroo "袋鼠" 的前两个音节),重音区别在两个语言里也都清楚。两个音节都长而且都有声调时(如汉语的"大路"、英语的 Red Cross "红十字"),重音区别在两个语言里都不清楚。

4 结　　语

语言之间既有共性也有任意性。共性需要探讨和挖掘,任意性却无需进一步探讨。不过,我们看到两个语言有不同表现时,往往不知道它们是否掩盖着共性——应该进一步探讨,还是体现了语言的任意性——无需进一步探讨。本文提出一个假设,即语言的任意性仅限于词汇的音义结合,在其他方面语言皆应该有共性可寻。

  本文通过两个实例来支持上述假设，一个是音步结构，一个是重音的体现。对于这两个音系问题，前人几乎都认为语言之间无共性，即每个语言可以选择自己的音步种类，每个语言还可以选择如何通过各自的方法来体现重音。本文的讨论却说明，音步结构可能只有一种，而不是有多种多样。而且，重音的实现可能也具有普遍性，而不是因语言不同而异。本文的假设有很高的"可证伪性"（falsifiability），即我们很容易证明它的错误，很容易发现它的缺点。从波普尔的角度来看（Popper，1959），一个理论的可证伪性越强，这个理论的价值就越高。我们希望学者们从各个角度对本文的假设进行验证，指出错误，使得理论能够进一步改进。

参 考 文 献

初敏，王韫佳，包明真. 2003. 普通话节律组织中的局部语法约束和长度约束//蔡莲红主编. 第六届全国现代语音学学术会议论文集（上）. 天津：天津人民出版社. 161-167.

川本皓嗣. 2004. 日本诗歌的传统——七与五的诗学. 王晓平，隽雪艳，赵怡（译）. 北京：译林出版社.

端木三. 2014. 重音理论及汉语重音现象. 当代语言学，（3）：288-302.

端木三. 2016a. 音步与重音. 北京：北京语言文化大学出版社.

端木三. 2016b. 从音系研究看语言的共性与任意性//沈阳，冯胜利，李亚飞主编. 甲子学者治学谈——学术研究心得和心路历程. 北京：北京语言大学出版社.

冯胜利. 1997. 汉语的韵律，词法与句法. 北京：北京大学出版社.

冯胜利. 2015. 汉语韵律诗体学论稿. 北京：商务印书馆.

高名凯，石安石. 1963. 语言学概论. 北京：中华书局.

林茂灿，颜景助，孙国华. 1984. 北京话两字组正常重音的初步实验. 方言，（1）：57-73.

吕叔湘. 1963. 现代汉语单双音节问题初探. 中国语文，（1）：10-22.

松浦友久. 1992. 关于中国古典诗歌的节奏结构——以"休音"（虚音）的功能为中心//中国唐代文学会，西北大学中文系，广西师范大学出版社主编. 唐代文学研究（第三辑）. 桂林：广西师范大学出版社：569-576.

王洪君. 2004. 试论汉语的节奏类型——松紧型. 语言科学，（3）：21-29.

王力. 1958. 汉语诗律学. 上海：新知识出版社.

游汝杰，钱乃荣，高钲夏. 1980. 论普通话的音位系统. 中国语文，（5）：328-334.

Abercrombie, D. 1965. *Studies in Phonetics and Linguistics*. Oxford: Oxford University Press.

Baayen, R. H., Piepenbrock, R. & Gulikers, L. 1995. *The CELEX Lexical Database: Release 2* (CD-ROM). Philadelphia: Linguistic Data Consortium, University of Pennsylvania.

Burling, R. 1966. The Metrics of Children'S Verse: A Cross-linguistic Study. *American Anthropologist*, 68(6): 1418-1441.

Chao, Y. R. 1933. Tone and Intonation in Chinese. *Bulletin of the Institute of History and Philology, Academia Sinica*, 4(2): 121-134.

Chao, Y. R. 1968. *A Grammar of Spoken Chinese*. Berkeley: University of California Press.

Chen, M. Y. 2000. *Tone Sandhi: Patterns across Chinese Dialects*. Cambridge: Cambridge University Press.

Chomsky, N. & Halle, M. 1968. *The Sound Pattern of English*. New York: Harper and Row.

Duanmu, S. 1999. Metrical Structure and Tone: Evidence from Mandarin and Shanghai. *Journal of East Asian Linguistics*, 8(1): 1-38.

Duanmu, S. 2000. *The Phonology of Standard Chinese*. Oxford: Oxford University Press.

Duanmu, S. 2007. *The Phonology of Standard Chinese* (2nd edn.). Oxford: Oxford University Press.

Duanmu, S. 2008. *Syllable Structure: The Limits of Variation*. Oxford: Oxford University Press.

Duanmu, S. Kim, H. Y. & Stiennon, N. 2005. Stress and Syllable Structure in English: Approaches to Phonological Variations. *Taiwan Journal of Linguistics*, 3(2): 45-77.

Fry, D. B. 1958. Experiments in the Perception of Stress. *Language and Speech*, 1: 126-152.

Goldsmith, J. A. 1976. *Autosegmental phonology* (Unpublished doctoral dissertation). MIT, Cambridge, Mass. Reproduced by the Indiana University Linguistics Club, Bloomington, Indiana.

Goldsmith, J. 1981. English as a Tone Language. In Didier L. Goyvaerts (Ed.), *Phonology in the 1980's* (pp. 287-308). Ghent: E. Story-Scientia.

Halle, M. & Vergnaud, J. R. 1987. *An Essay on Stress*. Cambridge, MA.: MIT Press.

Hayes, B. 1982. Extrametricality and English Stress. *Linguistic Inquiry*, 13(2): 227-276.

Hayes, B. 1985. Iambic and Trochaic Rhythm in Stress Rules. In Mary Niepokuj, Mary Van Clay, Vassiliki Nikiforidou & Deborah Feder (Ed.). *Proceedings of the Eleventh Annual Meeting of the Berkeley Linguistics Society* (pp. 429-446). Berkeley Linguistics Society, University of California, Berkeley.

Hayes, B. 1995. *Metrical Stress Theory: Principles and Case Studies*. Chicago: University of Chicago Press.

Hoa, M [华卫民]. 1983. *L'accentuation en Pékinois* [北京话轻重音]. Paris: Editions Langages Croisés. Distributed by Centre de Recherches Linguistiques sur l'Asie Orientale, Paris.

Hyman, L. 1977. On the Nature of Linguistic Stress. In Larry Hyman(Ed.), *Studies in Stress and*

Accent (pp. 37-82). Southern California Occasional Papers in Linguistics 4. Los Angeles: Department of Linguistics, University of Southern California.

Kager, R. 1993. Shapes of the Generalized Trochee. In Jonathan Mead (Ed.), *The Proceedings of the Eleventh West Coast Conference on Formal Linguistics* (pp. 298-312). Stanford: Published for the Stanford Linguistics Association by the Center for the Study of Language and Information.

Kager, R. 1995. The Metrical Theory of Word Stress. In John Goldsmith(Ed.), *The Handbook of Phonological Theory* (pp. 367-402). Cambridge, MA.: Blackwell.

Karlgren, B. 1918. *Ordet Och Pennan i Mittens Rike*. Stockholm: Svenska Andelsförlaget.

Karlgren, B. 1923. *Sound & Symbol in Chinese*. London: Oxford University Press.

Kenyon, J. S. & Thomas, A. K. 1944. *A Pronouncing Dictionary of American English*. Springfield, MA.: Merriam.

Ladefoged, P. 2001. *Vowels and Consonants: An Introduction to the Sounds of Languages*. Malden, MA.: Blackwell.

Leben, W. 1973. Suprasegmental Phonology (Unipublished Ph.D. dissertation). MIT, Cambridge, Mass.

Liberman, M. 1975. *The Intonational System of English* (Unipublished Ph.D. dissertation). MIT, Cambridge, Mass.

Mester, R. A. 1994. The Quantitative Trochee in Latin. *Natural Language & Linguistic Theory*, *12*(1): 1-61.

Pierrehumbert, J. 1980. The Phonetics and Phonology of English Intonation (Unpublished Ph.D. dissertation). MIT, Cambridge, Mass.

Pierrehumbert, J. & Beckman, M. 1988. *Japanese Tone Structure*. Cambridge, Mass: MIT Press.

Popper, K. R. 1959. *The Logic of Scientific Discovery*. New York: Basic Books.

Price, P. J., M. Ostendorf, S. Shattuck-Hufnagel & Fong, C. 1991. The Use of Prosody in Syntactic Disambiguation. *Journal of the Acoustical Society of America*, *90*(6): 2956-2970.

Prince, A. 1980. A Metrical Theory for Estonian Quantity. *Linguistic Inquiry*, *11*(3): 511-562.

Selkirk, E. & Shen, T. 1990. Prosodic Domains in Shanghai Chinese. In Sharon Inkelas & Draga Zec (Ed.), *The Phonology-syntax Connection* (pp. 313-337). CSLI, Stanford University, Stanford, Calif. Distributed by University of Chicago Press.

Steriade, D. 1999. Alternatives to Syllable-based Accounts of Consonantal Phonotactics. In Osamu Fujimura, Brian D. Joseph & Bohumil Palek (Eds.), *Proceedings of LP'98: Item Order in Language and Speech* (*Columbus, the Ohio State University, September 15-20, 1998*), *Vol. I* (pp. 205-245). Prague: Karolinum Press (Charles University in Prague).

Vijver, R. 1998. The Iambic Issue: Iambs as a Result of Constraint Interaction (Unpublished

Ph.D. dissertation). Vrije Universiteit, Amsterdam. Distributed by HIL Dissertations.

Wang, W. S-Y. 1962. Stress in English. *Language Learning*, *12*(1): 69-77.

Williams, E. 1976. Underlying Tone in Margi and Igbo. *Linguistic Inquiry*, *7*(3): 436-468.

Yip, M. 1980. Tonal Phonology of Chinese (Unpublished Ph.D. Dissertation). MIT, Cambridge, Mass.

Universal and Arbitrary Properties of Language: Perspectives from Foot Structure and Stress

San Duanmu

Abstract Some linguistic properties are universal and some are arbitrary or specific to a given language. When we see a difference between two languages, it is not always obvious whether the difference is an arbitrary one or whether it is only apparent, behind which a deeper universal can be discovered. Duanmu (2000) offers a hypothesis that arbitrary properties of language are limited to the sound-meaning association of words, and that beyond the lexicon language universals should dominate. In this paper I use evidence from foot structure and stress in support of the hypothesis. I also illustrate how to look for common properties among languages, despite their apparent differences.

Keywords: foot, stress, phonology, linguistic universals, arbitrariness of language

端木三

密歇根大学语言学系，教授

E-mail: duanmu@umich.edu

谈汉语焦点的韵律机制
——句法韵律界面的个案研究

蔡维天　李宗宪

摘要　本文宗旨在于结合语法理论和实验研究，厘清汉语焦点用法在句法、语义、韵律等部门之间错综复杂的关系。首先我们从句法韵律界面（the syntax-prosody interface）的角度切入，观察到汉语中"只"、"是"可对其范域（scope）内词组产生焦点量化的作用，同时造成高、低平调音域扩张且时长延长。此外，在位疑问词（wh-in-situ）也可运用焦点重音来避开孤岛效应（island effects）及阻断效应（intervention effects）。最后，我们藉由焦点韵律将限制性和非限制性关系句区分开来，并在声学实验上得到印证。凡此种种皆显示句法与韵律之间的确存在着系统性的对应关系，需要我们从理论建构和语音实验两方面双管齐下，才能得到较为周全的解释。

关键词　焦点韵律　"只"字句　"是"字句　在位疑问词　限制性关系句

1　焦点重音对语意诠释的影响

汉语的焦点有许多有趣的语意和韵律效应，有的用法有标（marked），有的用法无标（unmarked）。前者包括最常见的"只"字句和"是"字句，后者则以疑问词的宽域解释（wide scope interpretation）及修饰语的对比焦点（contrastive focus）为代表。

首先我们看有标焦点结构的语意性质，一为排他性（exclusiveness），一为穷尽性（exhaustiveness）（请参见 Kiss, 1998；徐烈炯，2002；蔡维天，2004）等）。一般的陈述句若含有并列结构，则可蕴涵（entail）其并列语（conjunct）中的任何一个；如（1a）蕴含（1b）或（1c）：①

---

① 本部分各例中，→表示具有蕴含关系，↮ 表示不具有蕴含关系。

（1）a. 阿Q吃了烧饼和油条。
　　　b. ⟶ 阿Q吃了烧饼。
　　　c. ⟶ 阿Q吃了油条。

若换成"只"字句和"是"字句，则完全没有这种蕴涵关系，如下例所示：

（2）a. 阿Q只吃了烧饼和油条（，没吃别的东西）。
　　　b. ⟶̸ 阿Q只吃了烧饼（，没吃别的东西）。
　　　c. ⟶̸ 阿Q只吃了油条（，没吃别的东西）。
（3）a. 阿Q是吃了烧饼和油条（，不是别的东西）。
　　　b. ⟶̸ 阿Q是吃了烧饼（，不是别的东西）。
　　　c. ⟶̸ 阿Q是吃了油条（，不是别的东西）。

再来看否定测试，一般陈述句如（4a）并不具排他性与穷尽性，因此无法接含有"也"的负面响应，如（4b）：（%表示后句不是前句的恰当响应）

（4）A：阿Q吃了烧饼。
　　　B：%不，阿Q也吃了油条。

而"只"字句和"是"字句刚好相反，可以接含有"也"的负面响应，分别有（5a，b）及（6a，b）为证：

（5）A：阿Q只吃了烧饼（，没吃别的东西）。
　　　B：不，阿Q也吃了油条。
（6）A：阿Q是吃了烧饼（，不是别的东西）。
　　　B：不，阿Q也吃了油条。

另一方面，蔡维天（2015）曾指出汉语的焦点作用必须和韵律上的条件配合才能运行顺畅。其中最明显的要属句调重音（intonation stress），我们要靠此类机制才能明确区分出各种不同层次的语意诠释和语用引申。下例中焦点算子"只"的量化对象是由韵律条件来决定的，这点在英语中也有极为类似的现象（Chomsky，1977）：（7a）的重音落在"烧饼"和"油条"，其焦点作用自然是比对两个宾语；同理，（7b）的重音落在"卖"和"买"，对比焦点也转移到两个动词之上。"是"字句的情况也差不多，如（8a，b）

的韵律和语意差别所示：

(7) a. 这家店只卖**烧饼**，不卖**油条**。　　［比对宾语］
　　 b. 这家店只**卖**烧饼，不**做**烧饼。　　［比对动词］

(8) a. 这家店是卖**烧饼**，不是卖**油条**。　　［比对宾语］
　　 b. 这家店是**卖**烧饼，不是**做**烧饼。　　［比对动词］

句调重音对焦点作用的影响还有一个很好的例子，亦即汉语疑问词孤岛（*wh*-islands）中的宽域解释现象（Huang, 1982）。以（9）中"想知道"所选择的间接问句为例，一共可以有三种解释：(9a) 表"谁"得到宽域解释，(9b) 表"什么"得到宽域解释，而 (9c) 中则是"谁"与"什么"均作窄域解：

(9) 你想知道[疑问词孤岛谁买了什么]？
　　 a. 是谁ᵢ你想知道他ᵢ买了什么？
　　 b. 是什么ₖ你想知道谁买了哪样东西？
　　 c. 你是不是想知道谁买了什么？

上述现象显示"谁"或"什么"都可在逻辑形式部门（Logical Form；LF）移出孤岛而得到宽域解释，但一定要有一个留在从句，满足"想知道"的选择限制，这也可以从下面三种解释的答句分别得到印证：

(10) a. 我想知道阿Q买了什么。　　　　　["谁"作宽域解]
　　　b. 我想知道谁买了那部车子。　　　["什么"作宽域解]
　　　c. 对啊，我想知道谁买了什么。　　["谁"与"什么"均作窄域解]

问题是当一般人听到（9）这个句子，又怎么知道问的是哪一个疑问词呢？其实此处韵律扮演了很重要的角色。我们可以先用句末助词"呢"排除（10c）的窄域用法，接着就轮到句调重音上场：要是重音落在"谁"上，就会得出主语的宽域解释，如（11a）；倘若落在"什么"，那就换成宾语作宽域解，如（11b）（请参阅蔡维天，2015）：

(11) a. 你想知道[疑问词孤岛**谁**买了什么]呢？　　["谁"作宽域解]
　　　b. 你想知道[疑问词孤岛谁买了**什么**]呢？　　["什么"作宽域解]

最后值得一提的是，Chao（1968）曾注意到重音可用来区分关系句

(relative clauses)的限制性用法(restrictive usage)和非限制性用法(non-restrictive usage)。首先比较下面这组内关系句(inner relatives;亦即在限定符、数词及量词之后出现的关系句):

(12) a. 那个[北京来]的学生很活泼。　　　[非限制性内关系句]
　　　　(≈那个学生很活泼,北京来的。)
　　b. 是那个[北京来]的学生很活泼,　　[限制性内关系句]
　　　　不是那个[上海来]的。

赵先生认为(12a)这类句调平铺直叙的内关系句其诠释偏向描述(descriptive),相当于我们现在所说的非限制性用法,在形式语意上等同于谓语。然而一旦运用句调重音凸显对比焦点,如(12b),那么其诠释也马上转为限制性用法。类似的区分也出现在外关系句(outer relatives;亦即在限定符、数词及量词之前出现的关系句):

(13) a. [北京来]的那个学生很活泼。　　　[非限制性内关系句]
　　　　(≈那个学生很活泼,北京来的。)
　　b. 是[北京来]的那个学生很活泼,　　[限制性外关系句]
　　　　不是那个[上海来]的。

诸如此类的现象不胜枚举,本文挑出上述三类焦点结构做声学测试(acoustic tests):我们认为唯有货真价实的句调重音,才能在句法韵律界面上产生画龙点睛的作用。

2　汉语焦点特色

在本文讨论焦点语音实验前,我们先讨论汉语焦点在传统声学的特色,首先,根据 Xu(1999),Chen、Wang 和 Xu(2009)及 Flemming(2008)的研究,汉语焦点在声学上有以下三种特色:

(14) 焦点的声学特色:
　　a. 音准(pitch):相较于平常非焦点情况,高平调(high tone)
　　　 音准会更高而使音域扩大(expanded pitch-range),而后焦点音域则会缩减（post- focus compression/PFC）[①]。

  b. 音强（loudness）：增大。

  c. 时长（duration）：增长。

本文并参照 Duanmu（2004）对汉语四个声调大致以高平与低平调区分以便于描述实验结果。

（15）汉语声调分别：

  a. 高平调（一声）：高平调

  b. 低升调（二声）：低平调+高平调　　　［顺序不可变］

  c. 低平调（三声）：低平调

  d. 高降调（四声）：高平调+低平调　　　［顺序不可变］

下图为 Xu（1999）标示男性受试者其汉语声调在焦点重音环境中音准的变化。图 1 中细线条为高平调（H）与重音互动情况，粗体线则为高、低平调（L）分别与重音互动情况。我们发现高平调音准会因焦点重音变高而使其与低平调音准的差距扩大（亦即音域扩大）；而后焦点的高、低平调音准则会骤减，连带使其音域缩减。

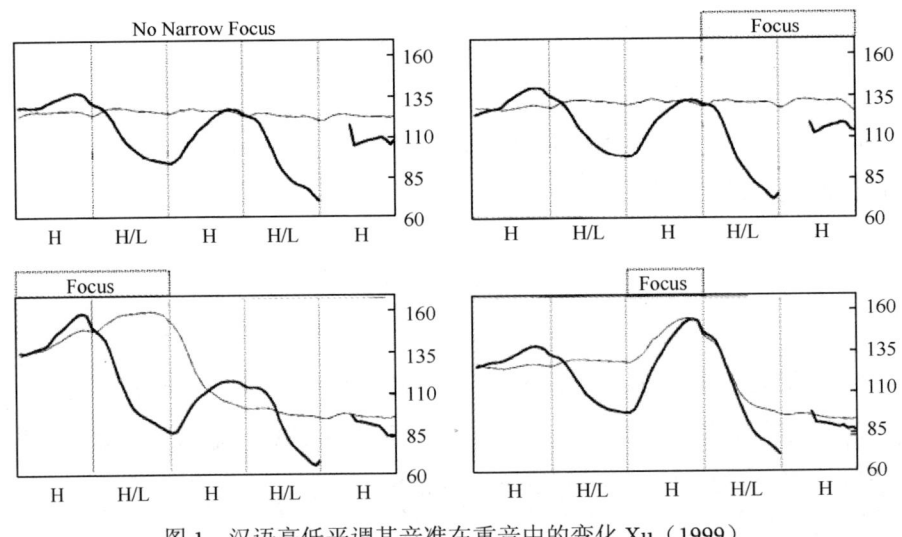

图 1　汉语高低平调其音准在重音中的变化 Xu（1999）

---

① 根据本文语音分析及先前文献如 Chen，Wang & Xu（2009）的研究，台湾华语中并没有显着的后焦点效应，因此相关现象就暂不列入讨论范围。此处感谢匿名评审提示。

3 研究方法

3.1 语料

关于语料方面，为了区别焦点与非焦点对比，我们分别用两次实验，第一次语料无任何焦点标记；第二次语料则是先给受试者适当情境。接下来我们用问答方式来导引出疑问焦点、"只"字焦点与"是"字焦点、疑问词焦点（WH-expressions focus）以及限制性关系句焦点（restrictive-clauses focus），碍于篇幅关系，部分语料如下所列：

(16) 疑问焦点、"只"字焦点与"是"字焦点：

语境：在一个乡村里有一家早餐店，卖的东西与开店时间如下：

a. **只卖烧饼**（这乡村里**别家店没有卖**；这家店也**不做烧饼**）。

b. 营业时间只有**周末**。

c. 答句：

　这家店卖烧饼。　　　　　　　　　　[无焦点]

　这家店卖什么？

　这家店卖**烧饼**　　　　　　　　　　[疑问焦点]

　这家店卖油条吗？

　这家店只卖**烧饼**；不卖**油条**。　　　["只"字焦点]

　这家店是卖**烧饼**；不是卖**油条**。　　["是"字焦点]

(17) 疑问词焦点：

　a. 你想知道谁买了什么？　　　　　　[非焦点]

　b. 你想知道**谁**买了什么？　　　　　　[谁-焦点]

　c. 你想知道谁买了**什么**？　　　　　　[什么-焦点]

(18) 限制性关系句焦点：

　a. 那个[北京来]的学生很活泼。　　　　[无焦点]

　b. 是那个上海来的学生很活泼吗？

是那个[北京来]的学生很活泼，不是那个[上海来]的。　[焦点]
　　　c. [北京来]的那个学生很活泼。　　　　　　　　　[无焦点]
　　　d. 是[北京来]的那个学生很活泼吗？
是[北京来]的那个学生很活泼，不是 [上海来]的那个。[焦点]

3.2　实验对象与录音过程

本次研究对象为三位以台湾华语为母语的人士，其中一位为35～40岁间男性（本文图表编号1），另外二位受试者皆为20～25岁男性（本文图表编号2-3）。实验前，必须使得录音人知道此次实验目的，并先与发音人讲解语料与语境，要求每位发音人正确陈述语句的内容与语气。如此一来，受试者可以更融入实验过程也大大避免掉受试者语句断续等问题。另外，若有漏字或者语句语气不顺，则会要求每位录音人重新念过。每个发音人总共念30（句）×2（每句2个焦点）×2（次）=120句。

本次录音地点在台湾清华大学语言学研究所语音实验室，背景噪音约为30dB～40dB。此次实验中，我们采用数字录音机（Edirol R09-HR）及单指向麦克风（Shure BETA54），采样率为44.1赫兹（16位），录音档案存成wav文件。

3.3　分析

语料录制好后，我们使用 praat 语音软件进行手工标注。为得到每个目标句中非焦点与焦点对比词组音准，我们以词组元音当切音分界。另外我们以 ProsodyPro 脚本（Xu，2013）引出音准。但根据先前文献（Shih 和 Lu，2015；Xu et al.，2003），子音（consonant）会影响元音音准，因此在使用 ProsodyPro 脚本引出非焦点与焦点对比词组音准时，本研究将每个音节取出十点音准值中第一点与最后一点音准删去以求准确值。另外，我们再次使用手工标记以每个音节为标界且再次使用 ProsodyPro 脚本来对比焦点与非焦点词组的音强（loudness）及时长（duration）。

3.4 结果

3.4.1 "只"与"是"焦点标记韵律现象

图 2 为我们实验下方语料每位受试者（编号 1-3）焦点词组测试，我们发现"只"与"是"的确会使其范域中的词组焦点化，其音准相较于非焦点化时产生了音域扩大现象。此外，虽音强（intensity）没相差很多，但焦点词组时长（duration）比非焦点句更为增强，因篇幅所限，本文要呈现实验语料重复如下：

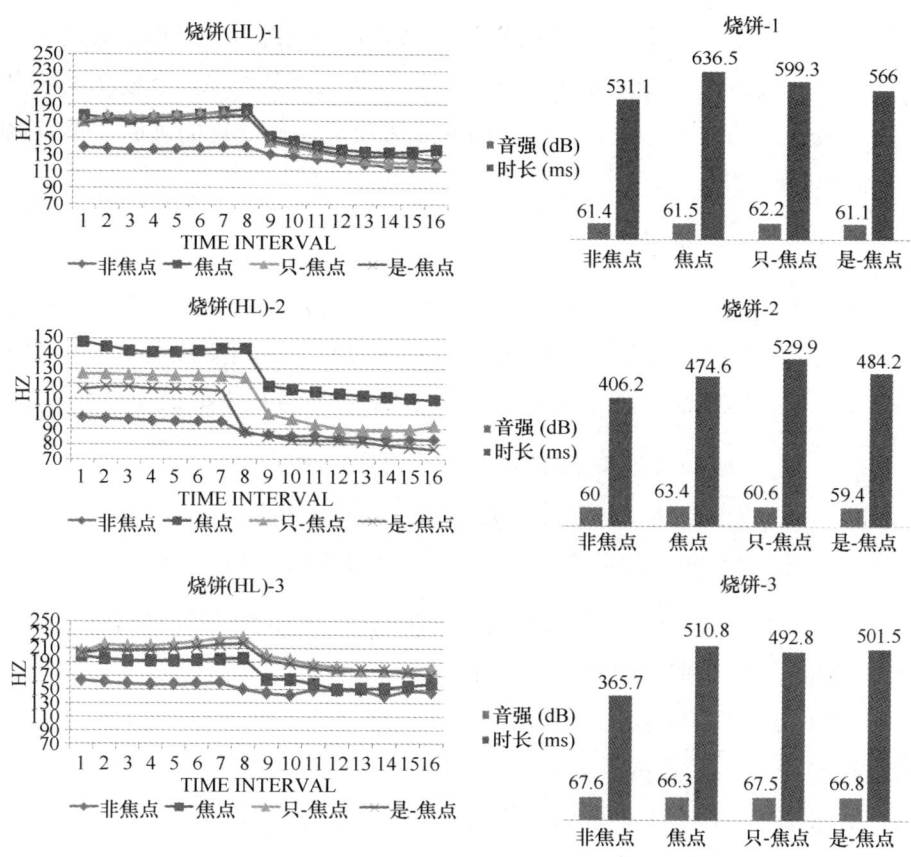

图 2 "只"与"是"焦点标记声学分析

（19）这家店卖烧饼。　　　　　　　　　[无焦点]

（20）这家店卖什么？
　　　这家店卖**烧饼**。　　　　　　　　[疑问焦点]

（21）这家店卖油条吗？
　　　a. 这家店只卖**烧饼**；不卖**油条**　　["只"字焦点]
　　　b. 这家店是卖**烧饼**；不是卖**油条**　["是"字焦点]

首先，测试词组"烧饼"是高平调与低平调所形成的双音节。在一般情况下，高平调与低平调其音准已有一定差距，如每张图中"非焦点"音准曲线图所示。然而当疑问焦点、"只"字焦点及"是"字焦点出现时，"烧饼"词组的高平调与低平调音准差距更大，也就是焦点词组音准音域扩大现象。

其次，我们也发现疑问焦点、"只"字焦点及"是"字焦点使其范域内词组"烧饼"的时长加大与增长。由此亦可反证这些标记的确起了焦点化（focalization）的作用。

3.4.2　疑问焦点与韵律效应

关于"焦点疑问词"方面，我们同样以询问方式来考察所谓"焦点化疑问词组"。本文要呈现的分析语料重复如（22）[①]。因篇幅所限，其中图3为其中一位台湾华语发音人（编号1）在Praat软件分析中的语句音准变化。

（22）a. 你想知道谁买了什么？　　　　[无焦点]
　　　b. 你想知道**谁**买了什么？　　　　[谁-焦点]
　　　c. 你想知道谁买了**什么**？　　　　[什么-焦点]

图4与图5为全部三人实验结果。我们可以清楚发现疑问词焦点词组会透过焦点重音来避开阻断效应（intervention effect）。

从图3、图4与图5可以得知,当疑问词想突破其孤岛效应（island effect）而得到宽域（wide scope）的解释时，焦点重音起了决定性的作用。那也就是，如图4，当（22b）的疑问词要问"谁"，此疑问词便加重了重音。也因

---

① 在录音过程中，我们发现到台湾华语中疑问词"什么"的"什"为低平调（L），而非低平调（L）加上高平调（H）。此处也要感谢与会者的问题与建议。

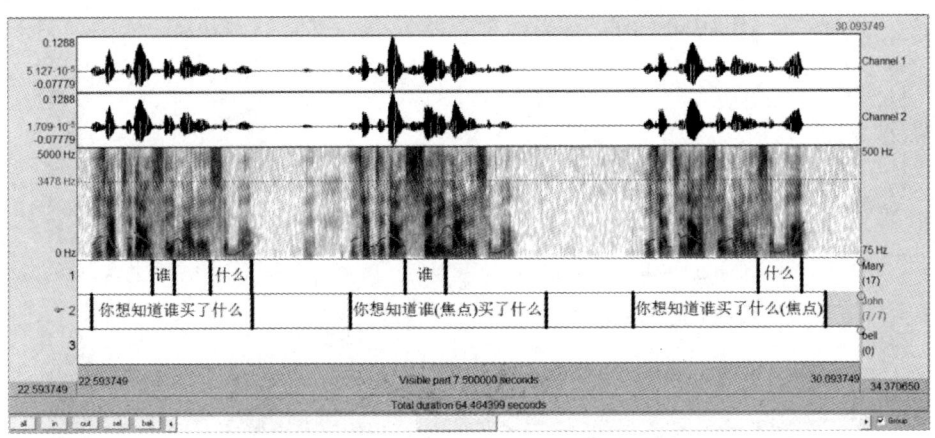

图 3 疑问焦点词组在句中的音准变异

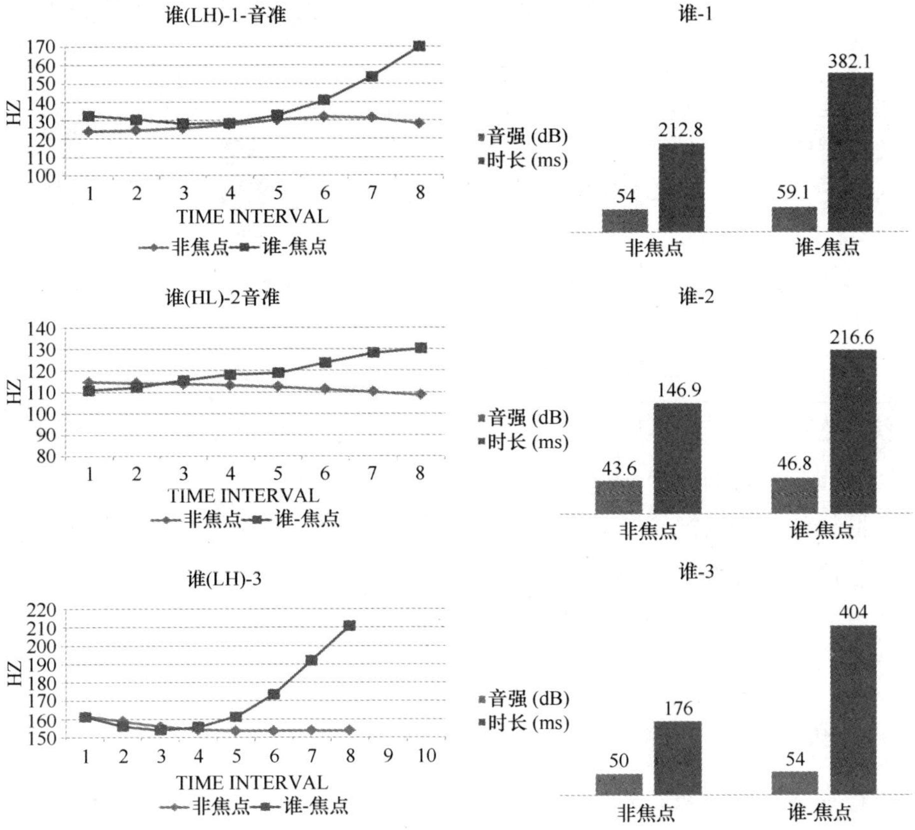

图 4 焦点与非焦点疑问词组-谁-声学分析

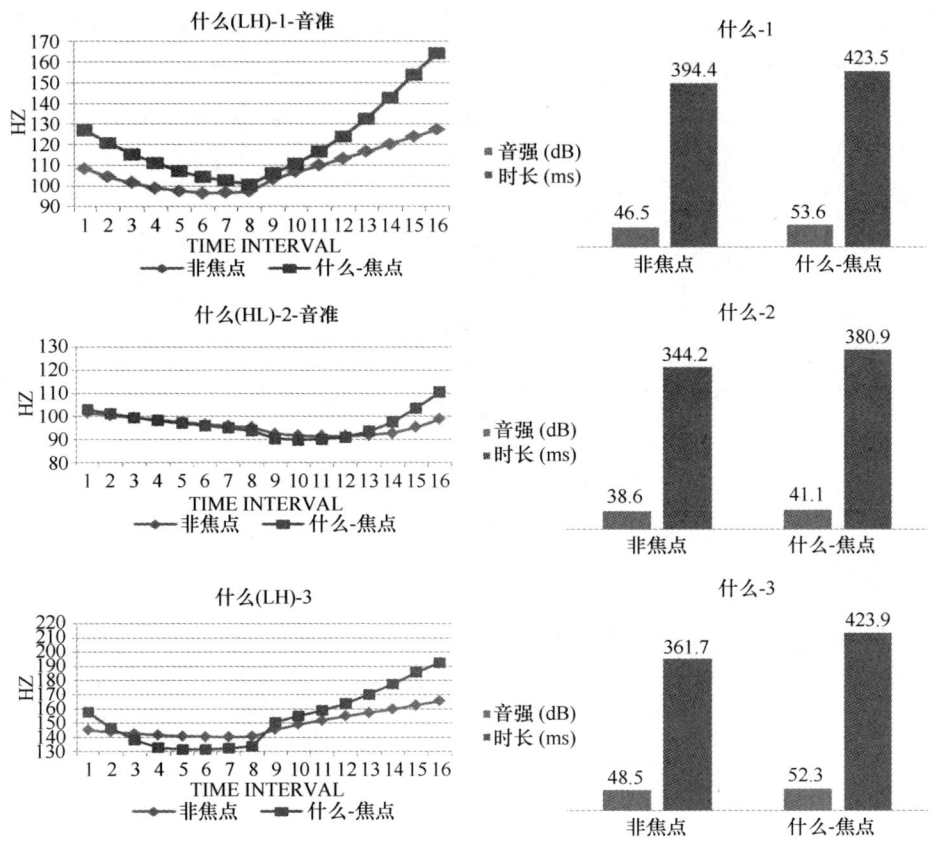

图 5 焦点与非焦点-什么-声学分析

此其高低平调音准差距拉大。另外从图 4 中,我们可以发现其音强及时长也比非焦点重音(22a)中的"谁"增大且拉长。

同样的,当(22c)问句要问"什么"时,疑问词"什么"在图 3 与 5 中也会产生焦点重音的情况;也就是音域扩大,音强拉高,时长增长。总而言之,焦点重音可以使得疑问词得到宽域解读,也就此避开句法上的孤岛效应及阻断效应。

3.4.3 关系句与韵律

根据我们的分析,对于限制性内关系句的重音诠释,我们得到了颇具兴味的结果,语料重复如(例 23-24)。在图 6 中,我们可以看到(24b)中限制性内关系句"北京来"承载了焦点重音;而(23)中非限制性关系句

"北京来"则无。

（23）那个[北京来]的学生很活泼。　　　　　　　　　　　　　　[无焦点]

（24）a. 是那个上海来的学生很活泼吗？

　　　b. 是那个[北京来]的学生很活泼，不是那个[**上海来**]的。[焦点]

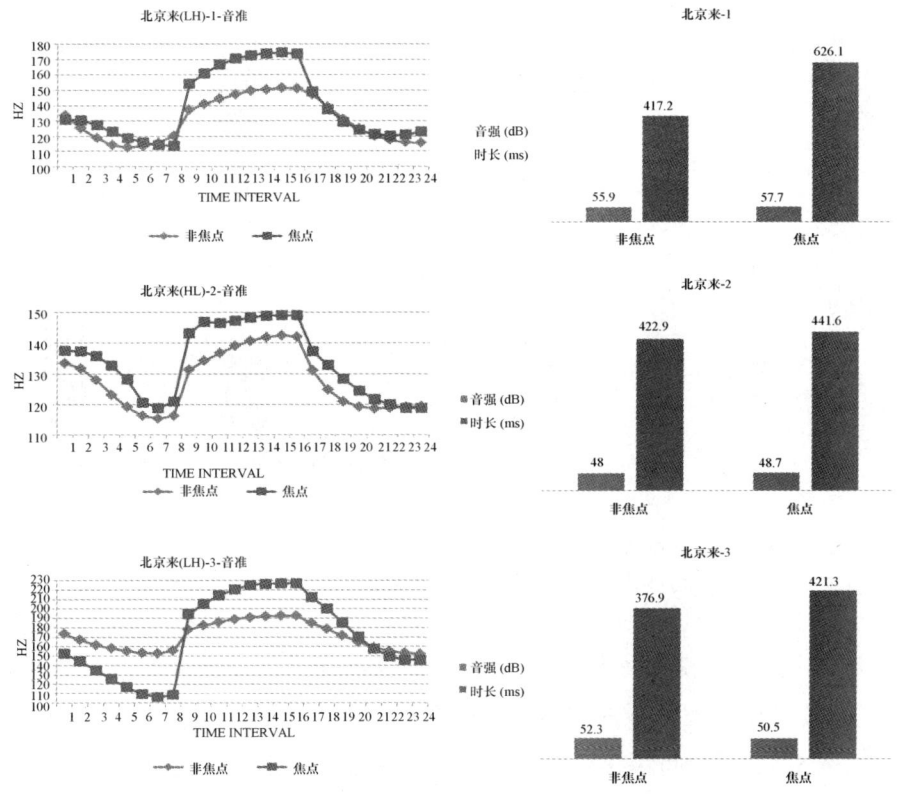

图 6　焦点与非焦点-北京来-声学分析（限制性内关系句）

同样的现象也适用于限制性外关系句，我们发现非限制性外关系句在一般情况下不会焦点化；相较之下，限制性外关系句则须承载焦点重音，语料重复如（例25-26），分析结果则如图7。

（25）[北京来]的那个学生很活泼。　　　　　　　　　　　　　[无焦点]

（26）a. 是[北京来]的那个学生很活泼吗？

　　　b. 是[北京来]的那个学生很活泼，不是 [**上海来**]的那个。[焦点]

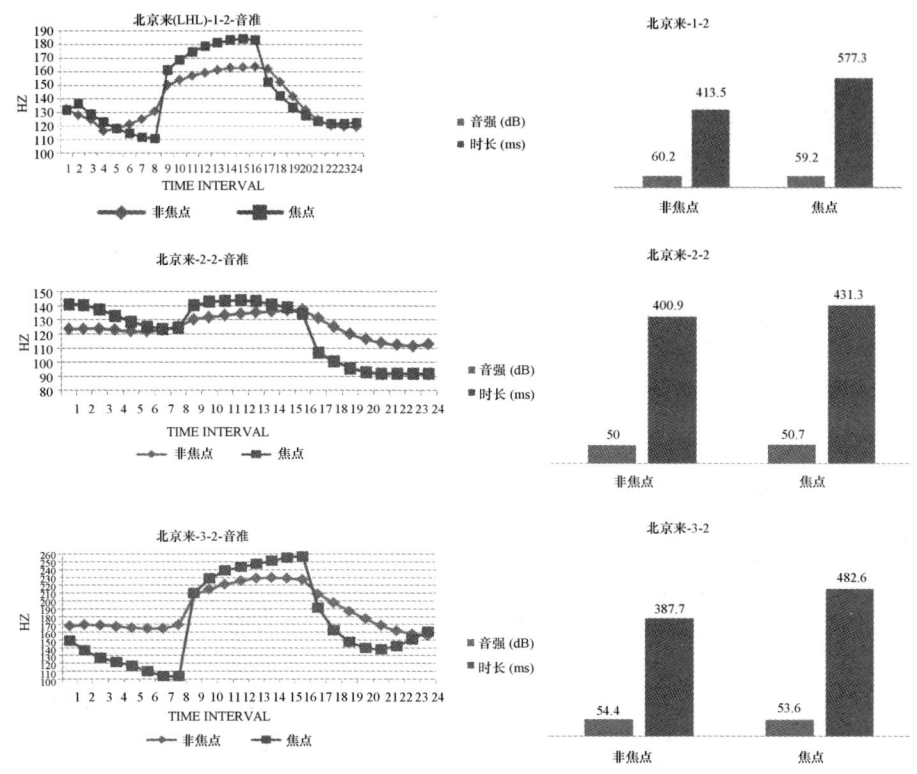

图7　焦点与非焦点-北京来-声学分析（限制性外关系句）

在图6与图7中，我们可以发现非限制性关系句中的修饰语"北京来"（23）与（25）特别在音准与时长与其在限制性内与外关系句产生极大的对比。这便证明了赵元任（1968）所提出的说法；重音起了很大的作用，只有非限制性关系句可用重音且会形成对比焦点，而限制性关系句不可。

4　结　　论

总结而言，本文通过语音实验得到下列结果："只"、"是"、在位疑问词及非限定性关系句的焦点用法都跟重音有极其密切的关联；这也显示句法部门与韵律部门之间的确存在着相辅相成的映射关系（mapping relation），值得我们继续深入探讨。

参 考 文 献

蔡维天. 2004. 谈"只"与"连"的形式语义. 中国语文,（2）：99-111.
蔡维天. 2015. 论句调重音对语法诠释机制的影响//冯胜利主编. 汉语韵律语法新探. 上海：中西书局：97-111.
徐烈炯. 2002. 汉语是话题概念结构化语言吗？中国语文,（5）：400-410.
Chao, Y. R. 1968. *A Grammar of Spoken Chinese*. Berkeley & Los Angeles: University of California Press.
Chen, S. W., Wang, B. & Xu, Y. 2009. Closely related languages, different ways of realizing focus. In *Proceedings of Interspeech* (pp. 1007-1010). Brighton, UK.
Duanmu, S. 2004. Tone and non-tone languages: An alternative to language typology and parameters. *Language and Linguistics*, 5(4): 891-923.
Flemming, E. 2008. The role of pitch range in focus marking. In Slides from a Talk Given at the *Workshop on Information Structure and Prosody*, Nijmegen: Studiecentrum Soeterbeeck.
É. Kiss, K. 1998. Indentificational focus vs. informational focus. *Language*, 71(2): 245-273.
Shih, C., & Lu, H.-Y. D. 2015. Effects of talker-to-listener distance on tone. *Journal of Phonetics, 51*: 6-35
Xu, Y. 1999. Effects of tone and focus on the formation and alignment of f0 contour. *Journal of Phonetics, 27*: 55-105.
Xu, Y. 2013. ProsodyPro—A tool for large-scale systematic prosody analysis. In *Proceedings of Tools and Resources for the Analysis of Speech Prosody (TRASP 2013)* (pp. 7-10), Aix-en-Provence, France.
Xu, C. X. & Xu, Y. 2003. Effects of consonant aspiration on Mandarin tones. *Journal of the International Phonetic Association, 33*: 165-181.

On the Prosodic Nature of Chinese Foci: A Case Study of the Syntax-Prosody Enterface

Weitian Tsai Zongxian Li

Abstract The article aims to combine grammatical theories and experimental studies so that the complex relationship among syntax, semantics, and prosody may receive proper treatment. We propose to tackle three relevant issues in terms of the syntax-prosody interface, backed up by solid acoustic experiments: Firstly, Mandarin focus markers such as *zhi*（只）and *shi*（是）may focalize certain constituents in their scope, which is accompanied by pitch expansion between high tone and low tone, as well as duration extension. Secondly, in-situ *wh*-expressions may employ intonational stress to escape from island/intervention effects. Finally, focus prosody is also needed to differentiate restrictive relative clauses from their non-restrictive counterparts. All these testify to the systematic correspondences between syntax and prosody, which in turn call for integrated research from the vantage point of both theoretical and experimental considerations.

Key words Focus prosody, *zhi*-construction, *shi*-construction, *wh*-in-situ, restrictive relative clauses

蔡维天

台湾清华大学语言学研究所、中国文学系，教授

E-mail：wttsai@mx.nthu.edu.tw

李宗宪

台湾清华大学语言学研究所及中国文学系，硕士

E-mail：tonyle29@hotmail.com

香港粤语句末助词声调与句调关系的初探*

张 凌 邓思颖

摘要 本文通过语音实验，论证香港粤语句末助词的超音段特征并非单纯的声调，而是句调，具有一定的语用意义，并具有一定的句法地位。根据粤语句末助词的声调分布，高平调（调值为55）、中平调（33）和低降调（21）可视为粤语基本的句末边界句调。两个上升调，即高升调（35）和低升调（23），可分析为疑问句上升调的同时叠加，或者不同基本句末边界调连续叠加的结果。本文的实验结果表明，句末助词可视为语段化的句调。本文进一步支持句末助词和句调关系的理论。

关键词 句末助词　句调　声调　粤语

1　香港粤语句末助词的声调

句末助词是用于句末，表达疑问、确认、建议、命令等意义的助词，如普通话里的"吗"、"呢"、"啊"、"吧"等。普通话中的句末助词数量不多，从声调分布来看，句末助词基本上都使用轻声调。与普通话相比，香港粤语（以下简称"粤语"）句末助词的数量要丰富得多。粤语的语音系统中无轻声调，从音高上说有六个声调，如表1所示。粤语助词的声调覆盖了这六个声调，如邓思颖（2015：342）所列，本文也转引为表2。

---

* 本文的初稿曾发表于"第二届汉语韵律语法研究国际研讨会"（香港中文大学2015年11月）、"第二十届国际粤方言研讨会"（香港中文大学2015年12月）、"第二届方言语法博学论坛"（中山大学2016年3月），感谢与会者的提问和意见。在写作的过程中，跟冯胜利教授的讨论非常有启发，特此致谢。

表 1　粤语声调系统

调类	描述	数字式	例子 舒声	例子 入声
T1	高平调/高降调	55/53	夫	福
T2	高升调	35	苦	鈪
T3	中平调	33	富	霍
T4	低降调/低平调	21/11	符	
T5	低升调	23	妇	
T6	（中）低平调	22	父	服

表 2　粤语助词的声调

调类		助词例子
1	高平调	添、啦、啰、咩、得；先、呢、啫、之
2	高升调	话、定、系、罢、好；喫、嘅、囄、啲、嘎
3	中平调	喇、噜、啩、吗、啊、喎；法、咋、嘛、嚩、喂
4	低降调	嚟、咧、嗱、呀、喝
5	低升调	咧、喎；吓
6	低平调	住、滞；未、嚟

不同声调的句末助词往往表达不同的情态和语义。如例（1）至例（3），句末助词都使用［la］音节，只是声调不同，三个句末助词表达了不同的情态语义。例（1）的"啦"是高平调，有显而易见之意。例（2）的"喇"是中平调，表示中性地陈述事实。例（3）的"嗱"是低降调，表示不确认，有疑问之意。

(1) 佢走咗啦［la⁵⁵］。他（显然）走了。

(2) 佢走咗喇［la³³］。他走了。

(3) 佢走咗嗱［la²¹］？他走了吗？

在粤语句末助词覆盖的六个声调之中，T6 的例子都能看到其实义词来源，由这个声调而衍生的句末助词较少，没有由常见的"maa"、"lo"、"le"[①]等助词音节构成的 T6 助词，可见其能产性很低，因此 T6 不在本文的讨论范

---

① 引用粤语助词例子时，本文采用香港语言学学会粤语拼音方案（简称"粤拼"）表示。

围之内。其余的五个声调，包括三个平调和两个上升调①，与句末句调有着紧密的关系，是本文重点研究的对象。

2 粤语句末助词与句调

句末助词和句调（intonation，也称语调）之间有紧密的内在联系。从语用上看，句末助词和句调有相似之处，两者都能表达语句的态度、意图、情感等微秒的意义，只是在语音形式上有所不同：句末助词一般具有独立的音段，如上面例（1）至例（3）的 [la] 音段。而句调一般没有独立的音段，以超音段（suprasegmental）的形式（如音高、时长、音强等韵律特征）附着在句子的音段上。如例（4），并无独立的音段表示疑问的意味，但是句子最后一个音节"过"的音高会受句调影响，其字调本为中平调 T3，调值为 33，但在这个句子里变读为一个高升调表示疑问，而此高升调即为句调。

（4）佢去过↗？他去过？

Fox et al.（2008）曾论述粤语句调在语句中的分布，主要分两个部位，一为句中（utterance-body）句调，二为句末（utterance-final）句调。粤语的句中句调主要体现为降势音高（declination）：若一个句子都由同一个声调的音节组成，那么音节在句中的位置越靠后，音高越低。这种降势音高在世界各语言中都很常见。另外，在词组边界会有音高重置（pitch reset）的现象，因而句中句调总体呈向下锯齿状。

句末句调也称边界调（boundary tone），主要影响句子最后一个音节。对陈述句而言，句子最后一个音节一般带有额外的降势音高（Fox et al, 2008；林建平 2002；Vance，1976）。这种额外的降势音高一般不会中和句末音节本身的声调，即句末音节的声调还是能被辨别出来。对一般疑问句而言，句子最后一个音节一般呈高升调形（林建平，2002；Ma，2007；Ma，Ciocca 和 Whitehill，2004，2006a，2006b，2011；麦耘，1998，2000；Xu 和 Mok，

---

① 在文献上，T5 的调值也有描述为 13。为方便讨论，本文把 T5 的调值标为 23。

2011),如例(4)提到的例子。这种高升调形甚至会中和句末音节的声调,即句末音节原有的声调无法辨认出来,都表现为高升调。

句末助词和句末句调除了从语用上有共通之处之外,在句中的分布位置也相同——同处句末。此前的理论研究也注意到这两者的紧密关系,提出不同的分析框架。Cheung(1986)、邓思颖(2006)、Zhang(2014)认为句末句调是一种无音段的句末助词。Zhang(2014)还注意到句末助词和句末句调呈互补分布:没有句末助词的句子,一般使用句末句调。有句末助词的句子,通过句末助词表达句子情态。Zhang(2014)进而提出可以假设粤语中所有句子都带有句末助词,传统所说的句末助词都是有音段的句末助词,而句末句调则是无音段的句末助词。

另一种分析框架则反过来,着眼于句末助词的声调,指出句末助词声调的实质是句调,如冯胜利(2015)。句末助词可视为句末句调附加于某些特定的音段上,逐渐固化成词(lexicalized)。这两种分析实际上是一个问题的两个方面,两者是共通的。

3　粤语句末助词声调分布与语义

过往对粤语句末助词声调分布与语义的研究,主要集中在三个平调 T1、T3 和 T4 上。Law(1990),Li(2006),Sybesma and Li(2007)和丁思志(2013)等研究都指出,粤语句末助词的三个平调(T1、T3 和 T4)皆与一定的语义有密切的关系。其中 T1 是高调(用"H"表示),表示听者导向(hearer oriented)的信息;T4 是低调(L),表示说者导向(speaker oriented)的信息;T3 是中调(M),表达的是中性、默认的语义。以我们上文提及的例(1)至例(3)的句末助词为例,例(1)用的是 T1,表达"他走了"这个信息是显而易见的,是听者应该知道的信息。例(3)用的是 T4,表达的意思是"他走了",这是说者不确定的信息,说者希望确定这个信息的真伪。例(2)用的是 T3,表达中性的语义,只是强调"他走了"这个信息是客观存在的事实。

如果句末助词只有三个平调具有一定的语用语义,那么还是难以建立一个统一的框架表明句末助词声调和句末句调的内在联系。研究的突破点在于句末助词的两个上升调 T2 和 T5。然而句末助词的这两个声调前人研究较少，也不够深入，不成系统。本文首次提出这两个上升调句调来源的理论假设，并提供语音实验的实证。

我们的理论假设是，句末助词的 T2 有两种句调来源，一种来源为中调 T3 和高调 T1 的叠加，如（5）所列；一种来源是从疑问句的句末高升调 R 而来。T5 的句调来源主要是低调 T4 和中调 T3 的叠加，如（6）所列。

（5）T2（3<u>5</u>）= T3（3<u>3</u>）+ T1（5<u>5</u>），或 M+H

（6）T5（2<u>3</u>）= T4（2<u>1</u>）+ T3（3<u>3</u>），或 L+M

接下来我们将通过语音实验证明以上理论假设。

4 语音实验

句末助词的语音实验与普通的声调实验相比，要顾及的因素更多，并不能采取传统的读单字表的方式，而是应该让发音人根据具体语境，尽量自然地说出句子，带出目标音节。为此，我们设计了一系列句子，它们的句末音节都是 T2 或 T5。T2 音节包括句末助词"嘅"（ge2）①、"吓"（haa2）、"嗬"（ho2）等（情景 1 至情景 4 的目标句），及非句末助词"水"在不同语气中的使用（情景 5 和情景 6 的目标句）。T5 音节包括句末助词"啊"（aa5）、"咋"（zaa5）、"喎"（wo5）、"咧"（le5）等（情景 7 至情景 10 目标句）。②

为与目标句匹配，我们设计了相应的语境，并设计了后接的句子，以便发音人能更自然地根据语境"说"出句子，而不仅仅是"读"出句子。以下是我们设计的十组语境和句子，下划线标示的是我们的目标音节。每组下面还列有相应的普通话表达方式。

情景 1：你带小朋友去玩，本来想提醒小朋友要饮水，小朋友话佢已经饮过啦，你话：

你带小朋友去玩，本来想提醒小朋友要喝水，小朋友说他已经

---

① 粤拼的数字表示调类，"1"至"6"分别指 T1 至 T6。
② 我们在实际实验中还包括了 T5 的非句末助词"嘢"，但经观察，它并无特别，在此不再赘述。

喝过了，你说：

饮咗嘅。怪之得你唔颈渴啦。

喝了（水）啊。难怪你不渴。

情景2：你买咗一樽可乐，叫朋友唔好饮住，等你打完波返来先饮，点知返到嚟发现朋友饮咗，你话：

你买了一瓶可乐，让朋友先不要喝，等你打完球回来再喝，谁知道回来时发现朋友已经喝了，你说：

饮咗嘅？唔系叫你留返俾我嘅咩？

喝了（可乐）呀？不是让你留给我喝的吗？

情景3：你带小朋友出去玩，你提醒小朋友要饮水，你话：

你带小朋友出去玩，你提醒小朋友要喝水，你说：

饮水吓。饮完再玩过。

喝水啊。喝了再玩。

情景4：你叫人送咗煲汤俾你朋友饮，佢过嚟还返个保温瓶俾你，你问：

你让人送了一锅汤给你朋友喝，他过来还你保温瓶，你问：

饮咗嚵？好不好味？

喝了吧？好喝吗？

情景5：你啱啱打完波返宿舍，朋友问你颈唔颈渴，你话：

你刚刚打完球回宿舍，朋友问你是否口渴，你说：

饮咗水。而家冇咁颈渴。

喝了水。现在没那么口渴。

情景6：你系医生，吩咐病人六个小时内禁水禁食，后尾去巡房嘅时候病人话俾你知佢啱啱饮咗水，你话：

你是医生，吩咐病人六个小时内禁水禁食，后来去巡房的时候病人告诉你他刚刚喝了水，你说：

饮咗水？唔系叫你唔好饮嘢食嘢嘅咩？

喝了水？不是让你不要喝东西或者吃东西的吗？

情景7：你同朋友玩游戏，要喺好短时间内完成一啲动作，开头你以为要两秒内，就话做唔到，后来你朋友话五秒内就得，你话：

你和朋友玩游戏，要在很短时间内完成一些动作，开始你以为
要两秒内，就说做不到，后来你朋友说五秒内就可以，你说：

五秒**啊**。我都可以试下嘅。

五秒啊。我也可以试试。

情景 8： 你朋友话佢跑 20 米用咗五秒，你话：

你朋友说他跑 20 米用了五秒，你说：

五秒**咋**。都唔系好快啫。

五秒而已。都不算很快啊。

情景 9： 你朋友问你几秒之内完成任务先得，你记得裁判话过系五秒，
你话俾你朋友知：

你朋友问你几秒之内完成任务才行，你记得裁判说过是五秒，
你告诉你朋友：

五秒**喎**。裁判话五秒之内完成都得。

五秒啊。裁判说五秒之内完成都可以。

情景 10： 你朋友话按比赛规定，要十秒内完成动作，你记得唔系十秒，
系五秒，睇返比赛嘅资料，果然系五秒，你指俾你朋友睇：

你朋友说按比赛规定，要十秒内完成动作，你记得不是十秒，
是五秒，看比赛的资料，果然是五秒，你指给你朋友看：

五秒**唎**。唔系十秒。

五秒啊。不是十秒。

  实验时由实验人员向发音人描述语境，发音人根据语境说出目标句及后接句。为了获得更多的数据量，每位发音人每个目标句及后接句都需要说三遍。若实验人员察觉到发音人发得不自然或者发出的并非目标句，会作出提示，让发音人重新说出正确的句子。测量的时候，只测量说得正确的句子。

  本实验邀请了 4 名香港中文大学的本科生当发音人，包括 2 名男生，2 名女生。实验使用 Marantz PMD620 专业录音机录音。录音后用 Praat 软件切分音节并测量基频 f_0 和时长 t。每个音节都测平均分布的 11 个音高点，这 11 个音高点把音高曲线平均分成 10 份。我们还对基频进行了归一化处理，先把基频 f_0 从赫兹转换为半音（Hart et al., 1990），再计算各音节的 Z-score

(Jassem，1971)。每个目标句末音节都有 12 个音节（4 个发音人×3 次发音），计算各音高点上的 Z-score 平均值及音高曲线的平均长度，连接各音高点，即为目标句末音节的平均音高曲线。

我们首先看看句末助词是 T2 的情况。图 1 画出声调为 T2 的句末助词音高曲线。这四条音高曲线前面一小段约占时长 20%的部分都呈下降趋势，这部分是过渡段，因为前面音节都是 T2，声调音高终点较高，因此图 1 所示的曲线前面都有一小段音高回落的过渡段。撇除了过渡段，我们现在重点来看音高曲线的主体部分。

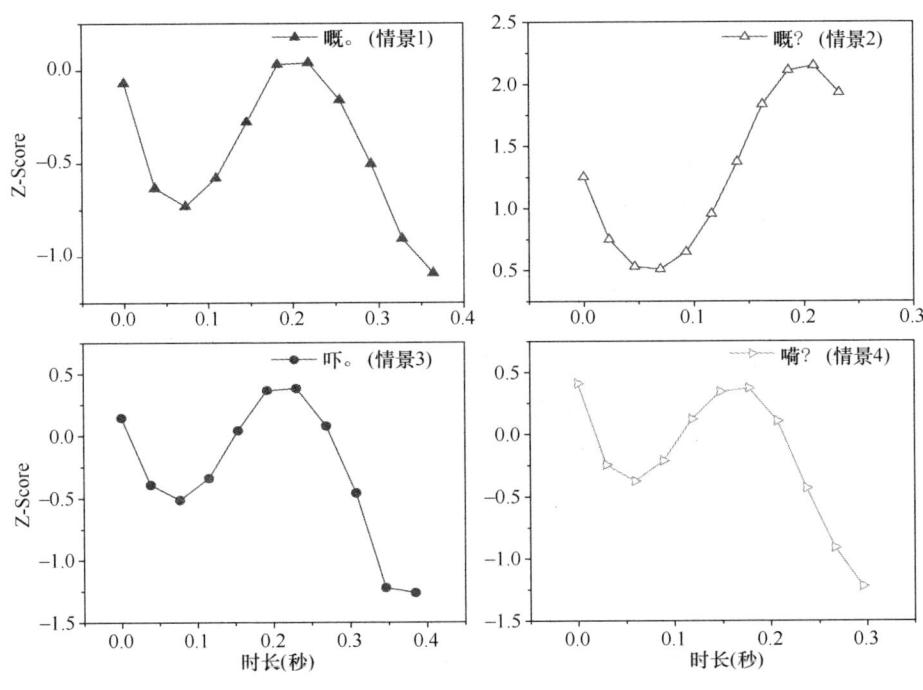

图 1 声调为 T2 的句末助词音高曲线

我们发现传统都记为"嘅"（ge2）的句末助词，在情景 1 和情景 2 中的音高曲线截然不同。情景 1 中的"嘅"（ge2），前 20%过渡段之后，从 20%至 60%是上升调形，这应该就是这个句末助词传统来说都标记为 T2 的原因。然而，从 60%至 100%都是下降调形，这是出乎我们意料之外的。这部分曲线占整条音高曲线时长约 40%，几乎与前面的上升部分等长，因此是不可忽略的，应该有其语言学意义。情景 2 中的"嘅"（ge2），则是绝大部分的音高曲线都是高升调形，只有头尾很小一部分有"弯头降尾"的现象。我们在图 2 的左图中将这两个"嘅"（ge2）并置，可以发现情景 2 中的"嘅"（ge2）所处的音高层明显要比情景 1 中的"嘅"（ge2）高。

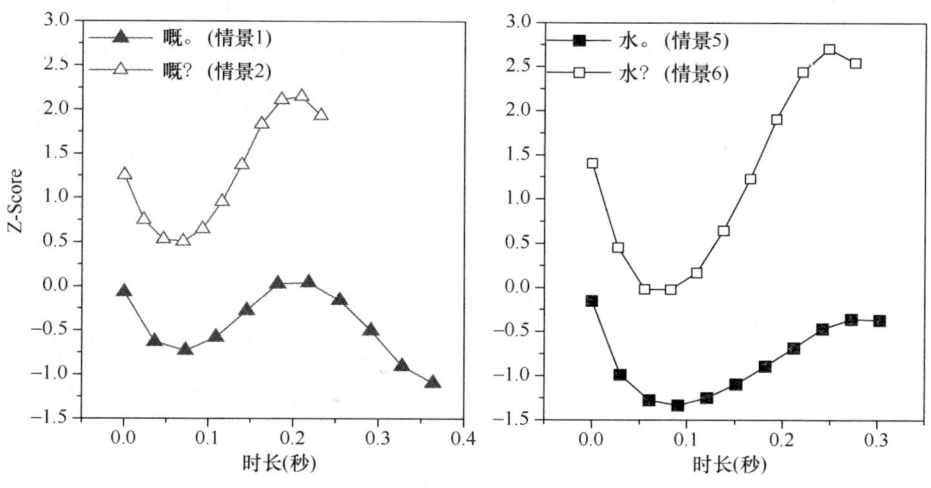

图 2　句末"水"和"嘅"（ge2）的音高曲线

　　这两个"嘅"（ge2）语音形式不同，是因为它们有不同的句调来源。我们应该综合运用语音实证与语义分析，揭示其背后的语言学意义。我们认为情景 1 中"嘅"（ge2）音高曲线的句调来源是"M+H+F"，即中调 M、高调 H 和降调 F 的连续叠加。从语音上看，中调 M 和高调 H 先叠加为音高曲线时长段 20% 至 60% 的上升调形；降调 F 则为最后 60% 至 100% 的下降音段。其中"M+H"的上升调形是我们能预计到的（与传统标记为 T2 相符），而"F"是我们通过语音实验揭示的重要组成部分。从语义上看，在情景 1 下，这个句末助词先是说明"喝了水"这个中性的、客观的事实，用 M 音高；然后这个信息对于听者来说是显而易见的，是听者导向的，用 H 音高；最后的下降调形 F 是一种陈述性降调，表示对信息的强烈肯定。因此，语音形式上的每个构成成分都能找到其语义上的构成因素，即语音形式和语义内涵一致，两者共同表明情景 1 中"嘅"（ge2）的句调来源是"M+H+F"。

　　与情景 1 中的"嘅"（ge2）相似，情景 3 中的"吓"和情景 4 中的"嗬"

也有类似的音高曲线。它们的句调来源也都是"M+H+F"。其中"M+H"都与中性意义和听者导向意义叠加有关,而"F"有不同的语义来源。情景3中"吓"(haa2)的"F"为祈使性降调。情景4中"嗬"(ho2)本为表达疑问的句末助词,但因为要表达期待肯定性的回答,因此音高曲线后半部分也是明显的降调调形F。

情景2中"嘅"(ge2)的句调来源是一般疑问句的句末高升调R。为方便大家理解句末高升调R的语音性质,我们设计了情景5和情景6的句末"水"作对比。图2的右图并行列出情景5和情景6中的"水"。我们可以看到,情景5目标句子是陈述句,句末的"水"虽然保持上升调形,但是所处的音高层(pitch register)不是那么高,上升的幅度不是那么大。情景6目标句子是一般疑问句,句末的"水"从音高层上看明显更高,从调形上看上升的幅度很大——这两点都是一般疑问句句末高升句调的显著特点。对比图2左图两个"嘅"(ge2)和右图两个"水",我们发现情景2中的"嘅"(ge2)与情景6中的"水"相似,它们的实质都是一般疑问句的句末高升调R。情景2中的"嘅"(ge2)的原调其实是"嘅"(ge3),句末高升调R的同时叠加覆盖,使其终为T2调。

我们接下来再看看T5的情况。图3画出声调为T5的句末助词音高曲线,即情景7至情景10的句末助词。观察图3,可发现情景7的"啊"(aa5)、情景8的"咋"(zaa5)和情景10的"咧"(le5)的模式相近。最前面20%至30%是音高回落的过渡段,后面的主体曲线为上升调形,只有最后约10%的音段不太稳定:情景7的"啊"(aa5)上升得更多;而情景8的"咋"(zaa5)和情景10的"咧"(le5)出现回落。总体来说,这三个T5的句末助词都是单纯的上升调,并符合我们在(6)中的推测,即它们的句调来源都是源自L(或低平调T4)和M(或中平调T3)的连续叠加,语义上都可以分解为先寻求信息的肯定(说者导向),再自我肯定(表示一种中性意义)。

情景9的"喎"(wo5)与另外三种情景中T5的句末助词有所不同,它并非一个单纯的上升调。前30%为音高回落的过渡段,30%至60%为上升调形,而60%至100%(占总时长40%)则为明显的下降调形,并非可以忽

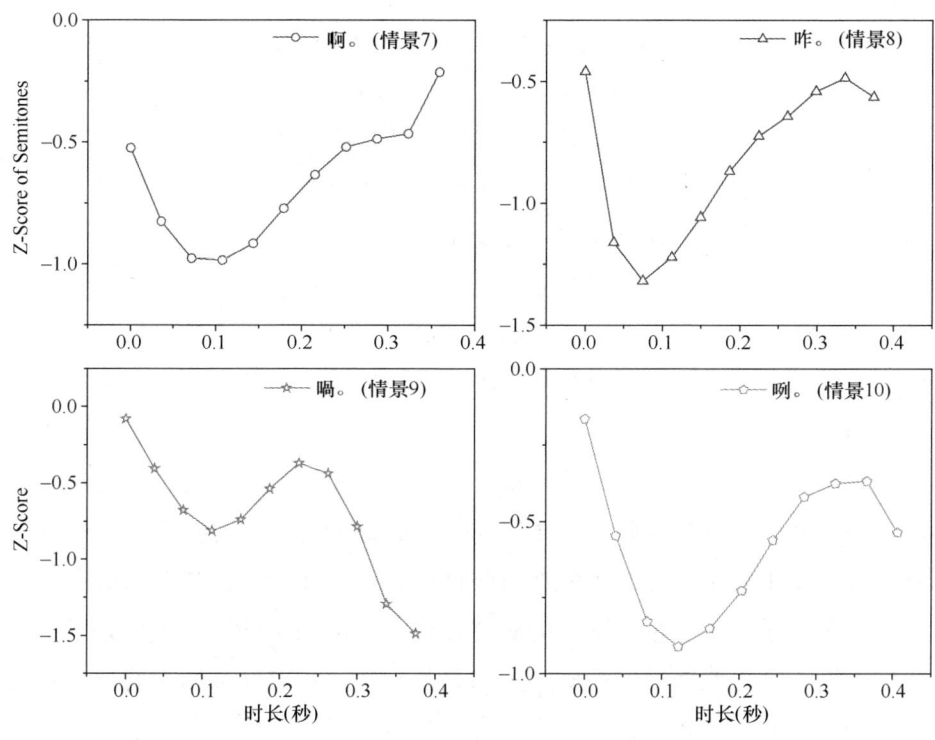

图 3　声调为 T5 的句末助词音高曲线

略的"降尾"。因此,"啹"(wo5)的句调来源除了"L+M"之外,还额外加了一个"F"表示强烈肯定,即其句调来源为"L+M+F"。"啹"(wo5)有转述他人话语之意,语义可以分解为先寻求信息肯定(L),再肯定信息(M),并且因为此信息有确切来源(他人话语),因此有额外的强烈肯定之意(F),语义的分解与句调上的音高变化吻合。

5　结　语

本文首次通过语音实验的方法研究粤语句末助词的声调,指出粤语句末助词的超音段特征与句调的关系。本文的研究重点在于两个上升声调 T2 和 T5,首次提出其句调上的来源及叠加机制,并提供了语音测量的实证。

赵元任先生曾将汉语里句调和字调的关系比喻为"大波浪"和"小波浪";提出汉语的音高是两者的代数和(Chao,1968)。他也曾提出句调和声调的叠加有两种方式：同时叠加（simultaneous addition）和连续叠加（successive addition）。本文分析的粤语句末助词两个上升调，也主要使用这两种叠加方式。本文中的大部分例子都使用了连续叠加，即句末助词的 T2 由 M 和 H 连续叠加而来；T5 由 L 和 M 连续叠加而来。我们还通过语音实验发现了处于音高曲线后半部分的降调 F，其占时长比例约 40%，是不可忽略的、具有语言学意义的音高曲线组成部分。它也通过连续叠加的方式，叠加到 T2 或者 T5 的上升调形后面。句末助词 T2 的另一个句调来源是一般疑问句的句末高升调，例如情景 2 中"嘅"（ge2），此例的句调和声调叠加方式为同时叠加。

朱晓农（2004）指出，语音跟语义之间的关系是任意的，这是语言学的一项通则。少见的例外情况是，句调上就是所有的语言都毫无例外地用高调或升调来表示疑问，用低调或降调来表示陈述。这是音高和语义之间的一种生物学上的关系。本文的研究发现，粤语句末助词的声调并不是任意的，而是与语义有一定的对应关系。若将粤语句末助词的声调视为普通的声调，则有违语音与语义关系任意的语言学通则。因为普通的声调只提供语音上的分类，并不指示语义，同一声调的词语，彼此之间并不会有语义上的联系，例如"标"、"诗"和"花"，同属阴平调，但三者之间并无语义上的共通之处。从本文的分析可见，粤语句末助词音高曲线主体的各个构成成分均能找到其对应的语义要素。因此，粤语句末助词的声调并不是普通意义上的声调（lexical tone），而是应该源自句调，是句调语段化并固化成词（lexicalized）后的结果。

因此，粤语句末助词的声调这一概念要从不同的层面去理解。从区别词义的角度看，不同音高的语段确实能区别不同的句末助词，如本文开头所举的例（1）至例（3），在这一点上，粤语句末助词的声调与普通的声调是一致的。然而，粤语句末助词的声调有其特殊性，即存在与语义的对应关系，有其句调语义方面的来源。本文的研究进一步支持句末助词和句调关系的理论（Wakefield，2010；Zhang，2014；冯胜利，2015；Tang，2015 等）。本文的发现，为人类语言韵律句法研究提供了新的佐证。

参 考 文 献

邓思颖. 2006. 粤语疑问句"先"的句法特点. 中国语文,（3）：225-232.

邓思颖. 2015. 粤语语法讲义. 香港：商务印书馆.

丁思志. 2013. 从语调到声调——以粤语句末语气助词"呀"、"喎"为例. 现代语言学,（1）：36-41.

冯胜利. 2015. 声调、语调与汉语的句末语气. 语言学论丛，51：51-77.

林建平. 2002. 香港粤语句调研究. 香港：香港中文大学博士论文.

麦耘. 1998. 广州话语调说略. 广州话研究与教学（第三辑）. 广州：中山大学出版社.

麦耘. 2000. 实验报告：广州话句末升语调对字调的影响//第七届国际粤方言研讨会论文集. 北京：商务印书馆.

朱晓农. 2004. 亲密与高调. 当代语言学,（3）：193-222.

Chao, Y. R. 1933. Tone and Intonation in Chinese. In Z. J. Wu & X. N. Chao (Eds.), *Linguistic Essays by Yuenren Chao* (pp. 198-220). Beijing: Commercial Press.

Chao, Y. R. 1968. *A Grammar of Spoken Chinese*. Berkeley & Los Angeles: University of California Press.

Fox, A., Luke, K.K. & Nancarrow, O. 2008. Aspects of intonation in Cantonese. *Journal of Chinese Linguistics, 36*: 321-367.

Hart, J., Collier, R., &Cohen, A.1990. *A Perceptual Study of Intonation: An Experimental-Phonetic Approach to Speech Melody*. Cambridge & New York: Cambridge University Press.

Jassem, W. 1971. Pitch and Compass of Speaking Voice. *Journal of International Phonetic Association*(12): 59 68.

Law, S. P. 1990. *The Syntax and Phonology of Cantonese Sentence-final Particles*. Ph.D. dissertation, Boston University, Boston.

Li, B. 2006. *Chinese Final Particles and the Syntax of the Periphery*. Utrecht: LOT.

Ma, J. K. Y. 2007. *The Interaction Between Intonation and Tone in Cantonese*. Ph.D. dissertation, The University of Hong Kong, Hong Kong.

Ma, J. K. Y., Valter Ciocca & Tara L. Whitehill. 2004. The Effects of Intonation Patterns on Lexical Tone Production in Cantonese. Paper presented at the *International Symposium on Tonal Aspects of Languages: With Emphasis on Tone Languages*, Beijing.

Ma, J. K. Y., Valter Ciocca & Tara L. Whitehill. 2006a. Effect of intonation on Cantonese lexical tones. *Journal of the Acoustical Society of America, 120*(6): 3978-3987.

Ma, J. K. Y., Valter Ciocca & Tara L.Whitehill. 2006b. Quantitative Analysis of Intonation Patterns in Statements and Questions in Cantonese. *Proceedings of the Third International Conference on Speech Prosody*, 277-280.

Ma, J. K. Y., Valter Ciocca & Tara L. Whitehill. 2011. The Perception of Intonation Questions and Statements in Cantonese. *Journal of Acoustical Society of America*, *129*(2): 1012-1023.

Sybesma, R. & Li, B. 2006. The Dissection and Structural Mapping of Cantonese Sentence Final Particles. *Lingua*, *117*: 1739-1783.

Tang, S.-W. 2015. A generalized Syntactic Schema for Utterance Particles in Chinese. *Lingua Sinica*, *1*(3): 1-23

Vance, T. J. 1976. An Experimental Investigation of Tone and Intonation in Cantonese. *Phonetica*, *33*: 368-392.

Xu, B. R. & Pik-KiMok, P. 2011. Final Rising and Global Raising in Cantonese Intonation. *Proceedings of the Seventeenth International Congress of the Phonetic Sciences*, 2173-2176.

Zhang, L. 2014. Segmentless Sentence-final Particles in Cantonese: An experimental study. *Studies in Chinese Linguistics*, *35*(2): 47-60.

Preliminary Studies on Tones of Sentence-Final Particles and Intonation in Cantonese

Ling Zhang Sze-Wing Tang

Abstract It is proposed in this paper that the suprasegmental features of sentence-final particles (SFPs henceforth) in Cantonese are intonational rather than simply lexical-tonal, i.e., they reflect pragmatic and syntactic features at the sentence level. Tones of SFPs cover the six-tone system in Cantonese, among which Tone 1 (55), Tone 3 (33), and Tone 4 (21) are basic sentence-final boundary tones, as discussed in previous literature. It is argued that the two rising tones, Tone 2 (35) and Tone 5 (23), are the results of simultaneous addition of the interrogative rising intonation or successive addition of the basic sentence-final boundary tones, as evidenced by the findings of phonetic experiments conducted in the present study, which suggests that the theoretical hypothesis of interrelationship between SFP and intonation should be on the right track.

Keywords sentence-final particles, intonation, tone, Cantonese

张 凌

香港中文大学语言学及现代语言系，副研究员

E-mail：lingzhang@cuhk.edu.hk

邓思颖，香港中文大学中国语言及文学系，副教授

E-mail：swtang@cuhk.edu.hk

先秦诗律探索[*]

施向东

> **摘要** 本文首先观察分析先秦诗歌诗句字数的实际状况，统计"四言句"在先秦韵文中的比重，并尽可能地观察其历史演变的过程；其次，分析其节律，观察字数和韵素、音步的关系，音步和押韵的关系，以及音步的演变脉络。
>
> **关键词** 先秦诗律　韵素　音步　押韵　演变脉络

先秦诗律固然可以从《诗经》的"风""雅""颂"诸体得出"四言诗为主"的结论，但是这个说法可以说是"大而化之"、"语焉不详"。《诗经》诗体确实是四言为主，但是非四言的诗句（二言、三言、五言、六言、七言等）所在皆是，而且《诗经》不是先秦诗的全部。"逸诗"而外，诸经（《周易》、《礼记》等）、传（《左传》）、诸子（《老子》、《庄子》、《荀子》等）、楚骚以及谚谣杂诗，都可以看出先秦诗体复杂多样，要总结出其韵律实属不易，更无可能"一言以蔽之"曰四言体。

本文首先统计"四言句"在先秦韵文中的比重，分析不同字数诗句的实际状况，并尽可能地观察其历史演变的过程；其次，分析其节律，观察字数和韵素、音步的关系，音步和押韵的关系，以及音步的演变脉络。

诗律的本质是利用语言本身的韵律特性造成诗歌的音乐之美，中国文学史上诗歌形式不论如何演变，这一艺术追求始终是不变的，只是因为汉语的语音系统发生了变化，构成诗律的要素产生变动，诗歌形式随之适应性地变化，这就是诗歌艺术的奥秘。

---

[*] 本文受到国家社会科学基金重点项目的经费资助（项目名称：乾嘉学者段玉裁《说文解字注》、王念孙《广雅疏证》中科学方法和理念研究。项目编号：15AYY009），特此致谢。

一、先秦韵文诗句的字数统计

谈到先秦韵文，人们首先想到的自然是《诗经》《楚辞》。要分析先秦的诗律，当然离不开分析《诗经》《楚辞》。但是，首先，诗、骚并非先秦诗歌的全部，我们无论如何不能忘记其他文献中保存的韵文韵语；其次，诗、骚的时代不同，其韵律形式差别巨大，诗、骚各自的内部，不同部分的诗体与韵律形式也不能等量齐观。这方面的例子随手就可以举出很多。但是我们不能满足于个别的例子，而必须从总体上进行分析统计。因此，这里首先将先秦韵文中每句诗的字数情况作一个统计。

（一）《诗经》

表1　《诗经》句子字数统计

类	二言	三言	四言	五言	六言	七言	八言
国风 2609 句	11	124	2233	164	55	19	3
	0.4%	4.8%	85.6%	6.3%	2.1%	0.7%	0.1%
雅 3942 句	6	20	3712	169	31	3	1
	0.15%	0.5%	94.2%	4.3%	0.8%	<0.1%	0.03%
颂 734 句	2	22	639	60	9	2	
	0.3%	3%	87%	8.2%	1.2%	0.3%	
总计 7285 句	19	166	6584	393	95	24	4
	0.3%	2.3%	90.4%	5.4%	1.3%	0.3%	0.05%

如表1所示，四言句在国风中的比例最低，在雅诗中的比例最高，在颂诗中的比例接近国风。各种类型的非四言句，在雅诗中均低于国风和颂诗。

（二）《周易》

《周易》有经、传之分，易传的年代争论颇大，这里只取经的部分即卦辞和爻辞中韵语进行统计（依据段玉裁《六书音均表五》）。

《周易》韵语中四言句的比例明显地低,二言、三言句的比例占了相当大的一部分(表2,图1):

表2 《周易》韵语句子字数统计

字数	二言	三言	四言	五言	六言	七言
句数合计 303	44	88	148	18	4	1
百分比	14.5%	29.0%	48.8%	5.9%	1.3%	0.3%

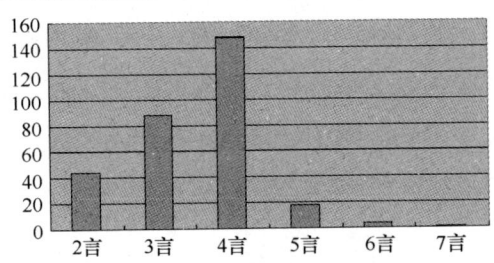

图1 《周易》韵语句子字数示意图

《周易》与《诗经》数据的差异,《诗经》内部数据的差异,与其体裁有关,更重要的是与时代有关。口语体的文本与文学性强的文本不同:卦辞、爻辞口语性强,非四言的句子多;《诗经》内部风诗与雅诗的差异,亦可以作如是观。《易经》的文本早于《诗经》的删定本,也是《周易》与《诗经》数据差异的一个重要的因素。为了证实我们的想法,我们分别统计了《左传》《国语》中引《诗》(包括《诗经》和"逸诗")和引谣谚筮辞等的数据。

(三)《左传》《国语》中引《诗》和引谣谚筮辞等的数据(表3,表4)

表3 《左传》《国语》中引《诗》的数据统计[①]

字数	三言	四言	五言	六言	七言	总计
句数合计	5	413	19	4	1	442
百分比	1.2%	93.4%	4.3%	0.9%	0.2%	100%

---

① 本文统计《左传》《国语》中引诗仅限于直接见到原文的,像"赋《某某》"或"赋《某某》之某章"(如《左传》闵公二年"许穆夫人赋《载驰》,郑人为之赋《清人》"、文公十三年"子家赋《载驰》之四章,文子赋《采薇》之四章")之类原文未出现的均不计入。若计入此类诗句,四言句的比例将更高。

表4 《左传》《国语》中引谣谚筮辞等的数据统计

字数	三言	四言	五言	六言	七言	总计
句数合计	15	146	9	5	4	179
百分比	8.4%	81.6%	5.0%	2.8%	2.2%	100%

《左传》《国语》引《诗》与引谣谚筮辞等韵语的数据统计的差异，同样反映了语体差异与时代差异。语体差别的对比如图2所示：

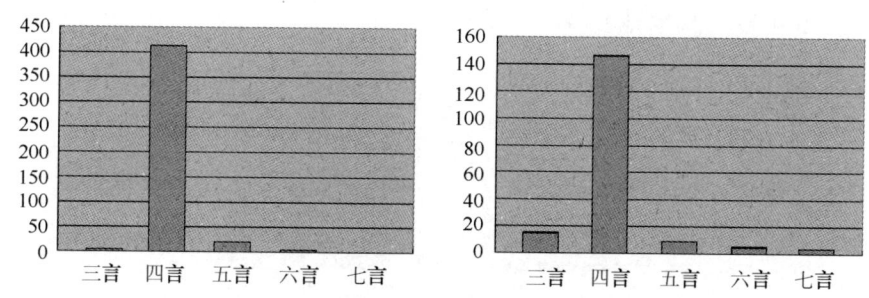

图2 《左传》《国语》中引《诗》、谣谚筮辞等的数据示意图

时代的差别如下例：

《周易·归妹》上六："女承筐，无实。士刲羊，无血。"而《左传·僖公十五年》："初，晋献公筮嫁伯姬于秦，遇《归妹》之《睽》，史苏占之曰"云云，引该段繇辞则作："士刲羊，亦无衁也。女承筐，亦无贶也。西邻责言，不可偿也。"不但两个二言句变成了四言句，还增加了两个四言句。

（四）《楚辞》句子的字数统计（表5）

《楚辞》我们只取屈原《离骚》《九歌》《天问》《九章》《远游》诸篇。

表5 《楚辞》句子的字数统计

类	题	三言	四言	五言	六言	七言	八言	九言	十言	总计
离骚	合计	1	0	7	160	176	25	5	1	375
	百分比	0.3%	0%	1.9%	43.2%	46.4%	6.7%	1.3%	0.3%	
九歌	合计			49	130	79	1	2		261
	百分比			19%	50%	30%	<1%	<1%		
天问	合计	19	286	50	14	3	1			373
	百分比	5%	77%	13%	4%	<1%				

续表

类	题	三言	四言	五言	六言	七言	八言	九言	十言	总计
九章	合计		86	74	231	245	30	2		668
	百分比		13%	11%	35%	37%	4%	0.3%		
远游	合计	1	8	10	72	78	9			178
	百分比	<1%	4%	6%	40%	44%	5%			
《楚辞》	合计 1855	21	380	190	609	579	66	9	1	
	百分比	1.1%	20.5%	10.2%	32.8%	31.2%	3.6%	0.5%	0.05%	

图 3 可以更形象地表现这一比例：

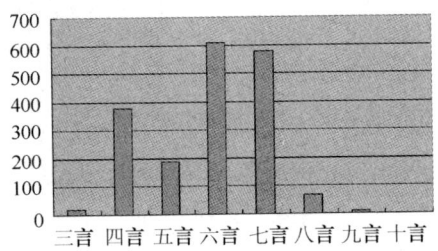

图 3 《楚辞》句子的字数示意图

《楚辞》中四言句整体式已经不占多数了（只在某些篇章如《天问》《橘颂》中占多数），而以六言、七言句为主，两者相加超过了六成。严格意义上已经没有二言句了，只有像"乱曰、倡曰、重曰"这些说明性的语句，我们没有把它们统计在内。

表 6 很可以看出不同时代诗句字数的变化：

表 6　先秦韵文句子字数示意图

	二言	三言	四言	五言	六言	七言	八言	九言	十言
易经	14.5%	29.0%	48.8%	5.9%	1.3%	0.3%			
《左传》、《国语》引谣谚筮辞		8.8%	81.9%	4.7%	2.6%	2.1%			
《诗经》	0.3%	2.3%	90.4%	5.4%	1.3%	0.3%	0.05%		
《左传》、《国语》引《诗经》		1.1%	93.4%	4.3%	0.9%	0.2%			
《楚辞》		1.1%	20.5%	10.2%	32.8%	31.2%	3.6%	0.5%	0.05%

如表 5 所列，早期的、口语性强的诗句二言、三言的句子多，晚期的、文学性强的或经过刻意修订的文献中二言、三言句逐渐减少以致消亡；四言句在《诗经》（尤其是雅诗）和《左传》所引亦即春秋会盟宴飨场合所引

用的诗句中达到顶峰,以后也逐渐走了下坡路。五言、六言、七言诗句早期绝少,到《楚辞》五言句成倍增长,六言、七言句子则占压倒性的多数。八言以上诗句,古之所无,诗骚中亦鲜见痕迹。

二、先秦韵文诗句的字数与韵素、音步的关系

我们之所以不厌其烦地统计先秦诗句的字数,目的是为了分析诗句字数与节奏、音步与韵律的关系。

冯胜利在《汉语韵律诗体学论稿》一书中对先秦汉语诗律有了开创性的论述,本文拟在此基础上作进一步的讨论。

(一)二言句

如上所述,二言句在先秦诗歌韵语中呈逐渐下降的趋势,多出现在先秦口语体的韵语中。如《周易·乾》初九:"潜龙,勿用";《屯》六二:"匪寇,婚媾"(又见于《贲》六四、《睽》上九);《蹇》九三:"往蹇,来反";六四:"往蹇,来连";《萃》上六:"赍咨,涕洟";《归妹》上六:"女承筐,无实;士刲羊,无血"。二言句的存在证明了上古存在单音节音步这一事实。单音节音步是一个音节中两个韵素构成的音步。冯胜利证明了上古一个音节中塞音韵尾与其韵腹元音这两个韵素可以构成一个音步(冯胜利,2015:137),其实,阳声韵的鼻音韵尾与其韵腹元音这两个韵素亦可以构成一个音步,上述《周易·蹇》九三、六四的"往蹇,来连"与"往蹇,来反"两段韵语中"蹇、反、连"三字就是如此。即使是阴声韵的平声字,据本人的研究,上古带有浊擦音韵尾-ɦ(施向东,2015:342-364),也是双韵素的音节,可以独自构成一个音步。二言句,就是一个双音步的诗句:

```
    潜            龙,         勿          用。
    zlom         b·roŋ        mɯd         loŋs      ——音节(σ)层=音步(f)层
   /\           /\          /\          /\
 (zl) o    m  (b·r) o    ŋ (m) ɯ     d (l) o     ŋs    ——韵素(μ)层
```

汉语音节的韵腹是强韵素（我们用 μ 表示），韵尾是弱韵素（我们用μ 表示），因此，诗句的韵律就是 μμ μμ，μμ μμ。

但是上古汉语的单音节后来随着其音节结构的简化而逐步丧失了独自成为音步的资格，双音节音步逐渐取代了单音节音步。我们知道，一般情况下，一个合格的诗句至少需要两个音步，独步不成句。二言结构因为只有一个音步而不能成为一个合格的诗句，因此二言诗句也就随之锐减而渐趋消亡。不过这一过程是渐进的，下面的分析会继续谈到这一点。

（二）三言句

《诗经》的三言句虽然总体上为数不多，只有 2.3% 的比例，但是在口语体较为显著的风诗中这一比例达到 4.8%，共有 124 句之多。在时代较早且口语性较强的《周易》卦辞、爻辞中，三言句达到 29%，其地位不容轻视。

《周易》《诗经》的三言句，有一些是二言句的变体，其中有一个音节从韵律上可以分析为其他音节的附属物，整个句子仍然必须分析为两个音节音步。如《周南·螽斯》：

螽斯羽，诜诜兮。宜尔子孙，振振兮。
螽斯羽，薨薨兮。宜尔子孙。绳绳兮。
螽斯羽，揖揖兮。宜尔子孙，蛰蛰兮。

整首诗 12 句，三言句 9 个，占了 75%。但是这里的三言句可以归为两个类型："螽斯羽"型和"诜诜兮"型，前者可以形式化为 AbC 型，后者可形式化为 ABc 型。假如我们把三章都有的"宜尔"两字视为"加言"，则此诗实际上的韵律形式就是：

螽斯羽，诜诜兮。（宜尔）子孙，振振兮。
螽斯羽，薨薨兮。（宜尔）子孙。绳绳兮。
螽斯羽，揖揖兮。（宜尔）子孙，蛰蛰兮。

它就是一首二言诗的变体而已。这里，"螽斯羽"仍然是一个双音步的诗句，"螽斯"是一个完整音节加上一个不能构成音步的词尾"-斯"的大音步（super foot）（tjuŋ-se）。语气词"兮"字在诗句中的作用主要是加强感叹的语气，并不参与句子句法成分的语义结构，也不单独构成音步，早期总是附着在独立音节的后面，一起构成一个大音步："诜兮"（srin-Ge）。大音步（我们用 **f** 表示）强于普通音步（我们用 f 表示），这样，此诗的韵律，我们可以表示为：

ff, **ff** 。（ ）**ff**, **ff** 。
ff, **ff** 。（ ）**ff**, **ff** 。
ff, **ff** 。（ ）**ff**, **ff** 。

《周易》也有这样的三言句，往往是两个实字加一个虚字或半虚字，可以看做由二言向三言过渡的形式，如《需》六四："需于血，出自穴"；《益》上九："莫益之，或击之"，等等。但是周代已经有不少真正的三言句，已经不能视作二言诗的变体了。如《周易·履》六三："眇能视，跛能履，履虎尾"；《噬嗑》九四："噬干肺，得金矢"；《鼎》九四："鼎折足，覆公餗，其形渥"，等等。《诗经》中亦多，如《召南·江有汜》"江有汜，之子归，不我以……江有渚，之子归，不我与……江有沱，之子归，不我过"；《小雅·庭燎》："夜未央"、"夜未艾"、"夜乡晨"；《周颂·桓》："绥万邦，屡丰年"，等等。真正三言句的产生，是诗歌节律的一大突破，是汉语诗律后来多次变化的基础。

为什么这么说呢？因为真正的三言句，无论分析为 1+2（噬-干肺，得-金矢；鼎-折足，覆-公餗），还是 2+1（其形-渥，良马-逐，之子-归）的节奏，都包含着一个矛盾，如果是单音节音步，则"2"已经是两个音步，"1"是韵律上多余的成分，如果是双音节音步，则"1"不够一个音步。事实上已经存在的三言句，迫使我们做出理论上的解释。

我们的解释是这样的：先秦时代是汉语从单音节音步（韵素音步）向双音节音步转变的时期，音节的地位还很微妙。一方面，一些不够一个音步的音节（语言中总是轻读的、句法上总是处于附属地位的虚词等）出现在诗歌中，形成 1-2 或 2-1 结构的诗句（就像上述"螽斯 羽"，"诜 诜兮"），造成 3 音节、2 音步的诗句，为后来真正的三言诗句开辟了道路；另一方面，汉语音节的简化，使一些实词字的读音（并不是全部和同时）逐渐丧失了可以分析为双韵素的资格，但是这个过程是渐进的，所以一定有一个韵素音步和音节音步并存或混乱的时期。先秦文献中三言诗句的存在，就是一个极好的证明。三言句"2+1"或"1+2"中的那个"1"，必须是一个完整的音步，在韵素音步时期，这不成问题，到音节音步时期，它就要借助"停延"的手段，使自己占有两个音节的时长，来获得一个音步的资格。而在诗歌中，这也是不难做到的。《毛诗序》说："言之不足，故嗟叹之；嗟叹之不足，故咏歌之。""咏"就是引而诵之，是诗歌创造音步的手法，自古有之。

三言诗句的存在，跟四言句的存在是同时的，互相补充的。《周易》《诗经》常常出现三言四言句连用的情况。《周易·蒙》："初噬告，再三渎，渎则不告"；《小畜》九三："舆说輹，夫妻反目"；《夬》九四："臀无肤，其行次且"；《困》九四："来徐徐，困于金车"；《艮》："艮其背，不获其身，行其庭，不见其人"，等等。《诗经·召南·摽有梅》："摽有梅，其实七兮。求我庶士，迨其吉兮！摽有梅，其实三兮。求我庶士，迨其今兮！摽有梅，顷筐塈之。求我庶士，迨其谓之"，又《郑风·大叔于田》："大叔于田，乘乘马。执辔如组，两骖如舞……叔于田，乘乘黄。两服上襄，两骖雁行……叔于田，乘乘鸨。两服齐首，两骖如手"，等等，也是三言四言混合存在的，其中的三言句，也是过渡的三言句跟真正的三言句混合存在的。

这些情况都说明，在从单音节韵素音步向双音节音步过渡的过程中，三言句的产生和存在是必然的，它在汉语诗歌史上具有重要的地位。

（三）四言句

先秦韵文中四言句数量最多，而且，观察四言句最多的文献和使用场合，可以知道它是一种典雅语体所追求的句式。《诗经》中，雅诗的四言句比例最大，达到94.2%，远超风诗的85.6%；《左传》中，诸侯大夫会盟赋诗，四言句的比例达到93.8%，远超其所引谣谚筮辞的81.6%。可见四言句在春秋时代是一种风雅的时尚和文学追求，那么它一定是一种逐渐取代旧事物的新生事物。新在何处？旧迹何存？我们分析先秦经典可以找到其清晰的证据。

首先，典型的四言句可以拆分为两部分："窈窕-淑女，君子-好逑"（诗经·周南·关雎》)、"我有-嘉宾，鼓瑟-吹笙"（小雅·鹿鸣）、"文王-陟降，在帝-左右"（大雅·文王），等等。每个部分两个音节，整齐，对称，凸显典雅庄严的风格气氛。但是我们尚不能断言四言句的产生就一定是双音节音步已经成立。这里仍然有两种可能：一是每句两个双音节音步，这是两步律，二是每句四个单音节音步，这是四步律。一般地说，诗句不能少于两个音步，但并不等于说一句诗只能有两个音步。四音步的诗句在世界诗歌史上是普遍存在的。经典梵语的诗歌，基本节奏称为 śloka（汉译为"颂"），每一颂由四个 8 音节的 pada（诗句）组成。比如古印度史诗《摩诃婆罗多》的诗句绝大部分就是四步律的：

  Śṛṇu rājankulastriṇāṁ

    mahābhāgyaṁ yudhiṣṭhira |

  Sarvametadyathā prāptaṁ

    Sāvitryā rājakanyayā‖

因此把《诗经》的四言句看成四音步的诗句并不是惊世骇俗、不可思议的。但是四言句的普及对双音节音步的定型一定具有重要的意义，这是毫无疑义的。因为由四言四音步转变为两个双音节音步是最自然不过的，比之三言句，更易为人们所接受：

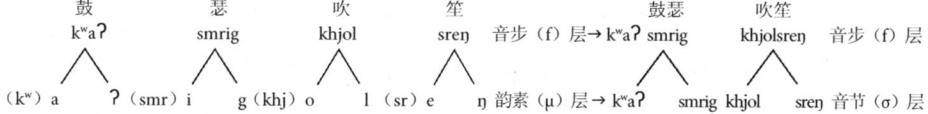

从认知心理的角度说，古人并没有"韵素、音节、音步"的自觉，他们能够感知的，只是四言句的两个偶丽的节奏段，正如《文心雕龙·丽辞》所谓："造化赋形，支体必双；神理为用，事不孤立。"这种双音节的节奏段究竟为何物，只是我们今人的分析。但是四言句的大量使用，无疑证明古人在心理上已经逐渐认可这种双音节组是一种节奏单位。我们之所以把这种逐渐定型的节奏单位认定为音步，是基于这样一个认识：春秋战国之际，汉语的声调逐渐产生，声调将一个音节"箍起来"成为语音流中一个明显的个体，与无声调时期相比，音节内部的韵素的对比已经不再是重要的关系，而音节之间的关系凸显为显性的关系。于是，两个音节成为一个音步

逐渐取代了单音节音步，成为汉语节奏的基本单位。

其次，先秦大量的四言句，还带着非四言句的过渡形式的痕迹。最典型的如《诗经·邶风·绿衣》：

> 绿兮衣兮，绿衣黄里。心之忧矣，曷维其已？
> 绿兮衣兮，绿衣黄裳。心之忧矣，曷维其亡？
> 绿兮丝兮，女所治兮。我思古人，俾无訧矣。
> 絺兮绤兮，凄其以风。我思古人，实获我心。

这种通过使用"兮、之"以及其他虚字将非四言句扩充成四言句的现象，充分体现了单音节音步向双音节音步的过渡。

再次，我们看诗经内部的差别，风诗2609句，"兮"字280见（不算题目中的兮字），平均9个句子中就有一个兮字；而雅诗3942句，兮字仅38见，平均104个句子中才见到一个兮字。可见典雅语体中更讲究节奏的均衡对称，尽量消除旧痕迹造成的韵律不整齐。

（四）五言句

春秋以前五言诗句很少，《诗经》中总共才393句，仅占5.4%。其中大量的是带有"兮、也、矣"等虚字的句子，如"西方之人兮"（邶风·简兮）、"终不可谖兮"（卫风·淇奥）、"乃如之人也"（墉风·蝃蝀）、"永以为好也"（卫风·木瓜）、"维其有章矣，是以有庆矣"（小雅·大田）等。此类五言句可以看成四言句的变体。但是也有一些五言句，不能分析为四言句的附庸，其中一部分，节奏为1-4式，如"在南山之阳"（召南·殷其雷）、"远兄弟父母"（卫风·竹竿）、"如松柏之茂"（小雅·天保）、"无此疆尔界"（周颂·思文）等，与后世五言诗句有异。但是也有一些节奏为2-3式的五言句，如"谁谓雀无角？何以穿我屋？谁谓女无家？何以速我狱"（召南·行露）、"宛在水中央"（秦风·蒹葭）、"九月筑场圃，十月纳禾稼"（豳风·七月）、"老马反为驹……毋教猱升木"（小雅·角弓）、"莫敢不来享，莫敢不来王"（商颂·殷武），等等。五言句在《诗经》虽为少数，但是其重要性不容小看。

《楚辞》的五言句已经占到10%强。大体可分为三类，一类是4-1（兮）

式，如"有鸟自南兮""聊以娱心兮"（九章·抽思）、"纷其可喜兮""姱而不丑兮"（九章·橘颂）等，其实是四言句的变体；一类是 1-4 式，如"曰遂古之初""而顾菟在腹""夫焉取九子"（天问）、"忽谓之过言"（九章·惜诵）等；还有一类 2-1-2 式，可以说是《楚辞》的发明，如"忍尤而攘诟""申申其詈予"（离骚）、"吉日兮辰良""扬枹兮拊鼓""石濑兮浅浅，飞龙兮翩翩"（九歌）等；也有一些 2-3 式的句子，如"名余曰正则兮，字余曰灵均"（离骚）、"登高吾不说兮，入下吾不能"（九章·思美人）、"鸟飞反故乡兮，狐死必首丘"（九章·哀郢）、"往者余弗及兮，来者吾不闻"（远游）、"高阳邈以远兮，余将焉所程"（远游），以上诸例下句都是 2-3 式的五言句，上句去掉"兮"的话，也是 2-3 式，与下句配合，音律之正，即使放到汉魏诗句中也可无惭。

五言句的出现，是双音节音步逐渐胜出的标志。即使我们可以勉强地说 4-1（兮）式和 2-1-2 式仍然是四个单音节音步的四步律诗句（包含一个大音步），但是 1-4 式就很难这样分析，尤其是 2-3 式，无论如何不能分析为单音节音步的"五步律"诗句。五言句一直到《楚辞》才有较大的增长，可以看出汉语双音节音步的胜出是一个异常艰难的历程。

2-3 式五言句的韵律可以分析为一个双音节音步和一个三音节大音步：

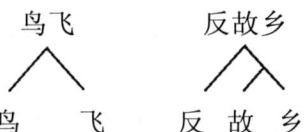

1-4 式五言句，有些其第一字是虚字，可以附着在后面的双音节音步上：

但是首字是实词的，其韵律却很难办。如"师何以尚之""媵有莘之妇"，或许勉强分析为

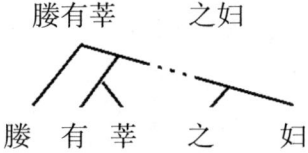

但是此种韵律后世辞赋骈文多用之，而为五言诗所不取。

（五）六言以上的诗句

《楚辞》之前，六言以上的诗句是很少见的，《周易》《诗经》所见均在2%以下，《左传》《国语》所引谣谚筮辞亦仅占5%，而到《楚辞》中忽然增长到68%以上。其中的原因，除了可用地方习俗、文体特性等来解释以外，最主要的，恐怕与汉语双音节音步的形成和发展分不开。

《楚辞》六言句占32.7%，是各种不同字数的句中最高的。《楚辞》六言句主要有以下句式：

5-1（兮）式，如"名余曰正则兮""女嬃之婵媛兮""理弱而媒拙兮""巫咸将夕降兮"（离骚）等。此式在节奏上多与3-3式相通，可读为"名余曰-正则兮""女嬃之-婵媛兮"等等。

1-5式，如"来吾道夫先路""羌中道而改路"（离骚）此式在节奏上亦与3-3式相通，如"哀-众芳之芜秽""恐-修名之不立"（离骚），读如"哀众芳-之芜秽""恐修名-之不立"亦顺。

3-3式，如"朕皇考曰伯庸""纫秋兰以为佩""既遵道而得路""偭规矩而改错"（离骚），"焉得彼嵞山女"（天问），等等。

2-2-2式，如"夕揽洲之宿莽""何不改乎此度""夕余至乎县圃""余犹恶其佻巧"（离骚）"夫何三年不施"（天问）"聊以舒吾忧心""反既有此他志"（哀郢）"蒙瞍谓之不章"（怀沙），等等。

3-1-2式，如"抚长剑兮玉珥""浴兰汤兮沐芳""帝子降兮北渚，目眇眇兮愁予"（九歌），等等。

六言句韵律，大多数可以分为两个音步，虚字附着在相邻的音步上，虽然音步的划分可能跟句法的划分不尽一致："聊以舒-吾忧心""余犹恶-其佻巧"。此种节奏后世多用于辞赋骈文，而为诗家所不取。少数2-2-2式句，如"夕揽洲之宿莽""夫何三年不施"等，无法分析成两音步句，我们只好承认它们是三音步句。六言三音步句在汉语诗歌中是存在的，汉魏以下，代有佳作，虽然不是汉诗的主流，但是也不绝如缕①。

先秦的七言句，与后世七言诗的七言句基本上没有关系。《楚辞》七言句的句式有如下几种：

6-1 式，如"帝高阳之苗裔兮""扈江离与辟芷兮""老冉冉其将至兮"，末字以楚辞最有特色的"兮"结尾，占了七言句的大多数。也有末字为其他虚字的，如"余不忍为此态也""今直为此萧艾也""羌众人之所仇也"，等等。

1-6 式，如"夫唯捷径以窘步""亦非余心之所志""孰两东门之可芜"，等等，首字以虚字为领。

3-1-3 式，如"恐年岁之不吾与""愿俟时乎吾将刈""驰椒丘且焉止息""览余初其犹未悔""谓幽兰其不可佩""历吉日乎吾将行""洞庭波兮木叶下""青云衣兮白霓裳""哀见君而不再得"，等等，两个三音节音步中间夹一个虚字。

以上三种七言句的韵律，就是六言句韵律加上一个虚字而已。

3-4 式，如"命灵氛为余占之""又何必用夫行媒""愿春日以为糇芳"，等等，此种节奏为后世诗家所不取。

4-3 式，如"愿依彭咸之遗则""谣诼谓余以善淫""吾将上下而求索""吾令謇修以为理""吾告堵敖以不长""固将愁苦而终穷""至今九年而不复"，等等。表面上看似乎与后世七言句一致，但事实上此类句子多含虚字，大多略去后成为六言句而意思不变，这一点为后世七言诗所忌。

3-4 式与 4-3 式亦可以分析为三音步句。冯胜利（2015：214-215）认为汉以后七言诗 4-3 式句子可以分析为两个节律单位，即一个四音节的复合音步和一个三音节的音步。但是在先秦，在单音节音步向双音节音步过渡的时期，恐怕还不能这样分析。

---

① 可参见 http：//baike.baidu.com/link？url=D_DuNFqq7jGKVMUqBNApa8gtWDkYMBZaK0UuoVwp6jkuaCDbu3zk4Gt-tIUnqjy3ACv8hms5D0CiPVI2LLa5L_；又，萧艾《六言诗三百首》，中州古籍出版社，1987 年。冯胜利主张"五言以后没有六言"（冯胜利，《汉语韵律诗体学论稿》，商务印书馆，2015：32），似可商量。

三、先秦韵文诗句的音步和押韵的关系

押韵是汉语诗歌的重要特征。现代诗歌押韵的方式是"韵脚",也就是"脚韵",即句末韵。先秦诗歌押韵的韵式却不限于脚韵。还有"腰韵"即句中韵。甚至还有学者说到"头韵"即句首韵。

押韵与诗歌的音步有密切的关系。

首先,先秦有单音节音步,因此有二言句,故二言一押韵的情况在先秦数见不鲜。《周易》多见二言韵语,如《乾》初九"潜龙,勿用",《屯》六二、《贲》六四、《睽》上九"匪寇,婚媾",《蹇》九三、六四"往蹇,来反……往蹇,来连",《萃》上六"赍咨,涕洟",等等。

其次,先秦句中韵的有无,学者之间有争论。句中韵的存在本是事实,比如《诗经·邶风·柏舟》和《诗经·邶风·日月》"日居月诸","居、诸"押韵,江永《古韵标准》就已经指出。段玉裁《六书音均表》五,指出《周易·小畜》上九"既雨既处"一句中"雨、处"押韵。王力《诗经韵读》没有接受句中韵的说法,但是在《卫风·硕鼠》篇,将"硕鼠硕鼠、乐土乐土、乐国乐国、乐郊乐郊"都拆开成两句,鼠与鼠、土与土、国与国、郊与郊分别押韵,等于变相承认了句中韵。这些都明显地透露出了句中韵和二言句的密切关系。

第三,王力《诗经韵读》中《王风·扬之水》篇,将"怀哉怀哉,曷月予还归哉"的"怀哉怀哉"拆开成两句,两"怀"字与"归"字入韵。这样,句首的"怀"字入韵。相同的情况,《周易·离》九四:"突如其来如,焚如,死如,弃如",段玉裁《六书音均表》五指出"死、弃"押韵。这也是句首韵。但是我们细致分析,这又跟一般意义上的句首韵不同。二言句押韵,本来韵字在后字,但是后字是虚字(哉、如),故韵脚前移,这就移到句首,才造成了句首押韵的现象。

第四,韵脚为什么前移?我们注意到,在诗歌的韵律现象中,虚字往往是不算数的,"名余曰正则兮,字余曰灵均"虽然六言,韵律实与下句五言同。所以许慎《说文解字》说:"词,意内而言外也。"一语道破"词"是不能算在"言"内的。也就是说,"意内而言外"的"词",不承担韵律

责任。因此句末是虚字的,"韵脚"的位置就前移。

第五,为什么上古韵文韵脚密度大,而到《楚辞》,韵脚就稀了?其实,"关关雎鸠,在河之<u>洲</u>",四个音步一押韵;"帝高阳之苗裔兮,朕皇考曰伯<u>庸</u>。摄提贞于孟陬兮,惟庚寅吾以<u>降</u>。"也是四个音步一押韵。外表的差别巨大,本质上仍然有相同的地方。汉语韵律特征的转变,决定了汉语诗律的面貌,这不是诗人个人的意志所能决定的。《史记·滑稽列传》载淳于髡说齐威王之穰田者祝辞:"瓯窭满<u>篝</u>,污邪满<u>车</u>,五谷蕃<u>熟</u>,穰穰满<u>家</u>。"这种祝辞二言一韵,韵中有韵,押韵密度奇大,一定是古老时代传承下来的,绝不可能是太史公的新创造。

四、结　　语

我们探讨先秦诗律,观察到汉语韵律特征的变化,其中关键的问题就是汉语音节的构成从先秦到汉以后发生了巨大的变化,汉语音节由无声调到有声调,由复杂到简单,有声调的、简化了的单音节,不能继续胜任音步的任务,因此汉语的音步由单音节向双音节转化,这个过程带动了汉语诗律的变化。

由于汉语的音步由单音节向双音节转化,二言已经不能成诗,先秦文献中的二言韵语到后代就没有余音。三言体是典型的过渡形式,曾经跟四言体一起活跃在过渡时期的舞台上。四言体在转变中是最佳形式,四个单音节音步变为两个双音节音步,仍然是很好的诗行,因此在《诗经》时代大放异彩。但是,随着双音节音步的胜出,五言、六言、七言等各种形式的诗句在战国时代纷纷涌现,各领风骚。《楚辞》中五言、六言、七言的各种节奏的诗句格式,有些被后代辞赋骈文所继承,只有2-3格式的五言句,因为其韵律模式适合诗歌的内在规律,得以在后代发展为绵延两千年的五言诗体。2-2-2格式的六言句,也曾经在诗歌园地获得一度的发展。先秦七言句,跟后代的七言诗体基本上没有关系。至于为什么适合汉语双音节音步的四言体汉代以后不能战胜五言体,这是一个引人入胜的问题,但不是本文的任务,这里就不讨论了。

参 考 文 献

段玉裁. 六书音均表//说文解字注. 上海：上海古籍出版社. 1981.

冯胜利. 汉语韵律诗体学论稿. 北京：商务印书馆，2015.

江永. 古韵标准. 北京：中华书局，1982.

施向东. 关于上古汉语阴声音节的韵尾、韵素和声调问题的探索//冯胜利主编. 汉语韵律语法新探. 上海：中西书局，2015：342-364.

王力. 诗经韵读. 上海：上海古籍出版社，1980.

萧艾. 六言诗三百首. 郑州：中州古籍出版社，1987.

朱熹. 楚辞集注. 上海：上海古籍出版社. 1979.

《国语》上海：上海古籍出版社，1982.

《诗经》《十三经注疏》本，北京：中华书局，1980.

《周易》《十三经注疏》本，北京：中华书局，1980.

《左传》《十三经注疏》本，北京：中华书局，1980.

Кочергина, В. А. 1955. *Начальный Курс Санскрита*. Ленинград: Издательство Академии Наук.

附录1　《诗经》诗句字数统计表

类	国/什	2言	3言	4言	5言	6言	7言	8言
国风	周南		12	143	2	2		
	召南		18	143	16	0		
	邶风	4	9	328	14	4		
	鄘风		3	153	17	0	3	
	卫风		3	188	12	0		
	王风		12	138	7	5		
	郑风		17	221	29	9	5	
	齐风		3	110	12	12	6	
	魏风		11	94	13	7	3	3
	唐风	6	20	167	11	2		
	秦风		14	161	4	2		
	陈风		2	110	2	0		
	桧风		0	33	10	2		
	曹风		0	68	0	0		
	豳风	1	0	176	15	10	2	

续表

类	国/什	2言	3言	4言	5言	6言	7言	8言
国风合计 2609		11 0.4%	124 4.8%	2233 85.6%	164 6.3%	55 2.1%	19 0.7%	3 0.1%
小雅	鹿鸣	3	3	302	5	1	1	
	南有嘉鱼			268		4		
	鸿雁	3	4	213	13			
	节南山			522	22	6	1	1
	谷风			339	15	2		
	甫田		3	278	12	3		
	鱼藻		2	295	5			
小雅合计 2326		6 0.3%	12 0.5%	2217 95.3%	72 3.1%	16 0.7%	2 <0.1%	1
大雅	文王			387	27			
	生民		6	390	30	7		
	荡		2	718	40	8	1	
大雅合计 1616			8 0.5%	1495 92.5%	97 6%	15 0.9%	1 <0.1%	
大小雅合计 3942		6 0.15%	20 0.5%	3712 94.2%	169 4.3%	31 0.8%	3 <0.1%	1 0.03%
颂	清庙	2	4	71	15	3	1	
	臣工			104		2		
	闵予小子		4	118	10	2	1	
	周颂合计	2	8	293	25	7	2	
	鲁颂		14	216	13			
	商颂			130	22	2		
颂合计 734		2 0.3%	22 3%	639 87%	60 8.2%	9 1.2%	2 0.3%	
《诗经》总计 7285 百分比		19 0.3%	166 2.3%	6584 90.4%	393 5.4%	95 1.3%	24 0.3%	4 0.05%

附录2　《易经》韵语字数统计表

周易	卦	2言	3言	4言	5言	6言	7言
	1. 乾	2		5			
	2. 坤	2	1	2	1		
	3. 屯	2		5	1		
	4. 蒙		2	1			
	5. 需		2	0			
	6. 讼			0			
	7. 师			2			

续表

周易	卦	2言	3言	4言	5言	6言	7言
	8. 比			0			
	9. 小畜	3	3	1			
	10. 履		3	0			
	11. 泰	3	2	0	3		
	12. 否	1		3			
	13. 同人		4	3			
	14. 大有			1		1	
	15. 谦			0			
	16. 豫			0			
	17. 随		1	1			
	18. 蛊			0			
	19. 临			0			
	20. 观			1	1		
	21. 噬嗑	1	3	0			
	22. 贲	2	1	5			
	23. 剥			3			
	24. 复			0			
	25. 无妄		2	4			
	26. 大畜		2	4			
	27. 颐			2			
	28. 大过			2		2	
	29. 坎	4	5	7			
	30. 离	3		5	3		
	31. 咸			2			
	32. 恒			0			
	33. 遁			0			
	34. 大壮		2	3			
	35. 晋	1	1	2			
	36. 明夷		1	6	1		
	37. 家人		2	0			
	38. 睽	5	2	6			
	39. 蹇	6	0	2			
	40. 解			0			
	41. 损			0			

续表

周易	卦	2言	3言	4言	5言	6言	7言
	42. 益		2	0			
	43. 夬		1	1			
	44. 姤		3	2			
	45. 萃	3	0	1			
	46. 升			0			
	47. 困		3	10	1		
	48. 井	2	3	7	1		
	49. 革			0			
	50. 鼎		8	3	1		
	51. 震		4	3	1		
	52. 艮		4	2			
	53. 渐	1	1	11	1	1	
	54. 归妹	2	5	6			1
	55. 丰		6	6			
	56. 旅		4	3			
	57. 巽			3	1		
	58. 兑			0			
	59. 涣		1	1			
	60. 节			0			
	61. 中孚	1	2	5	1		
	62. 小过			4			
	63. 既济			0			
	64. 未济		2	2	1		
周易合计303		44	88	148	18	4	1
百分比		14.5%	29.0%	48.8%	5.9%	1.3%	0.3%

附录3 《左传》《国语》引《诗》字数统计表

出处	来由	内容	三言	四言	五言	六言	七言
隐元	郑庄公/姜氏	公入而赋："大隧之中，其乐也融融！"姜出而赋："大隧之外，其乐也泄泄！"		2	2		
左隐1	君子曰	《诗》曰："孝子不匮，永锡尔类。"		2			
隐3	君子曰	《商颂》曰："殷受命咸宜，百禄是荷。"		1	1		
桓6	大子忽曰	《诗》云："自求多福。"		1			
桓12	君子曰	《诗》云："君子屡盟，乱是用长。"		2			
庄6	君子曰	《诗》云："本枝百世。"		1			

续表

出处	来由	内容	三言	四言	五言	六言	七言
庄22	敬仲辞卿	《诗》云："翘翘车乘，招我以弓，岂不欲往，畏我友朋。"（逸诗也）		4			
闵1	管敬仲言	《诗》云："岂不怀归，畏此简书。"		2			
僖5	士蒍曰	《诗》云："怀德惟宁，宗子惟城。"（大雅）……退而赋曰："狐裘尨茸，一国三公，吾谁适从？"（逸诗也）			5		
僖9	公孙枝对晋惠公	《诗》曰："不识不知，顺帝之则。"……又曰："不僭不贼，鲜不为则。"		4			
僖12	君子曰	《诗》曰："恺悌君子，神所劳矣。"		2			
僖15	韩简引诗	《诗》曰："下民之孽，匪降自天，僔沓背憎，职竞由人。"		4			
僖19	子鱼言于宋公	《诗》曰："刑于寡妻，至于兄弟，以御于家邦。"		2	1		
僖20	君子曰	《诗》曰："岂不夙夜，谓行多露。"		2			
僖22	富辰言于王	《诗》曰："协比其邻，昏姻孔云。"		2			
僖22	臧文仲曰	《诗》曰："战战兢兢，如临深渊，如履薄冰。"又曰："敬之敬之，天惟显思，命不易哉！"				6	
僖24	君子曰	《诗》曰："彼己之子，不称其服。"		2			
僖28	君子谓	《诗》云："惠此中国，以绥四方。"		2			
僖33	臼季对公	《诗》曰："采葑采菲，无以下体。"		2			
文2	且明曰	《鲁颂》："春秋匪解，享祀不忒，皇皇后帝，皇祖后稷。"……《诗》曰："问我诸姑，遂及伯姊。"				6	
文3	君子曰	《诗》曰："于以采蘩，于沼于沚"……夙夜匪解，以事一人……诒厥孙谋，以燕翼子。"				6	
文4	君子曰	《诗》曰："畏天之威，于时保之。"		2			
文4	君子曰	《诗》云："惟彼二国，其政不获，惟此四国，爰究爰度。"		4			
文6	君子曰	《诗》曰："人之云亡，邦国殄瘁。"		2			
文10	子舟曰	《诗》曰："刚亦不吐，柔亦不茹。"		2			
宣2	士季对曰	《诗》曰："靡不有初，鲜克有终。"又曰："衮职有阙，惟仲山甫补之。"	3			1	
宣2	赵盾曰	我之怀矣，自诒伊戚。（逸诗也）		2			
宣9	孔子曰	《诗》云："民之多辟，无自立辟。"		2			
宣11	郄成子曰	《诗》曰："文王既勤止。"	1				
宣12	随武子曰	《汋》曰："於铄王师，遵养时晦。"……《武》曰："无竞惟烈。"	3				

续表

出处	来由	内容	三言	四言	五言	六言	七言
宣12	楚子曰	武王克商。作《颂》:"载戢干戈,载櫜弓矢。我求懿德,肆于时夏,允王保之。"又作《武》,其卒章曰"耆定尔功。"其三曰:"铺时绎思,我徂求定。"其六曰:"绥万邦,屡丰年。"	2	8			
宣12	君子曰	《诗》曰:"乱离瘼矣,爰其适归?"		2			
宣12	孙叔曰	《诗》云:"元戎十乘,以先启行。"		2			
宣15	羊舌职曰	《诗》曰:"陈锡哉周。"		1			
宣16	羊舌职曰	《诗》曰:"战战兢兢,如临深渊,如履薄冰。"		3			
宣17	召文子曰	《诗》曰:"君子如怒,乱庶遄沮;君子如祉,乱庶遄已。"		4			
成2	宾媚人对晋人	《诗》曰:"孝子不匮,永锡尔类。"……故《诗》曰:"我疆我理,南东其亩。"……《诗》曰"布政优优,百禄是遒。"		6			
成2	子重曰	《诗》曰:"济济多士,文王以宁。"		2			
成2	君子曰	《诗》曰:"不解于位,民之攸塈。"		2			
成4	季文子曰	《诗》曰:"敬之敬之!天惟显思,命不易哉!"		3			
成7	季文子	《诗》曰:"不吊昊天,乱靡有定。"		2			
成8	季文子曰	《诗》曰:"女也不爽,士贰其行。士也罔极,二三其德。"……《诗》曰:"犹之未远,是用大简。"		6			
成8	君子曰	《诗》曰:"恺悌君子,遐不作人。"		2			
成9	君子曰	《诗》曰:"虽有丝、麻,无弃菅、蒯;虽有姬、姜,无弃蕉萃。凡百君子,莫不代匮。"(逸诗也)		6			
成12	郤至曰	故《诗》曰:"赳赳武夫,公侯干城。"……故《诗》曰:"赳赳武夫,公侯腹心。"		4			
成14	宁惠子曰	《诗》曰:"兕觥其觩,旨酒思柔,彼交匪傲,万福来求。"		4			
成16	申叔时对子反	《诗》曰:"立我烝民,莫匪尔极。"		2			
襄2	君子曰	《诗》曰:"其惟哲人,告之话言,顺德之行。"……《诗》曰:"为酒为醴,烝畀祖妣,以洽百礼,降福孔偕。"		7			
襄3	君子谓	《诗》云:"惟其有之,是以似之。"		2			
襄5	君子谓	《诗》曰:"周道挺挺,我心扃扃,讲事不令,集人来定。"(逸诗也)		4			
襄7	韩献子告老	《诗》曰:"岂不夙夜,谓行多露。"又曰:"弗躬弗亲,庶民弗信。"……《诗》曰:"靖共尔位,好是正直。神之听之,介尔景福。"		8			

出处	来由	内容	三言	四言	五言	六言	七言
襄7	穆叔曰	《诗》曰："退食自公，委蛇委蛇。"		2			
襄8	子驷曰	《诗》云："谋夫孔多，是用不集。发言盈庭，谁敢执其咎？如匪行迈谋，是用不得于道。"	3	2	1		
襄8	子驷曰	周诗有之曰："俟河之清，人寿几何。"（逸诗也）		2			
襄11	魏绛辞乐	《诗》曰："乐只君子，殿天子之邦。乐只君子，福禄攸同。便蕃左右，亦是帅从。"		5	1		
襄13	君子曰	《诗》曰："仪刑文王，万邦作孚。"……《诗》曰："大夫不均，我从事独贤。"		3	1		
襄13	君子曰	《诗》曰："不吊昊天，乱靡有定。"		2			
襄14	君子谓	《诗》曰："行归于周，万民所望。"		2			
襄15	君子谓	《诗》云："嗟我怀人，置彼周行。"		2			
襄21	叔向曰	《诗》曰："优哉游哉，聊以卒岁。"知也。……《诗》曰："有觉德行，四国顺之。"		4			
襄21	祁奚见宣子曰	《诗》曰："惠我无疆，子孙保之。"		2			
襄22	君子曰	《诗》曰："慎尔侯度，用戒不虞。"		2			
襄24	子产告宣子	《诗》云："乐只君子，邦家之基。"		2			
襄25	大叔文子曰	《诗》所谓"我躬不说，皇恤我后"……《诗》曰："夙夜匪解，以事一人。"		4			
襄26	声子对令尹子木	《诗》曰："人之云亡，邦国殄瘁。"……《商颂》有之："不僭不滥，不敢怠皇，命于下国，封建厥福。"		6			
襄26	国子赋	辔之柔矣（逸诗也）		1			
襄26	子展赋	将仲子兮		1			
襄27	君子曰	彼己之子，邦之司直。（郑风）何以恤我，我其收之。（逸诗）		4			
襄29	子大叔曰	《诗》曰："协比其邻，昏姻孔云。"		2			
襄29	裨谌曰	《诗》曰："君子屡盟，乱是用长。"		2			
襄29	子展曰	《诗》云："王事靡盬，不遑启处。"		2			
襄30	君子曰	《诗》曰："文王陟降，在帝左右。"（大雅）……又曰："淑慎尔止，无载尔伪。"（逸诗也）		4			
襄31	叔向曰	《诗》曰："辞之辑矣，民之协矣。辞之绎矣，民之莫矣。"		4			
襄31	冯简子	《诗》曰："谁能执热，逝不以濯。"		2			

续表

出处	来由	内容	三言	四言	五言	六言	七言
襄31	北宫文子言于卫侯	《诗》云:"靡不有初,鲜克有终。"…… 《诗》云:"敬慎威仪,惟民之则。"…… 《卫诗》曰:"威仪棣棣,不可选也。"…… 《周诗》曰:"朋友攸摄,摄以威仪。"…… 《诗》云:"不识不知,顺帝之则。"		10			
昭元	文子曰	《诗》曰:"不僭不贼,鲜不为则。"		2			
昭元	叔向对赵孟	《诗》曰:"赫赫宗周,褒姒灭之。"		2			
昭元	君子曰	"无竞维人"。		1			
昭元	叔向曰	《诗》曰:"不侮鳏寡,不畏强御。"		2			
昭2	叔向曰	《诗》曰:"敬慎威仪,以近有德。"		2			
昭3	君子曰	《诗》曰:"君子如祉,乱庶遄已。"		2			
昭3	君子曰	《诗》曰:"人而无礼,胡不遄死?"		2			
昭4	子产曰	《诗》曰:"礼义不愆,何恤于人言。"(逸诗也)		1	1		
昭5	仲尼曰	《诗》云:"有觉德行,四国顺之。"		2			
昭6	叔向诒子产书	《诗》曰:"仪式刑文王之德,日靖四方。"又曰:"仪刑文王,万邦作孚。"		3			1
昭6	左师曰	《诗》曰:"宗子维城,毋俾城坏,毋独斯畏。"		3			
昭6	叔向曰	《诗》曰:"尔之教矣,民胥效矣。"		2			
昭7	无宇曰	《诗》曰:"普天之下,莫非王土。率土之滨,莫非王臣。"		4			
昭7	晋大夫言于范献子	《诗》曰:"即鸰在原,兄弟急难。"又曰:"死丧之威,兄弟孔怀。"		4			
昭7	仲尼曰	《诗》曰:"君子是则是效。"		0		1	
昭7	伯瑕曰	《诗》曰:"或燕燕居息,或憔悴事国。"		0	2		
昭8	叔向曰	《诗》曰:"哀哉不能言,匪舌是出,唯躬是瘁。哿矣能言,巧言如流,俾躬处休。"		5	1		
昭9	叔孙昭子曰	《诗》曰:"经始勿亟,庶民子来。"		2			
昭10	桓子曰	《诗》云:"陈锡载周。"		1			
昭10	臧武仲曰	《诗》曰:"德音孔昭,视民不佻。"		2			
昭10	昭子曰	《诗》曰:"不自我先,不自我后。"		2			
昭13	仲尼谓	《诗》曰:"乐只君子,邦家之基。"		2			
昭13	刘献公曰	"元戎十乘,以先启行。"		2			
昭16	叔孙昭子曰	《诗》曰:"宗周既灭,靡所止戾。正大夫离居,莫知我肄。"		3	1		

续表

出处	来由	内容	三言	四言	五言	六言	七言
昭20	晏子曰	《诗》曰:"亦有和羹,既戒既平。鬷嘏无言,时靡有争。"……《诗》曰:"德音不瑕。"		5			
昭20	仲尼曰	《诗》曰:"民亦劳止,汔可小康。惠此中国,以绥四方。"……"毋从诡随,以谨无良。式遏寇虐,惨不畏明。"……"柔远能迩,以定我王。"……"不竞不絿,不刚不柔。布政优优,百禄是遒。"和之至也。		15			
昭21	昭子曰	《诗》曰:"不解于位,民之攸墍。"		2			
昭23	沈尹戌曰	《诗》曰:"无念尔祖,聿修厥德。"		2			
昭24	子大叔对范献子	《诗》曰:"瓶之罄矣,惟罍之耻。"		2			
昭24	沈尹戌曰	《诗》曰:"谁生厉阶,至今为梗?"		2			
昭25	乐祁曰	《诗》曰:"人之云亡,心之忧矣。"		2			
昭26	晏子曰	《诗》曰:"惟此文王,小心翼翼,昭事上帝,聿怀多福。厥德不回,以受方国。"(大雅)……《诗》曰:"我无所监,夏后及商。用乱之故,民卒流亡。"(逸诗也)		10			
昭26	晏子曰	《诗》曰:"虽无德与女,式歌且舞。"		2			
昭28	叔游曰	《诗》曰:"民之多辟,无自立辟。"		2			
昭28	成鱄对魏子	《诗》曰:"唯此文王,帝度其心。莫其德音,其德克明。克明克类,克长克君。王此大国,克顺克比。比于文王,其德靡悔。既受帝祉,施于孙子。"		12			
昭28	仲尼曰	《诗》曰:"永言配命,自求多福。"		2			
昭32	卫彪傒曰	《诗》曰:"敬天之怒,不敢戏豫。敬天之渝,不敢驰驱。"		4			
昭32	史墨曰	《诗》曰:"高岸为谷,深谷为陵。"		2			
定4	郧公辛曰	《诗》曰:"柔亦不茹,刚亦不吐,不侮矜寡,不畏强御。"		4			
定9	君子谓子然	《竿旄》"何以告之"……《诗》云:"蔽芾甘棠,勿翦勿伐,召伯所茇。"		4			
定10	君子曰	《诗》曰:"人而无礼,胡不遄死。"		2			
哀2	乐丁曰	《诗》曰:"爰始爰谋,爰契我龟。"		2			
哀5	子思曰	《诗》曰:"不解于位,民之攸墍。"……《商颂》曰:"不僭不滥,不敢怠皇,命以多福。"		5			
哀26	子赣曰	《诗》曰:"无竞惟人,四方其顺之。"		2			

出处	来由	内容	三言	四言	五言	六言	七言
国语	周语中 1	周文公之诗曰:"兄弟阋于墙,外御其侮。"		1	1		
	周语中 10	《诗》曰:"恺悌君子,求福不回。"		2			
	周语下 3	《诗》曰:"四牡骙骙,旟旐有翩,乱生不夷,靡国不泯。"又曰:"民之贪乱,宁为荼毒。"……《诗》云:"殷鉴不远,在夏后之世。"		7	1		
	周语下 4	其诗曰:"昊天有成命,二后受之,成王不敢康。夙夜基命宥密,於缉熙!亶厥心,肆其靖之。"……《诗》曰:"其类维何?室家之壶。君子万年,永锡祚胤。"	2	6	2	1	
	周语下 5	《诗》亦有之曰:"瞻彼旱麓,榛楛济济。恺悌君子,干禄恺悌。"		4			
	周语下 9	《周诗》有之曰:"天之所支,不可坏也。其所坏,亦不可支也。"(逸诗也)	1	2	1		
	晋语四 2	《诗》云:"上帝临女,无贰尔心。"……《周诗》曰:"莘莘征夫,每怀靡及。"……《郑诗》云:"仲可怀也,人之多言。亦可畏也。"		7			
	晋语四 8	曹诗曰:"彼己之子,不遂其媾。"		2			
	晋语四 24	《诗》云:"刑于寡妻,至于兄弟,以御于家邦。"……《诗》云:"惠于宗公,神罔时恫。"		4	1		
	楚语上 5	故《周诗》曰:"经始灵台,经之营之。庶民攻之,不日成之。经始勿亟,庶民子来。王在灵囿,麀鹿攸伏。"		8			
	楚语上 8	《周诗》有之曰:"弗躬弗亲,庶民弗信。"		2			
总计	442 句		5	413	19	4	1
			1.1%	93.4%	4.3%	0.9%	0.2%

附录 4　《左传》《国语》引谣谚筮辞等的字数统计表

出处	来由	内容	三言	四言	五言	六言	七言
隐 11	羽父请于薛侯	周谚有之曰:"山有木,工则度之;宾有礼,主则择之。"	2	2			
桓 10	虞叔曰	周谚有之:"匹夫无罪,怀璧其罪。"		2			
庄 22	懿氏卜妻敬仲	"凤皇于飞,和鸣锵锵,有妫之后,将育于姜。五世其昌,并于正卿。八世之后,莫之与京。"……"观国之光,利用宾于王。"		9	1		
闵元	士蔿曰	谚曰:"心苟无瑕,何恤乎无家。"		1	1		
闵 2	成季将生之卜	其名曰友,在公之右。间于两社,为公室辅。季氏亡,则鲁不昌。……同复于父,敬如君所。	1	7			
僖 4	晋献公卜骊姬为夫人	专之渝,攘公之瑜。一熏一莸,十年尚犹有臭。	1	2		1	

续表

出处	来由	内容	三言	四言	五言	六言	七言
僖5	宫之奇谏曰	谚所谓"辅车相依,唇亡齿寒。"		2			
僖5	卜偃曰	童谣云:"丙之晨,龙尾伏辰,均服振振,取虢之旗。鹑之贲贲,天策焞焞,火中成军,虢公其奔。"	1	7			
僖7	孔叔言	谚有之曰:"心则不竞,何惮于病。"		2			
僖15	秦伯伐晋筮	千乘三去,三去之余,获其雄狐		3			
僖15	晋献公筮嫁伯姬于秦	士刲羊,亦无衁也。女承筐,亦无贶也。西邻责言,不可偿也。	2	4			
僖27	赵衰曰:	《夏书》曰:"赋纳以言,明试以功,车服以庸。"		3			
文7	乐豫曰	此谚所谓"庇焉而纵寻斧焉"者也。		0			1
文17	子家告赵宣子	古人有言曰:"畏首畏尾,身其余几。"		2			
宣2	宋城,华元为植巡功	城者讴曰:"睅其目,皤其腹,弃甲而复。于思于思,弃甲复来"使其骖乘谓之曰:"牛则有皮,犀兕尚多,弃甲则那。"役人曰:"从其有皮,丹漆若何。"	2	8			
宣4	子文曰	谚曰:"狼子野心。"		1			
宣15	伯宗曰	谚曰:"高下在心。"		1			
宣15	伯宗曰	古人有言曰:"虽鞭之长,不及马腹。"		2			
宣16	羊舌职曰	谚曰:"民之多幸,国之不幸也。"		1	1		
成16	晋侯筮晋楚之战	南国蹙,射其元王中厥目。	1	0			1
成17	声伯梦食琼瑰而歌	"济洹之水,赠我以琼瑰。归乎!归乎!琼瑰盈吾怀乎!"		2	1	1	
襄3	君子谓	《商书》曰:"无偏无党,王道荡荡。"		2			
襄4	魏绛对晋侯	《虞人之箴》曰:"芒芒禹迹,尽为九州岛岛,经启九道。民有寝庙,兽有茂草,各有攸处,德用不扰。在帝夷羿,冒于原兽,忘其国恤,而思其麀牡。武不可重,用不恢于夏家。兽臣司原,敢告仆夫。"		13	1	1	
襄10	孙文子卜追之	兆如山陵,有夫出征,而丧其雄		3			
襄17	宋皇国父为平公筑台	筑者讴曰:"泽门之皙,实兴我役。邑中之黔,实慰我心。"		4			
襄25	武子筮娶妻	困于石,据于蒺藜,入于其宫,不见其妻,凶。	1	3			
昭元	刘子归以语王	谚所为"老将知而耄及之"者。		0			1
昭3	叔向曰	《谗鼎之铭》曰:"昧旦丕显,后世犹怠。"		2			
昭3	晏子曰	谚曰:"非宅是卜,唯邻是卜。"		2			
昭7	孟僖子曰	(正考父)鼎铭云:"一命而偻,再命而伛,三命而俯。循墙而走,亦莫余敢侮。饘于是,鬻于是,以糊余口。"	2	5	1		

先秦诗律探索   155

续表

出处	来由	内容	三言	四言	五言	六言	七言
昭 7	子产曰	抑谚曰"蕞尔国"。	1	0			
昭 13	子服惠伯曰	谚曰:"臣一主二。"		1			
昭 19	子产曰	谚曰:"无过乱门。"		1			
昭 19	令尹子瑕言	谚所谓"室于怒,市于色。"	2	0			
昭 25	师己曰	童谣有之,曰:"鸲之鹆之,公出辱之。鸲鹆之羽,公在外野,往馈之马。鸲鹆跦跦,公在干侯,征褰与襦。鸲鹆之巢,远哉遥遥。稠父丧劳,宋父以骄。鸲鹆鸲鹆,往歌来哭。"		14			
昭 28	魏子曰	谚曰:"唯食忘忧。"		1			
定 14	戏阳速曰	谚曰:"民保于信。"		1			
哀 6	孔子赞楚昭王	《夏书》曰:"惟彼陶唐,帅彼天常,有此冀方。今失其行,乱其纪纲,乃灭而亡。"		6			
哀 9	晋赵鞅卜救郑	是谓沈阳,可以兴兵。利以伐姜,不利子商。伐齐则可,敌宋不吉……是谓如川之满,不可游也。郑方有罪,不可救也。		9		1	
哀 17	卫侯贞卜	如鱼赪尾,衡流而方羊。裔焉大国,灭之将亡。阖门塞窦,乃自后逾。		5	1		
国语	周语中 1	古人有言曰:"兄弟谗阋,侮人百里。"		2			
	周语中 10	谚曰:"兽恶其网,民恶其上。"		2			
	周语下 3	人有言曰……"佐饔者尝焉,佐斗者伤焉。"		0	2		
	周语下 6	故谚曰:"众心成城,众口铄金。"		2			
	周语下 9	谚曰:"从善如登,从恶如崩。"		2			
	晋语二 5	童谣有之曰:"丙之晨,龙尾伏辰,均服振振,取虢之旗。鹑之贲贲,天策焞焞,火中成军,虢公其奔!"	1	7			
	晋语四 7	谚曰:"黍稷无成,不能为荣。黍不为黍,不能蕃庑。稷不为稷,不能蕃殖。所生不疑,唯德之基。"		8			
	郑语一 1	宣王之时有童谣曰:"檿弧箕服,实亡周国。"		2			
	吴语 1	夫谚曰:"狐埋之而狐搰之。"是以无成功。		0			1
	越语下 6	谚有之曰:"觥饭不及壶飧。"		0		1	
总计	193		17 8.8%	158 81.9%	9 4.7%	5 2.6%	4 2.1%

附录 5 《楚辞》句子的字数统计表

类	题	三言	四言	五言	六言	七言	八言	九言	十言
离骚	合计 375	1	0	7	160	176	25	5	1
	百分比	0.3%	0%	1.9%	43.2%	46.4%	6.7%	1.3%	0.3%
九歌	东皇太一			3	12				
	云中君			1	13				
	湘君			8	28		1	1	
	湘夫人			11	25	4			
	大司命			8	18	2			
	少司命			9	6	13			
	东君			6	12	6			
	河伯			0	14	4			
	山鬼			0	0	32		1	
	国殇			0	0	18			
	礼魂			3	2				
《九歌》合计 261				49	130	79	1	2	
	百分比			19%	50%	30%		<1%	
天问	合计 373	19	286	50	14	3	1		
	百分比	5%	77%	13%	4%	<1%			
九章	惜诵		0	5	32	44	7		
	涉江		14	5	17	18	4	2	
	哀郢		0	1	30	33	2		
	抽思		17	6	30	29	4		
	怀沙		25	40	12	3	0		
	思美人		2	9	27	24	4		
	惜往日		0	0	37	35	4		
	橘颂		28	8	0	0	0		
	悲回风				46	59	5		
《九章》合计 668			86	74	231	245	30	2	
	百分比		13%	11%	35%	37%	4%	0.3%	
远游	178	1	8	10	72	78	9		
	百分比	<1%	4%	6%	40%	44%	5%		
《楚辞》合计 1855		21	380	190	609	579	66	9	1
	百分比	1.1%	20.5%	10.2%	32.8%	31.2%	3.6%	0.5%	0.05%

A Research on the Versification in Pre Qin

Xiangdong Shi

Abstract This paper observes and analyzes the actual condition of character numbers of poetic lines in the Pre-Qin period, with statistics on "four- character lines" in Pre-Qin verse proportion. It also observes the possibility of historical evolution process as well. Secondly, this paper offers an analysis of the rhythmic structure, the lines of different number of characters in terms of relationships between mora and foot, as well as foot and rhyme, under which the changing of foot formation and versification in Pre-Qin will be explored in depth.

Keywords Versification in The pre Qin, mora, foot, rhyme, clue of the development

施向东
天津大学语言科学研究中心、南开大学汉语言文化学院，教授
E-mail：hyshixd@nankai.edu.cn

Under the Microscope of Prosody: The Serendipitous Revelation of the Poetic Power and Beauty of "Function Words"

Shudong Chen

Abstract The paper argues how contemporary theory of prosody helps significantly in revealing the otherwise eclipsed poetic beauty and meaning. It is particularly so in redefining *live* the concept of "function word," which usually indicates a limited number of conjunction, preposition, article, some adverbs, or typically any word with virtually little lexical meaning but mere syntactic function. The paper discusses how "function words" could also paralyze while enriching the context due to its syntactic-prosodic role, which is enlivened by the very syntactic-prosodic context that it enlivens at the same time, and function words, as a result, often tend to suggest a certain irreconcilable possibilities of reading. What does the word "still" often mean, as one of her favorite words, in the same poem by Emily Dickinson, for instance? Does it mean "motionless" as adjective or "in spite of that," "nonetheless," or "up to and during this time" as adverb? The paper demonstrates how function words in Chinese as in English, could likewise not only disrupt *a posteriori* the usual categorization or distinction of "function word" and "content word" *a priori* but also create thought-provoking ambiguity and pause, which cannot be merely interpreted in line with something of an authorial intention. Under the microscope of prosody, function words therefore reveal their otherwise often overlooked important meaning-making prosodic function. As crucial examples, the paper refers to the cases of *hai* 还 of Jia Dao's (贾岛) "On Visiting Li Ning at Midnight"〈题李凝幽居〉, zai 在 used in both Ma Zhiyuan's (马致远) "Tian Jing Sha"〈天

净沙-秋思〉and Jiang Kui's (姜夔) "Yang Zhou Man"〈扬州慢〉particularly in line with this most famous line of the poem "二十四桥仍在，波心荡，冷月无声," and the comparative reading of Liang Zongdai's and Fei Bai's translation of Paul Verlaine's "Il pleure dans mon cœur."①

The paper particularly refers to the indispensable role of *hai* in Jia's poem as the truly real but least noticeable "le mot juste." Whether with *tui* 推 (to push) or *qiao* 敲 (to knock), the poem could still be a poem, but without *hai* the poem cannot even *be* a poem in the first place, let alone to be in ways as it has been appreciated ever since. With prosody, it should make more sense now why "to understand a sentence," as Wittgenstein so emphasizes in *Philosophical Investigation*, "means to understand a language" but "to understand a language means to be master of a technique," which exactly means a vital technique to understand the "trivial" but crucial, often ambiguously hinge-like, "function words"; a function word in the text is thus often like a little unnoticeable common or "meanest flower" that for Wordsworth could evoke "Thoughts that do often lie too deep for tears." It is indeed such a vital technique for us to detect in the function words through prosody the same irreplaceable "lever long enough" and "fulcrum" as that Archimedes of Syracuse needs when he declares "Give me a lever long enough and a fulcrum on which to place it, and I shall move the world."

Key words   Prosody, Function words, Wittgenstein, Comparative literature

1　Introduction: The Power of the Trivial in Function Words with the Cases of "*Zai*"

"To understand a sentence," as Wittgenstein emphasizes, "means to understand a language" but "to understand a language means to be master of a technique" (1968, 199, 81e). The "technique" could often be exactly a one as vital

---

① All translations used in the paper thereafter are mine unless otherwise stated; all original classic texts employed in the paper, unless otherwise stated, are obtained online from sources of "public domain."

as prosody so indispensable for us to understand the trivial but crucial, often ambiguously hinge-like, meaning-making and life-making "function words." Whether reading in Chinese or other major modern languages, such as English, it thus often means an inevitable process of redefining *live* the concept of "function word," which usually indicates a limited number of conjunction, preposition, article, some adverbs, or typically any word with virtually little lexical meaning but mere syntactic function. There are indeed far too many possibilities of reading the same poem whether in Chinese or in English, especially in terms of the peculiar syntactic-prosodic pattern, which often simultaneously enlivens and is enlivened by function words; it is in this verbal environment where the meaning function words could become so versatile and chameleon-like as to appear utterly ungraspable but as much fully situated in the context whether right on the spot or behind the scene to suggest the power and beauty of the ever-present and irreducible human agency however elusive or illusive as it may often strike. The function word-facilitated or constructed metric pattern of the text could even occur in a critical moment to have an utterly unexpected dramatic or climatic effect by disrupting an otherwise quite predicable normal flow of the narrative mood. The function word's unique capability in the making function words of such a vital life-giving syntactic-prosodic verbal environment is ultimately often a simple matter that concerns not how much but how little the function word is actually used for a pure aesthetic of "less is more" as the case with "Tian Jing Sha"《天净沙·秋思》by Ma Zhiyuan (马致远 ca. 1260-1325).

枯藤-老树-昏鸦， A few withered vines, an old tree, a crow at dusk,
小桥-流水-人家， A small bridge, a flowing river, plus a cottage,
古道-西风-瘦马， An ancient road, the west wind, and a gaunt horse,
夕阳-西下， Down on the horizon is the evening sun, and,
断肠-人在-天涯. Alone, in the wild open field, stands a heart-broken man.

Of various other possibilities, one appropriate way of further appreciating this poem prosodically requires or depends on how and where we pause and stress, particularly with the last sentence, in ways permissible regarding the syntactic-prosodic verbal environment. This is the "environment" enlivened by the poem that it enlivens at the same time especially through the crucial variable ways of pausing mediated by the indispensable chameleon-like *zai* 在 with its multifunctional roles also at once activating and is being activated by the syntactic-prosodic verbal environment. Thus, varying with the key word *zai* 在 regarding whether it can be identified as a function word, i.e., a preposition (at, in, on, or by, etc.), or a verb within the given syntactic-prosodic verbal context, the poem's last line, which is undoubtedly the climax of the whole poem, suggests at least two possible ways of pausing and stressing with consequently different variations of meanings.

断肠人-在天涯
断肠-人在-天涯

With the first possibility, the pause is emphatically between the first and the second phrase, and the sentence thus becomes a judgment sentence 判断句. A pause indicates the absence of the auxiliary verb *shi* 是, and *zai* becomes in this regard a special verb that forms "noun of place" (处所名词) as a "prepositional phrase" and the "object" of the absent auxiliary verb. A pause therefore is not only grammatically necessary but also prosodically indispensable to activate empathically a particular metrical pattern and sentiments of the last line as well as the entire poem. The empty-verb structure thus grants an additional flexibility in Chinese in making parallelism for desirable metric/prosodic effect; it allows extra leeway for preposition to function in ways otherwise impossible. In contrast, with a slight pause between 断肠, 人在, and 天涯, the last line, however, could instantly become a narrative sentence 叙述句. The phrase "heart-broken" 断肠 also turns from an adjective for "*ren*" 人 into an adverbial phrase that describes the ways of the person "in the wild open field" and explains why or how the action or mood of "heart-broken" occurs. 在 in this regard should be a verb. Read this way, not only does the pause fall perfectly in line with the traditional "iambic" or *yi yang* 抑扬 pattern but the whole poem may also sound very "existentialistic" in flavor and processural in the sense that heart-broken is the result of the very situation of 在天涯 *a posteriori* rather than a case *a priori*. The mood of "heart-broken" is thus very much like the genuine flavor of a delicious home-cooked dish not prepared with any sauce ready-made and added on afterwards but truly "fixed" with ones that come naturally out of the actual process of cooking. Similarly, the very "essence" of *ren* is very much situational as revealed through the action or experience of being/becoming heart-broken that occurs upon the very situation. The heart-broken person is therefore not necessarily associated with any predetermined causes but with the peculiar mood that strikes him on the spot, and he, as a result, is no longer so centralized as the center of action that causes the situation but only a part of event who personifies the contextualized outcome. The person, in other words, may not necessarily sad or so sad, *a priori*, but the moment when he happens to be situated in the wild open field, he instantly or gradually becomes sad or heart-broken; he becomes so submerged in everything that touches his heart *a posteriori*; he becomes philosophically melancholic for no particular reasons. He is not sad for any trivial, immediate, and personal everyday life situation.

With the syntax so free or absent not only of verb but also of function words in defining specific relationship, either way of reading Ma's piece, there often appears a certain "museum effect," which suggests lyrically a sense of contemporaneity, so "spatiotemporal free" with a potentially infinite arrays of variation for imagination, as if everything in the world often remains in the mode of timely timelessness and motionless motion with all the elements in the poem or artwork *live* in a pure relationship of interdependent independence. By "museum effect," it means that artworks otherwise utterly unrelated to one anther are put together in a group for special exhibition in the museum; they are juxtaposed in such a way as if each were born exactly for the other within this particular group, whereas, at the same time, any one of them can also be so easily dissembled either for individual exhibition the way each deserves or for another grouping under a different exhibition theme. The same is certainly also true with Jiang Kui's "Yang Zhou Man" 〈扬州慢〉 particularly with regard to this most famous line "二十四桥仍在，波心荡，冷月无声." With the hinge-like "*zai*," the poem also reveals at least three possibilities of reading the same line and thus of the whole text. With the first, even if we must pause as suggested by the comma, the "twenty-four bridge" is still the subject, "*zai*" is a preposition that forms a prepositional phrase 在波心 modifying the verb 荡 "*dang*," with 仍 "*reng*" (still) as an adverb describing 在波心, and 冷月无声 is then an adverbial phrase. The second possible reading is inherent in the first. While the twenty-four bridge remains the subject, "*zai*," however, is no longer a preposition but a verb with 波心荡 and 冷月无声 as two "subordinate" sentences describing the ways of how the bridge "is still there." With the third possibility, the poetic line thus reveals its hidden "museum effect"; there instantly appear three subjects and three sentences in the same line, that is, "the twenty-four bridge is still there," "the lake center ripples," and "the moon remains cold in silence." With this peculiar "museum effect" that suggests the otherwise hidden meaning-making and beauty-making power of the "spatiotemporal freedom" behind, beneath, between, and beyond each juxtaposed discrete and concrete image, both poems yield special sense of lyrical contemporaneity with everything so immediately, immensely, and immeasurably so real, present, but so timely timeless, and motionlessly in motion, contemporary and ancient, perpetually *a priori* and infinitely *a posteriori*.① Of this lyrically "creative syntax," everything, however insignificant as dried vines or "meanest flower" could, as a result, appear so impeccably live and perfectly frozen up in motion, so lyrically with not just emotion but also images subtly recollected in tranquility or awakened live from within "thoughts that do often lie too deep for tears." From within this "creative syntax" that generates the power of "spatiotemporal freedom," everything however discrete by itself, could also come to suggest the power of "informed imagination" reminiscent of a process of transformational-generative aesthetic that yields or facilitates the museum effect. Therefore, as if of a certain quintessential "museum effect," each otherwise discrete and concrete image juxtaposed in the "creative syntax" of the poems so referred to should certainly be appreciated as a one completely *of* itself and *by* itself; it It means, in other words, however each is so naturally positioned along with others in a group under a particular theme for the special occasion; each piece's group value for the museum effect lies exactly within its original merit regardless of how perfectly each fits in the group in terms of a certain perceived new relation and theme—simply because it is utterly impossible to redo any single piece to make it fit in a new group if it is not "naturally" or

---

① With "museum effect" understood with a comparative reference to the concepts of "spatiotemporal free expression and imagination" 超时空想象 and "creative syntax" the way they so appear in Feng Shengli's most recent works, the issue immediately concerns one of the most crucial arguments that Feng developed in these works, such as Feng & Henson (2015). Feng's endeavor stands for a fresh but restrained or self-consciously disciplined reinterpretation from a clear-cut prosodic perspective, which is based, first and foremost, solely and solidly, as in Wittgenstein's words, upon the tangible evidence *from within* "the rough ground" of "actual language," At the same time, as in Feng's (2015, 160-161) book, this endeavor also suggests how to transcend any possibly innate or inevitable structural limits of such an approach by bringing in the "spatiotemporal freedom" evoked *a posteriori* in reader's mind by means of any creative-turning syntactic-prosodic elements *from within* the text itself, such as the trivial and thus invisible but indispensable function words. Ultimately, the new prosodic approach or venue to literature based solidly and solely upon the significant studies on the syntax of classic Chinese literature could be equally applicable if, or when, it could also be adequately fine-tuned for us to understand likewise the classic literary texts in languages other than Chinese however these languages may appear so different from Chinese as from one another.

unpremeditatedly so in the first place. Everything, after all, however, must also *be* and should be fully grasped as one of the group in terms of the creative syntax.

2 The Cases of 而 and Instances of *Yijing* 易经

There are certainly subtle variations with regard to function words' actual level of indispensability in each literary text because function words may appear from time to time in the text with nothing more than a purely rhetorical or decorative element to play in ways to resemble something of an "architectural ornament," which is, as Wittgenstein would put it, like "architectural [decoration …] a kind of ornamental coping that supports nothing.) (Wittgenstein, 1968, 217, 85e). In the poem "*Nishang Zhongxu Diyi*" (霓裳中序第一) by Jiang Kui (姜夔) "沉思年少浪迹，笛里关山，柳下坊陌……漂零久，而今何意，醉卧酒垆侧，" which describes how the poet or personas hopelessly misses his love and ends up drunk in sleep, the role of the function word *er* 而 is indeed very subtle. Even if it is not the kind of "architectural ornament," neither is it as indispensable as *zai* in the poems above nor is it simply dispensable. *Er* is there not only to make it crystal clear the "transition," which is both grammatically adequate and prosodically necessary, but also to emphasize a hidden contrast of situations that suggests so much of a keenly felt irony. Sometimes, a certain otherwise quite mundane looking verses or poems with added "decorative" elements could also instantly turn out to be as much original and organic in ways as a grand of salt in water—to borrow this quite frequently used analogy from the *Upanishads*. This particular case and issue could be further understood especially in terms of Sun Deqian's(孙德谦, 1869-1935) theory of "internalized transition of *qi*" (潜气内转 *qianqi neizhuan*) and it could be so useful for us to understand various unique ways that function words play their role in Chinese.[①] It is because that compared with other major languages,

---

[①] For further relevant discussion on the issue, see Feng Shengli(2010b).

such as English, French, German, and Japanese, Chinese may not appear to depend upon function words as much. This phenomenon however does not mean that function words have fewer roles to play in Chinese; it may just indicate that function words have instead a more flexible but invisible role to play in Chinese not only with its presence but also with its absence or, often, its indispensable but implied presence. In this poem also by Jiang Kui, "疏疏雪片，[却]散入溪南苑。春寒锁、旧家亭馆。有玉梅几树，背立怨东风，高花未吐，[而]暗香已远" (Flakes of snow several in the sky float/Into the garden of Xinan they all go/Chill comes with Spring/And emptied of all visitors sit the ancient pavilion alone/Scattered are only a few jade-colored plum trees/In the east wind shivering/With their elegant flowers yet to bloom/And their delicate fragrance far off blown), there is, for instance, the indispensable but implied presence of *que* and *er*. As *ji* 几 could be added for both syntactic and prosodic reason (since 树 as a single syllable cannot stand by itself prosodically as Feng would so argue here), the function words *que* or *er* could also be absent for purely technical reasons, that is, for being metrically short of space. Even so, the two function words would still be considered as indispensable; their indispensable presence, however, could be considered as semantically or thematically implied or internalized in accordance with the given syntactic-prosodic context. The function words *que* and *er* could then still be *seen* as surreptitiously being there and smoothing out the transition with further theatrical implications along the way. It is because *que* could also mean *que pian pian* 却偏偏 (why just this way or me…), which may thus further suggest a thematically crucial sentiment of surprise, be amazed, or be mystified; likewise, *er* may indicate subtle but strong feeling of "regret," "resignation," or a sense of "hopelessness" and "helplessness" with what occurs. With such an understanding, we can further appreciate the meaning of the poem in ways otherwise impossible. With such an understanding of the implied sentiments as indicated by implied function words, we may thus, in other words, come to have a better reading of the poem especially in terms of the key content word *yuan* 怨 (to complain, to become sad or unhappy), which suggests in such a subtle but strong way the sentiment even in a seemingly quite objective description of the scenery with trees quietly personified as a person feeling sadly abandoned with the coming of all-too-soon wintry season. With their indispensable presence so "internalized" as 潜气内转 (*qianqi neizhuan*), these function words do appear so effective and elusive in ways described in Chinese idioms "as instantaneously traceless as an antelope in full speed" or "as ungraspable as the phantom like dragon, the elusive presence of which would could only be felt but not seen except for an occasional glimpse of its head without the appearance of full body" (羚羊挂角，无迹可寻；神龙见首不见尾，感其神而不见其形).

But for such a "miracle" to happen, it is often contingent upon how we read with what adequate amount of sensitivity to subtle but crucial "suggestions," which we could obtain at any time from the common but often so crucial function words, such as *zai* and *er* in terms of how they are actually "situated" in the text. These function words thus usually also function like the indispensable "hinges," "switches," or to borrow one of most frequently used analogies from The *Upanishads*, "salt in the water" in making the ordinary extraordinary. One of the particular cases in point is this special poem or one of several hexagram texts from *Yijing*, which is, however, so quintessentially "poetic" to be compared with any piece of poetry from *Shijing*.①

鸣鹤在阴，	There is a crane calling on the shady northern slope
其子和之。	Its offering answers it
我有好爵，	We have a fine beaker (of wine)
吾与尔靡之。	I will empty it together with you.

(Kunst, 1985, 53)

---

① While talking about how the cases of using *bi* 比 (metaphorical comparison) and *xing* 兴 (poetic mood and sentiment setting) are equally abundant in both *Shijing* and *Yijing*, Li Jingchi (李镜池, 1902-1975) emphasizes that this verse is just one of these "very beautiful and poetic of poetry" in *Yijing* (很美很有诗意的诗歌) but no one seems to pay attention to it as such(38).

Compared with any piece from *Shijing*, the hexagram text often appears more aesthetic not only in terms of its visual but also audible imaginary with a rich and intimate theme on friendship, love, and sharing. Its rhyming pattern is definitely so instrumental in bringing the hexagram all the poetic flavor or making it a poem par excellence. So instrumental are particularly the function words in constructing an aesthetically and meaningfully rhythmic syntactic-prosodic pattern that gives a sense of well-sounding coherence to things that may not seem to be so connected, if at all, in the natural sequence of events. The function word "*zhi*" 之 (it, this) of the last line, for instance, is syntactically and prosodically indispensable in the context. Along with *qi* 其 (this, that), *wu* 吾 (we; I), *er* 尔 (you), and *yu* 与(and, with) not only is *zhi* so instrumental in helping hexagram text to rhyme so poetically for the aesthetic coherence but also in making the text pause in ways that its syntactic-prosodic structure encourages and facilitates for the utmost poetic flavor. What makes this hexagram text particularly poetic, however, are the two key words *wu* and *er*. While *wu* could certainly be omitted, the omission of *wu* nonetheless could apparently make the hexagram text more smoothly of *regular* sounding especially in terms of how everything of the last line could then be so evenly well-rhymed with the whole poem. But when *wu* is kept the way it is, a slight and yet emphatic pause might be required or necessary on both *wu* and *yu* but especially on *er*. The line may thus sound like it is *you*, no one else, whom *I* would like to enjoy sharing the wine and the moment—regardless of *who* we are, *where* you are, *whether* we like each other or not previously, *whether* we will ever meet again in this or other world. But to make such a reading with *wu* and *er* even possible in the first place a hinge-like function word *yu* is irreplaceable because it must be there not only to make the required syntactic connection but also to mete out adequate amount of duration and stress that *wu* and *er* must work out along with itself to ensure a successful full landing on *zhi* at the most stressed end position (重中之重). Thus, within this specific context, the addition of *wu* in this regard becomes so crucial in making the hexagram text truly a poem the way it deserves especially regarding its entire subtly extraordinary visual and addible flavor.

3 The Indispensable but "Invisible" *Hai* 还

The indispensable and yet "invisible" power and beauty of the word *hai* 还 (again, still) in one of historically most famous poems and literary anecdotes, such as Jia Dao's most well-known poem "On Visiting Li Ning at Midnight"《题李凝幽居》, is another case in point. This poem describes how Li Ning, the poet's friend, lives by himself in seclusion with no neighbor nearby and how the poet attempts an impromptu visit there at night. Even though the poet does not find his friend at home, he experiences the wild beauty of nature along the way and around his friend's house. The live scene depicted in the poem implies more of life so quietly perfect in its scenic stillness than in its rolled out action.

闲居少邻并，	A house sits idly alone,
草径入荒园。	A weed path leads to the deserted garden.
鸟宿池边树，	While birds rest on the pond side trees,
僧推月下门。	Pushes a monk at the door under the moonlight.
过桥分野色，	Wild scene varies its beauty over the pond,
移石动云根。	Rock-shaped in motion are the clouds floating.
暂去还来此，	I will be back again after a brief leave today,
幽期不负言。	And this is a promise for me to keep.

(My translation)[①]

Like Ma Zhiyuan's "Tian Jing Sha," in which no function words appear until the last line with the ambiguous appearance of *zai* 在. The poem uses no function words until the second next to the last line. But unlike Ma's poem, which uses

---

① For clarity, I replace the original "And weeds run over the garden" and "the moon-shaded door" of the second and third line with these suggested versions from Dr. Baihua Wang, Associate Professor of Comparative Literature and World Literature at the Department of Chinese Language and Literature, Fudan University.

no verbs but nouns as if interested only in the stillness of life, this one uses verb in each line along with nouns as if in an attempt to catch a live scene in action and in process. Regardless, the stillness of life captured in Ma's verb-less depiction often suggests live motion, moment, and mood in contrast with Jia's poem that reveals more of a motionless picture of perfect stillness amidst motion.

Here the scenic quietness and stillness could indeed be perfectly suggested in the verb *qiao* 敲 (to knock), for which the poem becomes so famous. The word *qiao* suggested by Han Yu (韩愈, 768-824), in other words, does sound better than the original *tui* 推. Even if *qiao* could be so crucial for the success of the poem, there still remains serendipitously hidden a real but least noticeable "le mot juste," that is, the "function word," *hai*. No matter how often the synaesthetic phenomenon of the poem is suggested in the classical debate regarding how or which "content word" should be used, i.e., whether it should be the verb *tui* 推 (to push) used as in the original or *qiao* 敲 (to knock) as is suggested by Han Yu to the poet himself, the synaesthetic phenomenon, however, is mainly enhanced by the crucial but overlooked "function word" *hai* 还. Without the quiet assistance of *hai*, *qiao* would not be as effective in ways as it is so frequently referred to or praised for. Whether with *tui* or *qiao*, the poem can still be a poem, but without *hai* the poem cannot even *be* a poem in the first place, let alone to be in ways as it has been appreciated ever since. It is because *hai* is needed here in the crucial position to fulfill its indispensable syntactic and prosodic function to make the line become the organic part of the metric pattern of the poem with two full feet 暂去-还来此. With these two full feet, the line thus flows smoothly within the whole metric pattern especially in terms of coherence. Literally, without *hai*, neither can the line have two indispensable feet, which is a MUST prosodically, nor can it even be a sentence grammatically, let alone for the line to be the most important synaesthetically theme-revealing of the poem. The word *hai* emphasizes how only when the poet comes *again* can he then literally reassert and confirm the crucial moral value of promise-keeping and simultaneously prove, as claimed, how aesthetically intoxicating this midnight experience really is. The function word *hai* thus emphasizes, in other word, along with the value of friendship and sentiments for nature, the value of keeping promise, which also testifies whether the sentiment revealed at the moment is genuine enough to touch the heart of the reader. While fulfilling its syntactic, prosodic, and thematic function with visual and sound impact, *hai*, as a simple function word, brings out all these possible human sentiments and values along with the heart-touching scenic beauty. Only in this way can we then hear and visualize the scene and understand the meaning as if "we were literarily there" 身临其境 on the spot with the poet or even as the poet himself. This is why understanding function word regarding its syntactic-prosodic structure is important for us to grasp the literary situation as such; it is also important thereby for us to understand how one key content word, such as *qiao*, or function word, such as *hai*, must be used or thus also understood as "le mot juste" for both syntactic prosodic values as well as for all its implied visual and sound impact, which are in fact so mutually reversible, interchangeable, or concurring to make a poem a poem at once thematically and aesthetically.

Even if Chinese, unless for the particular stylistic and rhetorical purposes, does not rely as much on function words as English, French, German, and even Japanese, function words in Chinese, such as *hai*, also function in as much a crucial role as in English often with further surreptitious influences. As indicated by this practically word-by-word translation below, which "mimics" the original text, for the benefit of those who do not read in Chinese, it is almost self-evident how the original text can be literally function word free and how any literal translation, in other words, would utterly impossible whatsoever if without using any function word as in the original. Thus, to make any sense of even the most literal "mimic" of the original, some of the functions words, such as articles, proposition, and conjunction, must still be used as those marked in the brackets.①

闲居/少邻并，　Idly live/no neighbors are nearby,
草径/入荒园。　A weed path /leads to the deserted garden.
鸟宿/池边树，　Birds/nestle pond-side trees,
僧推/月下门。　[A] monk/ pushes/knocks [at] door under the moonlight.
过桥/分野色，　Wild scene varies beauty [over/across] bridge,
移石/动云根。　Floating clouds move rock-shaped.
暂去/还来此，　Leave temporarily still be back,
幽期/不负言。　"Come again" is [a] promise never [to] break.

This "literal" version should therefore further clearly indicate how the Chinese language could be so less dependent on function words, but, at the same time, how it could be so dependent on them once they become truly indispensable, as the case of *hai* shows here.

4　The Power of "That" and "Still" with Additional Cases

However English, French, German, and Japanese, may appear quite different from Chinese as they may appear from one another, their dependence on the indispensable but invisible function words are quite compatible. Function words can help capture the unheard melodies, which, as John Keats would argue here, is serendipitously "sweeter" but hidden even in our most familiar texts. This is the case with James Wright's "A Blessing,"

---

① This word-by-word version would not be possible without my colleague and friend, Dr. Tom Patterson's sensible advice that I should show the audience who do not read Chinese how the original could be literally function-word-free.

in which, with emphatic pauses, the function words *that* and *into* punch, with the emphatic pensive pauses, at such strategic positions and critical moments, the Zen-like "*sea changing*" experience or revelation in the last sentence of "*satori*" (悟り) as in Japanese or "dun wu" (顿悟) as in Chinese.

> Suddenly I realize
> That if I stepped out of my body I would break
> Into blossom

So is the most common の "*no*" in Matsuo Basho's. 松尾芭蕉(1644-1694) haiku in additional to the standard ya, such as his most famous jumping frog that strikes the similar "sea changing" moment, which in a split second transforms the sound of water into the sound of universe.

古池や(furu ike ya)	The ancient pond
蛙飞び込む(kawazu tobikomu)	A frog jumps in—
水の音(mizu no oto)	Sound of water.
	(Bashô, 1995: 417)

Indeed, in Basho's most famous frog piece, for instance, not only is *ya* や so instrumental as the special "cutting word" *kireji* (切れ字), which is always there at this strategic position suggesting or requesting an emotional and reflective pause but also is the function word "*no*" の so indispensable both syntactically and prosodically as "that" in Wright's "A Blessing"; other than its syntactic function, の demands a crucial "pensive pause" in very much the same way as *ya* however subtle or thereby often unnoticeable. Actually, somewhat *ya* also carries an implicit and irreplaceable syntactic role as a usual topic mark は *wa* also in ways compatible with "that" in Wright's text. No matter how crucial as it is, the importance of the function word ya, however, often emerges as not sufficiently noticeable as in the above English when is simply not even translated.① Even in the little piece of pure beauty, such as Goethe's "*Wandrers Nachtlied*" as below, the seemingly insignificant function words, such as "*über,*" "*im,*" "*du,*" "*auch,*" appear to provide so timely the key support in rhythmically activating the crucial syntactic-prosodic verbal pattern that enlivens each content word at the crucial vantage positions regarding *where* and *how* things truly are and *will* soon be thereafter.

---

① The unique poetic flavor of this haiku, however, could certainly be considered as simultaneously the result of the strategic absence and presence not only of the content words but also of function words that make a "creative syntax" with its poetic spatiotemporal free expression and imagination. Should the haiku be returned to the corresponding prosaic syntaxes (refined as below, thanks to Kazuyo Rumbach, a colleague and friend) out of the numerous possibilities, it is clear not simply what or how many content words are omitted to make room for a "creative syntax" indispensable for the spatiotemporal free expression and imagination or "beauty of ambiguity" that this little poem is famous for; it should also be clear how crucial but barely noticeable is role that function words play in the scheme of making creative syntax, i.e. *ya* and *no*.

   a. 古池で蛙が飛び込む音がした (In the ancient pond, there was a sound of frog jumping in the water).
   b. 古池で蛙が飛び込む音が聞こえた (In the ancient pond, I heard the sound of frog jumping in the water).
   c. 古池の方から蛙が飛び込む音がした (From the (direction of) ancient pond, there was a sound of frog jumping in the water).

What does it mean by the sound of water? Does it mean there is sound of water or there is sound of water to be heard, seen, or simultaneously heard and seen in ways as another case of synesthetic phenomena so characteristic of Basho's haiku in general and this one particular? In fact, to recover the "missing verb," which is possibly "omitted" but "recoverable" only in terms of whatever spatiotemporal free imagination that may appear awakened in reader's mind, instead of "there is a sound" (音がする), there could also be as many other possible verbal choices that equally fit the syntactic position to result in different aesthetic/synesthetic meanings or impacts. It could be "to hear" (聞こえる), "to feel" (感じる) or simply "to appear or to reveal" (見える) with subtle synaesthetic implication as the cases with William Blake or Joseph Conrad. In his poem "London," Blake suggests that he not only hears, but also sees "... the hapless soldier's sigh/Runs in blood down palace walls" (Kirszner, 1991: 899).

Uberallen Gipfeln ist Ruh'	<u>On</u> all <u>the</u> hilltops there is peace
In allen wipfeln Spurest du	<u>In</u> all the treetops you feel
Kaum **eine** Hauch	Hardly any breeze
Die Voglein schweigen **im** Walde,	The birds are quiet <u>in</u> the woods
Warte nur, balde	Just wait, soon
Ruhest du auch	You too will be in peace.

Of the amount of twenty four words that makes up the poem, the six function words, approximately thirty three percent, literally emerge as the crucial relay points where rhythmic pause and stress occur right at the moment in making the little piece a lyric marvel for the unusual visual and audial pleasure aesthetically.

Quite often, as the case "still" below shows, Dickinson's poems also redefine *a posteriori* the concept of "function word," which usually indicates a limited number of conjunction, preposition, article, some adverbs, or typically any word with virtually little lexical meaning but mere syntactic function.

> Embarrassment of one another
> And God
> Is Revelation's limit,
> Aloud
> Is nothing that is chief,
> But still,
> Divinity dwells under a seal (Johnson, 1960: 662)

The life or power of this poem also appears to be determined by a function word of a certain dubious or ambiguous nature. In this syntactic-prosodic context, "still" could be simultaneously an adjective, an adverb, or a "conjunction." it functions like a "hinge" that allows meaning to go around in all possible directions. In this regard, "still" is very much like "that" as "demonstrative pronoun" *and* "subordinating conjunction" in the previous pieces. However barely noticeable as if with a slight pause over a speed bumper, "still" also like "that" functioning in such ways to occasion a subtle or serendipitous turn or shift; this occasion also suggests a releasing or quiet explosion of serious energy at a critical moment by disrupting a seemingly normal or mundane process, which runs, as if wholly in inertia, to the conclusion in a regular iambic metrical pattern. In the context, "still," for instance, could be simultaneously or respectively a "content word" meaning "silent, quiet, or motionless," a "conjunction" meaning "but, and yet, nonetheless," and/or an "adverb" indicating "at this or that time; as previously" or "up to this or that time; as yet." Which one therefore could be possibly decided on with regard to Dickinson's authorial intention? Whatever our "surmises" could be in line with the assumed "authorial intention," one possible way of reading the poem is to read it as Dickinson's attempt to explore divinity as the "un/graspable phantom" of life regardless of whether divinity becomes such an issue for its own reason or the way we approach it. The poem explores in other words whether divinity remains as something real or something as real as "glorious nothings" under a seal, simultaneously invisible and visible, revealed and hidden, substantial and illusive, or, Seng Zhao would so put it here, somewhat of a state between "*you* (there is)" and "*wu* (there is not)," a state of the real unknown, which we might have to stay quiet or silent about. In "Embarrassment of one another" as in many others, the word "still" thus not only disrupts the usual categorization or distinction of "function word" and "content word" but also creates thought-provoking ambiguity and pause, which cannot be merely interpreted in line with something of an authorial intention.

5 Verlaine, Liang Zongdai 梁宗岱, and Fei Bai 飞白

Such an understanding of the use of function words may also help us significantly in detecting or discovering the hidden common ground beneath and behind the observable differences amidst Chinese and other major languages, such as English, French, and Japanese; it would certainly be quite helpful not only for us to detect the subtle beauty in the poems, such as Wright's "A Blessing" and Basho's haiku, but also for us to make better translation. The obvious superiority of Fei Bai's(飞白) version to Liang Zongdai's (梁宗岱, 1903-1983) in translating Paul Verlaine (1844-1896) "Il pleure dans mon cœur." for instance, should be a supreme example in this regard.

Paul Verlaine	(Fei Bai)	(Liang Zongdai)
Il pleure <u>dans</u> mon Coeur	泪水流<u>在</u>我<u>的</u>心底,	泪流在我心里,
<u>Comme</u> il pleut <u>sur</u> la ville;	恰似那满城秋雨。	雨在城上渐沥,
Quelle est cette langueur	一股无名<u>的</u>愁绪	哪来的一阵凄楚
Qui pénètre mon coeur ?	浸透到我<u>的</u>心底。	滴得我这般惨戚?
Ô bruit doux <u>de la</u> pluie	嘈杂而柔和<u>的</u>雨	啊, 温柔的雨声!
<u>Par</u> terre <u>et sur</u> les toits !	<u>在</u>地上、<u>在</u>瓦上絮语!	地上和屋顶应和。
<u>Pour</u> un coeur <u>qui</u> s'ennuie,	啊, 为一颗柔和的心	对于苦闷的心
Ô le chant <u>de la</u> pluie !	而轻轻吟唱<u>的</u>雨!	啊, 雨的歌!
Il pleure <u>sans</u> raison	泪水流得不合情理,	这样无端地流,
<u>Dans</u> ce coeur <u>qui</u> s'écoeure.	这颗心啊厌烦自己。	<u>流得我心好酸</u>!
Quoi ! nulle trahison ?...	怎么? 并没有人负心?	怎么? 全无止休?
Ce deuil est <u>sans</u> raison.	这悲哀说不出情理。	这哀感也无端!
C'est bien <u>la</u> pire peine	这是最沉重的痛苦,	可有更大的苦痛
<u>De</u> ne savoir pourquoi	当你不知它<u>的</u>缘故。	教人慰解无从?
<u>Sans</u> amour <u>et sans</u> haine	既没有爱, 也没有恨,	既无爱又无憎,
Mon coeur a tant <u>de</u> peine !	我心<u>中</u>有这么多痛苦!	我的心却这般疼。

Fei's version is apparently superior to Liang's because it brings authentic flavor not only so naturally out of French but also out of Chinese. The superiority of Fei's version suggests a crucial syntactic-prosodic structure so compatible in both French and Chinese, which explains the version's secret of success. It is this crucial syntactic-prosodic structure that not only accounts for the important choice of content words but also indicates the indispensable role of function words that makes Fei's a better version than Liang's. This crucial syntactic-prosodic structure, in other words, literally demonstrates how instrumental the role of function words plays in successfully setting up a rhythm-making and meaning-making coherent poetic pattern so suggestive of the rich sound and visual imagery as in Fei's superior version compared with Liang's. In this way, Fei's version becomes as much palpable in translation as in the original, even though in the original French version the visual imagery seems to be not as much emphasized as its musical quality.

The sound and visual imagery of Fei's translation, nonetheless, still appear to be so mutually sustaining and interchangeable due to this syntactic-prosodic structure that enables function words to be fully functional both visually and in sound. Compared with Fei's smooth and rhythmically aesthetic version, which matches the original in various ways especially prosodically, Liang's translation, however, does appear so uneven with its often quite expediently mixed literary and colloquial vocabulary, such as "雨在城上淅沥" (Like the rain over the city drizzling) with "流得我心好酸" (My heart aches with the endless rains). This second line simply sounds far too colloquial especially in line with 淅沥 *xi li* (to drizzle), the highly literary sounding and never orally spoken vocabulary, neither does this part even seem to deliver the meaning of the original line in French. Also quite expediently treated is the other literary vocabulary, such as *qi can* 戚惨 (sad), which appears so artificially or forcefully reversed into *can qi* 惨戚 to fit the given metric pattern or to make *qi* 戚 rhyme with *li* 沥 of 雨在城上淅沥. In contrast with such expediently extended "poetic license," Fei's version does strike particularly smooth, natural, and authentic with the original flavor very much well-kept – not just in terms of its verbal choice but with regard to its prosodic pattern and resounding imagery as well. The word 浸透 (to soak or to be soaked), for instance, sounds more suggestive of an endless and profound sense of melancholy than Liang's 滴得 (drizzle to such a degree) not only in meaning but also in sound; it is because *tou* 透 (to penetrate) apparently sounds longer and louder than *de* 得 (particle used after a verb to show effect; degree or possibility) in terms of each word's sound quality. Fei's version "这颗心啊厌烦自己" (Inside the heart sobbing in grief) is also definitely more elegant and lyrical than Liang's "流得我心好酸."

But the strength of Fei's version, most certainly, must be further appreciated prosodically. The words 泪水 (tear), for instance, undoubtedly sound better than 泪 (also tear). It is because, as Feng would explain here, 泪水 makes a full foot that can thus stand by itself without being "awkwardly tongue-twisting" (拮据唇吻), whereas Liang's 泪 with single syllable (单音) simply cannot stand by itself as a prosodically self-sufficient foot ("单音不成步").① For the same reason 秋雨 (autumn rain) does sound better than 雨 as a full prosodic foot with the word 秋 obviously added to make a full foot. For exactly the same reason, the exclamation *a* 啊, which is apparently overused in Liang's translation to cause it often sound unnecessarily sentimental, is adequately used in Fei's especially with accurate timing to make the line sound so rhythmically heart touching through four perfect "iambic" feet; one of these perfect feet 这颗心啊厌烦自己 is unquestionably formed by one content word *xin* (heart) paired up with the exclamation *a* 啊. Another exemplified case in point regarding how skillful Fei is in exploring the inherent syntactic-prosodic capacity of each function word is the use of *de* 的 (of) in the whole text to create an indispensable syntactic-prosodic environment or context that enables both function word *and* context word to function as fully as possible not only for meaning but also for meaning-making beauty of prosodic rhythms. In the line of 泪水流在我的心底, (My heart is weeping), for instance, *de* may seem utterly unnecessary from a sheer grammatical point of view; it is, however, so indispensable prosodically for the crucial rhythmic pause that *de* mediates within the syntactic-prosodic pattern of four full perfect "iambic" feet, of

---

① This proves to be one of Feng's basic prosodic rules as it often thus appears emphasized in his earlier publications of 1997 and 2005.

which *de* is also one of the irreplaceable components. Along with another function word *zai* 在 (in, at), *de*, in other words, appears not only so instrumental in punctuating the poetic line with rhythmic and meaning-making pace but also decisive in setting up the coherent rhythmic pattern throughout the whole poem; *de* is literally repeated at each crucial moment that the poem needs for a melancholically pensive pause. Such a vital moment of pause, from time to time, is clearly—not there in Liang's version, which is so deficient in terms of effective use of function word for critical life-making poetic rhythms the way Feii does, especially with regard to Fei's thoughtful exploration with full feet for the purpose and effect.

Similarly, those otherwise utterly innocent function word, such as *qia* 恰 (just) in "恰似那满城秋雨" (Just as the rain over the city drizzling), also provide the vital text-enlivening rhythms especially because 似 *shi* (as, like) simply cannot stand by itself prosodically as a self-sufficient full foot. In addition, with the phrase 恰似 *qia shi* (just as), this line also comes to enrich the poem with the subtly evoked meaning-making and image-making allusions to the other famous poetic lines, such as the ones from Li Qingzhao's (李清照, 1084-1151). So exemplary of Fei's masterful use of the function words for aesthetically visual imagery through sound are also these two lines "在地上、在瓦上絮语！" (On the ground and on the roofs whispering), in which the repetition of *zai* makes the line so rhythmically lyrical, and "嘈杂而柔和的雨" (O drizzles the gentle and noisy rain), in which the function word *er* 而 (and, but) provides smooth transition so regretfully missing in Liang's version. Even though *er* may seem as grammatically unnecessary as *de* in this context, they both are prosodically irreplaceable in creating more rhythmic sounding; the line would certainly not sound as subtly or gently rhythmic as now without *er* in between mediating for a contrasting and complementary symbiosis of imagery that two content words *cao za* 嘈杂 (noisy) and *rou he* 柔和 (gentle) may evoke at once visually and in sound. It is because the phrase 嘈杂 (noise) *cao zao* in Chinese may indicate such a mixed or concurring synaesthetic experience with *cao* likely referring to sound experience and *zai* a visual one; the phrase thus suggests that one sees the noisy sound as well as hearing it. Fei's translation of "Ô bruit doux de la pluie" as "嘈杂而柔和的雨" thus does bring out the full flavor and meaning of the original missed in Liang's version "啊，温柔的雨声！" (Ah, gentle sounds of the rain!); it brings out the original flavor in such a synaesthetically poetic way because "bruit" in French does not just mean sound but rather "noises of sound" or "noisy sound." Along with *de* fulfilling its indispensable syntactic-prosodic function in the context, this particular line therefore does touch the reader's heart and imagination with its gentle and soothing rhythms so mediated by these two key function words *er* and *de*. Actually the second stanza, in which these two lines appear, are the most exemplary of Fei's art or mastery of translation. Thus with such skillful use of function words in creating this quite crucial syntactic-prosodic environment, Fei's version has so far stood for the best possible Chinese version of this famous poem by Verlaine; his version makes the poem "transplanted" in Chinese but with as much authentic vivacity both visually and in sound as in the original. All is done, nonetheless, not via forcefully matched rhymes as is often the case with Liang's text, but through the actual rhythmic motion, moment, movement, and mood so timely mediated or punctuated via the creative use of the meaning-making, rhythm-making, image-making, and thus life-making function words; all the function words in the text appear so motivated to function fully in accordance with the live syntactic-prosodic environment or verbal context, which they also simultaneously enliven and are enlivened by in turn.[①]

[①] This syntactic-prosodic approach thus also helps solve the "unsolved mystery" regarding why I have been so personally taken with Fei's version, which literally never fades away in my mind since I happened to read it, most likely, in "*Yili*" 译林 around 1980's. However much in my heart I respect Liang as a translator, Liang's translation of Verlaine never aroused my interest or curiosity in the original; Fei's version, however, did. My curiosity started like a wild fire. My love affair with Verlaine and then with French symbolists afterward never seems to stop.

6   Conclusion: Catching the Indispensable and Invisible through the Microscope of Prosody

Our appreciation of the literary texts thus often means our involuntary appreciation of the magic power of function words if we are not quite conscious of such a trivial but crucial role that function words play in the scheme of our reading. With prosody, it is however not only necessary but also possible for us to grasp the meaning-making and beauty-making power of function words through the crucial syntactic-prosodic structure that each function word so at once immensely and intimately enlivens and is enlivened by; within this very environment, the function words, each in its own way, become the indispensable nexuses, hinges, or catalysts that makes literary texts alive. The function words along with the syntactic-prosodic structure thus becomes, in other words, the "plain" green leaves that set off the beauty of the flowers; it could be as plain or simply as much unnoticeable but indispensable as the nutritious dirt or soils that yields the beauty of the daffodils; it could also be like the invisible dew and air that nourish the appealing beauty of roses. Whether observable as the results of self-conscious "internalization" or "naturalization" or as seemingly a mere magic "coincidence" as in the cases with "*that*" of Wright's "A Blessing," "*no*" of Basho's haiku, or "*zai*" of both Ma's and Jiang's poems, these prosodically explainable thematically and aesthetically crucial functions of the function words all suggest a certain road not taken for reading within the roads frequently trodden regarding our common classical texts and our habitual ways to read them. We may thus find the meaningful and beautiful where least noticeable when we pay attention not only to the content words but also to the function words. Along with the syntactic-prosodic structure, the function word, in other words, is likely where the "sweeter" unheard melody is hidden. As a result, the issue in question indicates not only a crucially "local" but also "global" phenomenon yet to be further understood; it also indicates how reading across cultures should no longer be a distant goal but attainable practice as long as all our lofty ideas for cross-cultural dialogue could thus be, as Wittgenstein would suggest here, so solidly landed on the real "rough ground" of "actual language" so real or so enlivened via all its trivial but crucial "mechanics" or "frictions" (1968, 107, 47e). Indeed, no matter how much there might be difference from one language to another, i.e., Chinese, English, French, German, and Japanese, the function word, together with the syntactic-prosodic structure, is the indispensable common ground, which not only makes all the differences meaningful but also comparable and compatible for better mutual understanding. The function word thus also exists as the common ground of interdisciplinary and cross-cultural dialogue not only in terms of translation but also in terms of how prose or "non-literary" texts could equally be poetic; the hexagram texts of *Yijing*, for instance, could come to reveal so serendipitously and so much aesthetic quality or hidden literary values to rival even those in the *Shijing* other than their practical use for divination, regardless of the seemingly unbridgeable compartmentalization of genres between poetry and prose, literary and non-literary texts. The function word now holds the key to the sweeter and hidden melodies of words.[①]

References

Bashô, M. 1995. Frog. In P. Davis et al. (Eds.), *Western Literature in a World Context: The*

[①] For the paper, I want to thank my colleagues and friends Drs. Tom Patterson, Dennis Arjo, Michael Robertson, and Allison Smith in addition to Janette Jasperson and Janet Brooks, for all the indispensable logistical support and help whether in the form of travel funds that enabled me to deliver the paper last November in Hong Kong, travel arrangements, or library research assistance, whether as the chairpersons of the Departments they each head, i.e., International Education, Philosophy and Religions, Humanities, and Art History, or as the coordinator *extraordinaire* or librarian *extraordinaire*. Ultimately, I am grateful to Dr. Shengli Feng, the Editor-in-Chief, for having literarily initiated my now steadily deepened interest in prosodic research as early as his tenured years at Harvard.

Enlightenment through the Present. Vol. 2 (p. 417). New York: St. Martin.

Berlin, I. 1997. *The Proper Study of Mankind: An Anthology of Essays*. New York: Farrar, Straus and Giroux.

Chen, S. 2015. Emily Dickinson, Function Words, and Dao: A Prosodic and Philosophical View from Across Cultures. *Journal of Comparative Literature and Comparative Cultures*, (1): 42-87.

Chen, S. 2012. Reading Prosodically, Reading Serendipitously: Fine-tuning for the Unheard Melodies of *Dao*. *The Tsing Hua Journal of Chinese Studies*, *42*(3): 379-400.

Dickinson, E. 1960. In T. H. Johnson (Ed.), *The Complete Poems of Emily Dickinson*. Boston: Little, Brown and Company.

Feng, S. 1997. *Interactions between Morphology Syntax and Prosody in Chinese*. Beijing: Peking University Press.

Feng, S. 2005. *Studies on Chinese Prosodic Grammar*. Beijing: Peking University Press.

Feng, S. 2010a. On Principles of Prosodic Stylistics. *Contemporary Rhetoric*, (1): 25-36.

Feng, S. 2010b. The Annotation of the Rhythm of Liuchaolizhi. *Han Yu Shi Xue Bao*, (2): 86-89.

Feng, S. 2011. A prosodic explanation for Chinese poetic evolution. *Tsing Hua Journal of Chinese Studies*, New Series, *42*(2): 223-258.

Feng, S. 2015. *Hanyu Yunlü Shixue Lungao* [*Poetic Stylistics of Chinese P*rosody]. Beijing: The Commercial Press.

Feng, S. & Henson, A. 2015. Parallel Prose and Spatiotemporal Freedom: A Case for Creative Syntax in 'Wucheng fu'. *Journal of Chinese Literature and Culture*, *2*(2): 444-480.

Feng, Y. (Fung, Yu-Lan). 1953. *History of Chinese Philosophy*. Trans. Derk Bode. Vol. II. Princeton: Princeton University Press.

Kunst, R. A. 1985. *The Original Yijing: Texts, Phonetic Transcription, Translation, and Index, with Samples Glosses* (Unpublished Ph.D. dissertation). University of California, Berkeley.

Liang, Z. 1984. *Poetry and Truth*. Beijing: Foreign Literature Press.

Li, J. 2007. *Zhou Yi Tan Yuan*. Beijing: Zhong Hua Shu Ju.

Miller, C. 1987. *Emily Dickinson: A Poet's Grammar*. Cambridge, MA.: Harvard University Press.

Sun, D. 1923. *Liu Chao Li Zhi*, Zhu Ying Ping (Ed.). Yi Huan Kan Ben.

Wittgenstein, L. 1961. D. F. Pears & B. F. McGuinness (Trans.), Bertrand Russell (Introd.), *Tractatus Logico-Philosophicus*. London: Routledge & Kegan Paul.

Wittgenstein, L. 1968. G. E. M. Anscombe (Trans.), *Philosophical Investigations* (3rd ed.). New York: Macmillan.

音韵学显微境下的惊喜发现:"功能词"诗的力与美

陈曙东

摘要 通过音韵学去发现功能词隐藏的、不可或缺的"足够长的杠杆"和"支点"无疑是一门重要的技术。本文旨在表述当代音韵学理论有助于揭示诗歌中藏而不露的美和意义,尤其是有助于根据实际语境重新定义功能词,即一些数量有限的连词、介词、冠词或任何除语法功能外并无实际词义的词。本文还探讨了功能词如何因其音韵学及语法功能,既授予文本生命力,丰富了文本;又因存之于文本而增强自身的生命力。在汉语中,功能词同英语中一样,不仅打破了词先时而定的一般属性,或区别功能词和实义词的基本特征,而且产生了一种后时而定的模糊性及停顿的实际效果。这种实际效果无法依据某种所谓的作者意图而判定,只有在音韵学的显微镜下,方能揭示功能词常被忽视而又十分重要的特殊表意功能。

关键词 音韵学 功能词 维特根斯坦 比较文学

Shudong Chen

Professor, Department of Humanities, Johnson county community college

E-mail: schen@jccc.edu

《韵律研究》

来稿须知

一、来稿请使用电子本，请同时用 word（doc）格式和 pdf 格式各寄一份，请勿上传压缩文件（投稿邮箱：prosodicstudies@126.com）。来稿审读时间一般为 6 个月，半年内未接到备用通知，可自行处理。

二、如果文章用到特殊字体，请用附件形式把相应的字体文件发送过来；如果文章用到自造字、图表或其他特殊形式，请做成图像文件发送过来，或者另附上一份说明文件。

将 word 文件转换成 pdf 文件时，请确认文章内容可以在 pdf 文件中正确显示。

如果文章中有手写的内容，也可以扫描或拍照后做成 pdf 文件，请确认 pdf 文件内容可以清楚显示。

三、所有论文需要提供英文题目。八千字以上的稿件请提供二百字以内的中英两种文字的提要和关键词。

四、本刊体例如下，务请按此体例上传稿件。

（一）论文题目：

正题：二号标宋，占 4 行。

副题：三号仿宋，另占一行，前加破折号（——）。

题注：在正题末右上角加星号（*）。题注注文排当页下，与正文之间加一细线。注文小五号宋体，起行空一格。前加星号做注码，后空一格。

（二）摘要和关键词

摘要：小五号黑体，后空一字空，接排摘要正文。摘要正文居中，左右空 3 字符，小五号宋体，回行齐"摘要"。

关键词：小五号黑体，后空一字空，关键词小五号宋体，各词之间空一字空，回行齐"关键词"。

（三）正文

1. 正文，通栏，五号宋体。如例句较短，可排分栏。

2. 二级标题（文章分节小标题），用 4 号宋体，占 2 行，居中。

3. 三级标题，用小 4 黑，占 1.5 行，齐左顶格。二、三级标题可选用汉字序码或阿拉伯数码，二者要统一。

4. 例句：

有序码例句：序码用阳文码排序，后空半字空。起行空 2 字空，回行齐汉字。序码原则上一排到底，酌情可分节编排。如果例句接排，例句间空二字空。

无序码例句：起行空 3 字空，回行空 3 字空。较短的可接排，中间用竖线隔开。

5. 引文：起行空 4 字空，回行空 3 字空。

6. 例句、引文等的出处（书名、报刊名）一律用书名号，外加圆括号。

书名依次为：作者、书名、出版社、时间。例：

（吕叔湘《汉语语法论文集》（修订本），35 页）

报刊名依次为：作者文章、报刊名称、时间。例：

（周培红《今生今世》，《收获》1991 年第 1 期）

古文依次为：朝代、人名、书名、篇名、章节。例：

（唐·李白《古风·十九》）、（《诗经·硕鼠》）

7. 国际音标括号用直方括号"[ ]"声调一律用数码标在右上角。

8. 数字：公历年、月、日用阿拉伯数字，其他参考《出版物上数字用法的规定》视情而定，一篇文章内要统一。

9. 正文中引述文献标注顺序：作者、年代，中间加逗号，外加圆括号。例：

（朱德熙，1986）

10. 文中图表一律小五号宋体，图表名用小五号仿体，位于表格上端，齐表头。

(四）附注与参考文献

1. 附注请用页脚注，每页重新编码，序号为圈形符号。

2. 参考文献请采用"科学出版社语言分社学术专著参考文献格式"。

（五）英文稿件格式，请参阅 *Prosodic Studies* Style Sheet（可在我刊网站下载，网址 https://www.arts.cuhk.edu.hk/~jclal/journal/）

其他未尽事宜，请来函咨询。

五、本刊投稿邮箱：prosodicstudies@126.com。

图书在版编目(CIP)数据

韵律研究. 第一辑 / 冯胜利主编. —北京：科学出版社，2016.9
ISBN 978–7–03–049930–1

Ⅰ. ①韵… Ⅱ. ①冯… Ⅲ. ①汉语–韵律(语言)–文集
Ⅳ. ①H116.4-53

中国版本图书馆 CIP 数据核字(2016) 第 220210 号

责任编辑：阎　莉　王洪秀 / 责任校对：郑金红
责任印制：张　倩 / 封面设计：铭轩堂

科学出版社 出版
北京东黄城根北街16号
邮政编码：100717
http://www.sciencep.com

三河市骏杰印刷有限公司 印刷
科学出版社发行　各地新华书店经销

*

2016 年 9 月第 一 版　开本：720×1000 1/16
2016 年 9 月第一次印刷　印张：12 1/2
字数：250 000

定价：48.00 元
(如有印装质量问题，我社负责调换)